Romanticism and

Children's Literature in

Nineteenth-Century England

Romanticism and Children's Literature in Nineteenth-Century England

Edited by

JAMES HOLT MCGAVRAN, JR.

The University of Georgia Press

Athens and London

© 1991 by the University of Georgia Press
Athens, Georgia 30602
All rights reserved

Designed by Kathi L. Dailey
Set in Linotron 202 Linotype Walbaum by
Tseng Information Systems, Inc.
Printed and bound by Thomson-Shore
The paper in this book meets the guidelines for permanence and
durability of the Committee on Production Guidelines for Book
Longevity of the Council on Library Resources.

Printed in the United States of America

95 94 93 92 91   5 4 3 2 1

Library of Congress Cataloging in Publication Data

Romanticism and children's literature in nineteenth-century
    England / edited by James Holt McGavran, Jr.
        p.   cm.
    Includes bibliographical references and index.
    ISBN 0-8203-1289-4 (alk. paper)
        1. Romanticism—England.   2. Children's literature, English—
History and criticism.   3. English literature—19th century—
History and criticism.   4. Children—England—Books and
reading—History—19th century.   I. McGavran, James Holt.
PR457.R458' 1991
820.9'9282'09034—dc20   90-36157
                                                            CIP

British Library Cataloging in Publication Data available

Title page illustration by Arthur Hughes from *At the Back of the
North Wind*, George MacDonald (London: Blackie and Son
Limited, n.d. [1899?]). Courtesy of Rare Book Collection, Atkins
Library, University of North Carolina at Charlotte.

CONTENTS

JAMES HOLT MCGAVRAN, JR.

Introduction

A little child, a limber Elf
Singing, dancing to itself;
A faery Thing with red round Cheeks,
That always *finds*, and never *seeks*—
Doth make a Vision to the Sight,
Which fills a Father's Eyes with Light!
And Pleasures flow in so thick & fast
Upon his Heart, that he at last
Must needs express his Love's Excess
In Words of Wrong and Bitterness.
Perhaps 'tis pretty to force together
Thoughts so all unlike each other;
To mutter and mock a broken charm;
To dally with Wrong, that does no Harm—
Perhaps, 'tis tender too & pretty
At each wild Word to feel within
A sweet Recoil of Love & Pity;
And what if in a World of Sin
(O sorrow & shame! should this be true)
Such Giddiness of Heart & Brain
Comes seldom, save from Rage & Pain,
So talks, as it's most used to do.—

A very metaphysical account of Fathers calling their children rogues, rascals, & little varlets—&c—"; thus Samuel Taylor Coleridge mock-seriously appraised the foregoing expression of his contradictory feelings towards his four-and-a-half-year-old son Hartley, after copying it into a letter to Robert Southey in 1801 (*Collected Letters* 2: 728–29). Coleridge's comment to Southey belies the importance he attached to the poem, for he printed it in 1816 as the "Conclusion" to part 2 of his disturbing Gothic fragment *Christabel*

1

(*Poems* 235–36). Thematically, the dramatic division between mental image and spoken language—specifically from "Vision," "Light," "Pleasures," and "Love's Excess" to "Words of Wrong and Bitterness"—holds a central and crucial place in Coleridge's wintry Inferno of the Romantic Imagination (Knight, in Abrams 202–3); it also helps to explain his much-criticized inability to finish the poem. "Love's Excess," as exemplified in Christabel's dead but supernaturally hovering mother, and "Wrong and Bitterness," in her spiritually dead father, freeze both parents into their respective roles of ineffectual guardian angel and misanthropic prophet of death, defining an intergenerational ethic in which caring is inseparable from betrayal and in effect calling forth Geraldine as Christabel's seductive, silencing, spellbinding shadow. It was not that Coleridge lacked any means to thaw the icejam of *Christabel*'s plot; he could easily enough have ended the poem in either of the ways he alluded to in his later comments on the subject. Given a "World of Sin," which is also a world of possible Christian redemption through suffering, Christabel could sing her song of desolation and, as her name suggests, sacrifice her innocent self to save the depraved Geraldine. Alternatively, the "Rage & Pain" of parents and children could be dissolved in an essentially pagan comedy through a series of supernatural transformations.[1] Coleridge, however, seems to have found in neither possibility an acceptable resolution of the conflict; instead, he deliberately restates and clarifies the conflict itself in the non-concluding passage on Hartley.

But this paradigmatic passage prophesies far beyond its contextualization in *Christabel*. The "Giddiness of Heart & Brain," originating in adults' simultaneous idealization of the child and lament over the loss of their own childlike innocence, anticipates William Wordsworth's better-known evocation of the theme in the "Immortality" ode and frames a Romantic dilemma of consciousness and expression that is equal parts beauty and fear, exaltation and abuse, love and "pretty" hypocrisy. It is this tension, expressed repeatedly in Romantic texts, that both lovingly engendered and relentlessly shadowed the efflorescence of imaginative children's literature in the Victorian period. Moreover, Coleridge's 1801 letter-poem to Southey alludes to three areas of late eighteenth-century culture where conflicts arose that helped to bring about the Romantics' dilemma: economic and medical conditions, theories of child development and education, and basic philosophical concepts of adult and child. A brief review of these major areas of change will prove the breadth and depth of Coleridge's "meta-physical account"; it will also orient the reader to the perspectives of the writers of this collection. The first five essays (by Jeanie Watson, Alan Richardson, James McGavran, Ross Woodman, and Mitzi Myers) focus on writings of the Romantic Period; and the remaining six (by Patricia Demers, Roderick McGillis, Judith Plotz, Michael Hancher, Phyllis Bixler, and Anita Moss) explore Victorian literature and document further development and complication of the Romantic conflict over childhood.

In his letter Coleridge introduces Southey to the lines on Hartley with an affecting expression of parental concern: "—Dear Hartley! we are at times alarmed by the state of his Health—but at present he is well—if I were to lose him, I am afraid, it would exceedingly deaden my affection for any other children I may have—"(*Collected Letters* 2: 728). There is more than self-indulgence here: the Coleridges had already lost a second son, Berkeley, in infancy in 1799. In his mortal fears and bitter words—in *Christabel* the line becomes "words of un-meant bitterness"—as in his doting descriptions of the "limber elf," Coleridge illustrates an attitude towards the life and death of children that had greatly changed during the eighteenth century, when vacci-nation, the gradual elimination of the practice of wetnursing in favor of maternal nursing at home, improvements in obstetrical techniques, and better personal hygiene brought a decrease in child mortality suf-ficient to foster the beginnings of a modern sense of family planning and family caring (Ariès 43; L. Stone 9, 20, 72–73, 426–27). Living more isolated, protected lives, parents of the upper and middle classes could plan smaller families, hold more realistic hopes for the survival of both their children and their families' fortunes, and permit them-selves to care more deeply for their offspring (Ariès 415; L. Stone 8). An increase in the perceived value of formal education, especially for boys, as a preparation for an economically and morally sound life was another result of the lower mortality rate that tended to set childhood apart as a special time (Ariès 58, Pickering 6).

Although medical improvements became increasingly available and accepted, child mortality rates remained far higher than in our own time. Ironically, Berkeley Coleridge died of complications after re-ceiving a faulty smallpox vaccine (Lefebure 104); among the families of the other major Romantic poets alone, the Wordsworths and the Shelleys lost two or more children (Moorman 2: 213–14; Holmes 281, 446, 518). Throughout the nineteenth century poorer parents continued to have more children and to lose more of them. Further, as Judith Plotz documents in her essay on Victorian comfort books, the dramatic decline in child mortality from mid-eighteenth to mid-nineteenth centuries affected older children first; infants' survival rates did not improve significantly, and sometimes seemed to worsen, until after 1900. Thus the painful separation of adult and child in death was only exacerbated by Romantic child-worship; Victorian parents, like the Coleridges, Wordsworths, and Shelleys before them, too often needed comfort.

The conflict between the "Vision" Coleridge sees—leading to the "Love's Excess" he feels—and the "Words of Wrong and Bitterness" he apparently speaks to little Hartley gains another sort of significance when viewed in the context of the great debate over education that flourished at the turn of the nineteenth century. Coleridge expresses Romantic sympathy with the child's intuitive way of knowing; he also reveals older doubts, both religious and materialistic, about children's souls and minds; and he touches on the controversy over the value to children of fairy tales. His first eight lines clearly establish Hartley as the innocent, spiritual child of the *Lyrical Ballads* and William Blake's *Songs of Innocence*; radiant with what Wordsworth was later to call "the visionary gleam" ("Ode: Intimations of Immortality from Recollections of Early Childhood" 56, in *Selected Poems* 187), little Hartley dances seemingly unconscious of either his own joy or his father's notice. In fact Coleridge's first phrase, "A little child," recalls the opening lines of "We Are Seven," "A simple Child, / That lightly draws its breath," in a stanza Coleridge wrote for Wordsworth (*Selected Poems* 49, 506). Trailing clouds of glory from heaven, how could Hartley learn anything important from his parents or any other adult teacher? In addition, Coleridge anticipates Wordsworth's negative opinion of contemporary pedagogical schemes (*Prelude* [1805] 5.290–345) when he asserts that Hartley "always *finds*, and never *seeks*": consciously to seek to expand one's knowledge will not foster, and may actually impede, the sudden imaginative recognitions, the discoveries of what is hidden, that constitute real education. Influenced by Jean-Jacques Rousseau's insistence in *Emile* on the natural goodness of man and the evils of society, Wordsworth in the *Lyrical Ballads* exceeds Rousseau in his radical rejection of pedagogical structuring: children, like adults, must be given time to feel the "impulse from a vernal wood" that will tune their souls ("The Tables Turned" 21, in *Selected Poems* 107). They must not be held to "years of toiling reason" either in or out of school ("To My Sister" 26, in *Selected Poems* 48), and they will best grow in both knowledge and virtue if they are least bound to any sort of imposed schedule, least constrained by thou-shalt-not's written over the door (Blake, "The Garden of Love" 6, in Blake 86).

Nevertheless, Coleridge lashes out at Hartley with "Words of Wrong and Bitterness," calling him—to Southey at least—a rogue, a rascal, and a little varlet and probably warning him to use his time more profitably than in dancing like a leaf in the wind. Thus Coleridge seems to revert from the Romantic idealization of childhood to the older view, a somewhat unlikely but powerful blend of Puritan morality and John Locke's empirical psychology (Pickering 211–14), whereby children were found in great need of both religious and secular instruction because, being smaller, weaker, and less developed than adults, they were inherently both more subject to temptation and more stupid (Coveney xii–xiii, 1–6). Almost as old as Christianity itself was the debate as to whether Jesus suffered the little children to come unto him because of their innate goodness or their innate corruption (Pattison 9–20). At the time Coleridge wrote his lines about Hartley, the Puritan Isaac Watts's gently worded but relentlessly scolding *Divine Songs Attempted in Easy Language for the Use of Children*, which I examine later as an influence on Wordsworth's *Lyrical Ballads*, was still a very popular children's book though nearly a century old; and a number of English writers— among them not just Christians like Mrs. Barbauld, Mrs. Trimmer, and Mrs. Sherwood (see Patricia Demers's essay) but also an influential group of secular rationalists like Thomas Day and Richard and Maria Edgeworth (see Mitzi Myers's essay)—supported themselves by producing stories that offered children practical moral advice about learning to do good and get ahead in the world.

In *The Prelude* Wordsworth encouraged the exposure of children to those types of literature—fairy tales, folk myths, ballads, romances— that would best stimulate their innate imaginative powers ([1805] 5.364–69, 475–77). Similarly, writing about Hartley, Coleridge too makes implicitly clear his belief in the value of imaginative literature for children: when he calls his son "a faery thing," it is as if the real child had taken on the supernatural aspect of "a limber elf" from a fairy tale. In the first essay below, Jeanie Watson examines Coleridge's belief in "Faery," relating it to his belief in the One Life, and ultimately to a Christian resolution of child-adult conflict; for Coleridge fairy tales *were* moral—even more deeply moral than overtly moralistic writings, since they led children to the world of Spirit. Watson argues that in "The Raven: A Christmas Tale" Coleridge unites fairy-tale elements with a "tongue-in-cheek, yet serious" tone to emphasize the need for morality while parodying the moral tale. Until recently it has been taken for granted that just as the Romantic visionaries rejected the overt didacticism of the moralists, so both the religious and rational peda- gogues eschewed the appeal to children's imagination as an invitation to sinfulness or self-indulgence: their deep, basic antagonism has been likened to that between Don Quixote and Sancho Panza (Summer- field x). However, as Coleridge's conflicting commentary on Hartley, his belief in the morality of fairy tales, and the intertextual relationship of Watts and Wordsworth illustrate in their diverse ways, there was no absolute dichotomy between visionary and moralist. In "We Are Seven" and the "Anecdote for Fathers," I further show, Wordsworth presents dialogues in which the catechizing adult and the innocent child both speak, leaving the work of synthesis to the reader. And in his essay Alan Richardson comments, "The relation of didactic writers to the fairy tale might better be described as one of appropriation than one of censorship." Richardson further shows that both the moralistic real- ists and the Romantics adapted fairy tales to their own purposes, and that these purposes were as much political as they were either spiritual or moral; thus the "Whig" moralists adapt fairy-tale elements to show children that by doing good they will rise in the world, and Words- worth's championing of fairy tales becomes for Richardson part of the poet's Burkean anti-revolutionary agenda. Similarly, for Mitzi Myers, Maria Edgeworth's rationalistic moral tale, ironically titled "Simple Susan," inscribes a complex "interplay of the generic and the generic" where the moral tale is interwoven with a pastoral romance, where paternal and maternal narrative strategies are united, and where the girl hero creates a strong identity for herself and her female readers. Part-child, part-adult at age twelve, Susan succeeds not by being an- gelic but by being necessary, acting in "a literary space where dream reward and active endeavor come together."[2]

"The Child is father of the Man" ("My Heart Leaps Up" 7, in *Selected Poems* 160); Wordsworth's epoch-making oxymoron embraces aspects of Locke's empty slate (Pickering 7) and Rousseau's natural goodness (Coveney 4) yet transcends both, as—to paraphrase Coleridge—the adult's eyes are filled with light from the child. Blessed with such vision, the adult can find beauty and joy in the natural world. Significantly, the 1801 letter-poem to Southey ends all the internal conflict over Hartley with an ecstatic postscript on the near-Edenic fecundity of the Coleridges' garden: "P. S. We shall have Pease, Beans, Turneps (with boiled Leg of mutton), cauliflowers, French Beans, &c &c— endless!—We have a noble Garden!" (*Collected Letters* 2: 729) Coleridge's epistolary exuberance here would perhaps have been repeated in poetry had he concluded *Christabel* happily in marriage and reconciliation and springtime. Celebrating a similarly primitive, chthonic power in Wordsworth, Ross Woodman argues that the poet's achievement began with the discovery, prompted by his sister Dorothy, that the true "country of romance" was not revolutionary France but his own childhood (*Prelude* [1850] 11.112). Wordsworth's ultimate "portrait of the artist as an infant," Woodman demonstrates, is "The Idiot Boy," a radical poem that celebrates "a healing nature bathed in maternal love under the rule of an eternal child" so powerful he can elude his adult narrator and wander the forest independently. Unlike Hartley Coleridge, a child like Johnny, who can never grow up intellectually, can never be entrapped or corrupted by the horrors of the intellect that caused Wordsworth's post-revolutionary crisis and Coleridge's post–Sara Hutchinson dejection. Yet as both Coleridge and Wordsworth well knew, most children do grow up into adult consciousness: thus, to invert another Wordsworthian oxymoron, nature always betrays the heart that loves her ("Tintern Abbey" 122–23, in *Selected Poems* 110). It is the "Rage & Pain" attendant upon this realization that, independently of either mortal fears or educational controversy, would still lead Coleridge to the "Love's Excess" and "Words of Wrong and Bitterness" he expresses in the lines on Hartley. The Romantic idealization of childhood leads paradoxically to child abuse and exploitation; the tender, "sweet Recoil of Love & Pity" felt after "each wild Word" approaches in its careless self-indulgence the glib hypocrisy of "innocent" Blakean aphorisms such as those concluding "Holy Thursday" and "The Chimney Sweeper": "Then cherish pity, lest you drive an angel from your door"; "So if all do their *duty*, they need not fear harm" (Blake 60, 53). And, like Christabel, the naughty, poor, sick, or dying children of Victorian fiction thus have the potential not just to disturb but perversely to gratify their adult readers—while enthralling and threatening child readers.

Further, as we have seen with the unfinished *Christabel,* there is a potential textual entrapment attendant upon the Romantic splitting of the child's and the adult's consciousnesses. Although it begins with the adult's bright "Vision" of the child as a supernatural being, Coleridge's unresolved dilemma over Hartley brings a sense of claustrophobia to the reader because the text keeps reversing and recoiling back upon itself, finally talking lightly but cynically, "as it's most used to do," because it cannot transcend the contrarieties it has itself established. Nor does Coleridge escape his dilemma in texts of more overtly harmonious tone. In the gently loving conversation-poem of February 1798, "Frost at Midnight," having recalled his own childhood pain of loneliness and homesickness while at boarding school in London, Coleridge can imagine Hartley, here less than eighteen months old, going forth blessed by God, happy at all seasons of the year, in lines that seem to open on practically infinite new possibilities:

> Therefore all seasons shall be sweet to thee,
> Whether the summer clothe the general earth
> With greenness, or the redbreast sit and sing
> Betwixt the tufts of snow on the bare branch
> Of mossy apple-tree, while the nigh thatch
> Smokes in the sun-thaw; whether the eave-drops fall
> Heard only in the trances of the blast,
> Or if the secret ministry of frost
> Shall hang them up in silent icicles,
> Quietly shining to the quiet Moon.
>
> (lines 65–74, *Poems* 242)

But Coleridge's bright imagined future for the infant Hartley here, like his vision of the "limber elf" dancing three years later, excludes the adult from direct participation in the child's joy just as, instead of freeing the child, it consigns him to the cycles of nature almost in the manner of Wordsworth's dead Lucy. Once again, as in *Christabel,* both adult and child are caught in Coleridge's frosty adult perception and "pretty" adult words that "mutter and mock a broken charm" without affording anything charming to put in its place.

While appealing to the innocent, spiritual receptivity that children were assumed to possess, Victorian children's books had to speak simultaneously to adult readers who were increasingly anxious, as they grew older, to recover their own childhood selves, lost in time, in the children about and to whom they were reading. As Coleridge's lines on Hartley prophesy, not just the content of children's literature but also its psychological power and its narrative structure were fundamentally affected by the Romantic concept of childhood.[3] Many Victorians, though influenced in varying degrees by Romanticism, continued, like Coleridge, to incorporate Christian teachings about sin and redemption; indeed some of these writers trusted faith sufficiently to see earthly life as a divine comedy, and thus to write stories with endings that looked beyond suffering. In the works of other Victorian children's writers, however, Romantic idealism met with the material realities of nature, society, and language to effect profoundly secular resolutions of the conflict, although the relationship of both child and adult to the text remains, as it was for Coleridge, crucial.

As Patricia Demers demonstrates below, Mrs. Sherwood and "Hesba Stretton" (Sarah Smith)—two Evangelical writers for children, two generations apart, whose work spanned the nineteenth century—combine differing degrees of Romantic sympathy for children with stern religious teachings about good and evil. Their texts often contain heavenly visions, Christianized "spots of time" that serve to enlighten both characters and readers and lead them to a resolution of conflicts between earthly and heavenly life (Wordsworth, *Prelude* [1805] 11.257). Demers shows that "Hesba Stretton," writing after Sherwood and more thoroughly influenced by the Romantic ideal of childhood, portrays her poor children both more concretely and more lovingly, and threatens her readers far less, than Sherwood. And similarly, Roderick McGillis argues below that in his stories for children George MacDonald—in the gentler, more sympathetic manner of "Hesba Stretton"—takes Wordsworth's belief in the sanctity of childhood and the healing sublimity of nature and Christianizes them. Nature for MacDonald does not entrap adult or child reader in the past, as it tends to do for Wordsworth, because spirit, while immanent in Nature, has ultimately a heavenly home. Childhood, like Blake's Innocence, is for MacDonald a condition to which adults must continually aspire, and which they may eventually attain through the faith that makes one as a little child—ultimately as the Christ Child.

This churching of Romantic childhood may have provided some Victorian writers and readers with a solution for the Coleridgean dilemma. Nevertheless, as Judith Plotz demonstrates, commenting on Victorian childhood death, religious consolation was not enough to comfort be-reaved parents, given the symbolic weight attached to childhood by Romanticism. Lip service is paid in these books to Christian piety, but, Plotz argues, the deeper purpose of a book like Juliana Ewing's *Story of a Short Life* is to make the child's "death bearable by making his life meaningful." It is not enough that the dying children possess the inno-cent wisdom of the Wordsworthian "Seer blest!" ("Immortality" ode 114, in *Selected Poems* 189); they must be shown to have left their mark on their surroundings, so they are portrayed as heroes in their personal struggles, in their family relationships, and in their larger communities as well. Plotz further shows that some of the comfort writers, including MacDonald, create unorthodox, morbid heavens in their stories where the souls of children sing in heavenly choirs while waiting for their parents to join them in eternity.

For Michael Hancher, writing of Lewis Carroll's Victorian won-derland, Alice surprisingly points the way towards escape from the Romantic labyrinth of time and text. Hancher takes his reader through the intriguing but entrapping looking-glass of speaker-listener, author-reader relationships, showing us reflection after reflection of Alice's dream-narrative: first, as she and it are alternately dispersed and re-newed by Carroll himself, his narrator, and Alice's fictional sister; next, as she is seen by the other characters of the stories, the real Alice Liddell, the son of George MacDonald who heard the text before pub-lication, the publisher Alexander Macmillan, and the illustrator John Tenniel; and then finally as the larger Victorian and twentieth-century reading and viewing public perceive her. For Hancher, both because of and in spite of this multiplicity of perspectives, Alice finally becomes so empowered that she breaks free to achieve a mythic status that is no longer textually determined—like Johnny wandering through the night in Wordsworth's "Idiot Boy," and unlike poor Christabel, spellbound and rejected.

Contrasting with Hancher's Alice, Frances Hodgson Burnett's Mary Lennox disappears *into* the text, apparently abandoned in the final chapters of *The Secret Garden*, because of the author's choice to em-phasize the regeneration of Mary's cousin Colin and his father rather than continuing to focus on Mary herself. Responding to Burnett's ap-parent slight and to recent feminist criticism that Mary retreats from assertive contrariety into passive conventionality, Phyllis Bixler argues below that the garden, not Mary, is the novel's main character. In leading her male relatives to the renewed garden from the labyrinthine Misselthwaite Manor, symbol of patriarchy in both its power and its cold isolation, Mary completes the final stage of a process which the whole novel records—that of permeating both garden and manor house with a nurturing power that is both Romantic and feminine, and that is symbolized in, but not limited to, the revived spiritual presence of the dead Mrs. Craven. Herself become a Romantic child of nature but with an adult's awareness of the pains of loss and separation, Mary has absorbed "the magic" of the garden into herself, has become part of a community of nurturers both male and female, and thus has no further need of her author's or her reader's notice.

In a final case for the secularization of Romanticism, Anita Moss argues that a new Romantic vision of the child emerged at the turn of the twentieth century in the works of the Edwardian writer E. Nesbit. Nesbit's vision answers the inevitable Romantic nostalgia for lost childhood with the creation of an ideal human world in which children participate not only as characters but also as their own storytellers. In her great fantasies, *The Enchanted Castle, The House of Arden, Harding's Luck*, and *The Magic City*, Nesbit endows children with her deeply held belief in the arts as the center of civilization and the imagination as the center of the self. While influenced by Christian Platonists such as MacDonald, Nesbit in effect reverses the Platonic view to emphasize that in the union of imagination with language, and of childhood's dreams with adulthood's rationality, the holy city *can* be built on earth. Armed with what Moss calls a "profoundly optimistic belief in the human capacity for transformation," Nesbit thus points in directions explored by some of the most compelling authors for children of the twentieth century—writers otherwise as disparate as Philippa Pearce, Virginia Hamilton, and Maurice Sendak—who continue to be haunted by, and thus to redefine, the Romantic figure of the child.

NOTES

1. In a notebook entry in 1823, Coleridge wrote, "Were I free to do so, I feel as if I could compose the third part of Christabel, or the song of her desolation" (qtd. in Beer 198); and according to Dr. Gillman, in whose house Coleridge lived the last sixteen years of his life, the poet once said that Christabel's suffering was "founded on the notion, that the virtuous

of the world save the wicked" (qtd. in Perkins 414). The long, magically
delightful ending, also recorded by Dr. Gillman, goes as follows:

> Over the mountains, the Bard, as directed by Sir Leoline, "hastes"
> with his disciple; but in consequence of one of those inundations
> supposed to be common to this country, the spot only where the
> castle once stood is discovered,—the edifice itself being washed
> away. He determines to return. Geraldine being acquainted with
> all that is passing, like the Weird Sisters in Macbeth, vanishes. Re-
> appearing, however, she waits the return of the Bard, exciting in
> the mean time, by her wily arts, all the anger she could rouse in
> the Baron's breast, as well as that jealousy of which he is described
> to have been susceptible. The old Bard and the youth at length ar-
> rive, and therefore she can no longer personate the character of
> Geraldine, the daughter of Lord Roland de Vaux, but changes her
> appearance to that of the accepted though absent lover of Christabel.
> Next ensues a courtship most distressing of Christabel, who feels—
> she knows not why—great disgust for her once favoured knight.
> This coldness is very painful to the Baron, who has no more con-
> ception than herself of the supernatural transformation. She at last
> yields to her father's entreaties, and consents to approach the altar
> with this hated suitor. The real lover returning, enters at this mo-
> ment, and produces the ring which she had once given him in sign
> of her betrothment. Thus defeated, the supernatural being Geraldine
> disappears. As predicted, the castle bell tolls, the mother's voice
> is heard, and to the exceeding great joy of the parties, the right-
> ful marriage takes place, after which follows a reconciliation and
> explanation between the father and daughter. (qtd. in Beer 198–99)

2. See also *Charles Dickens and the Invisible World*, where in a fine summary of the "fairy-tale heritage," Harry Stone emphasizes that although
   Dickens's heart lay with fairy tales and the imaginative writers, "he was
   also influenced by some of the very doctrines he would reject—moral
   teaching, for instance" (31).

3. Several recent critical studies have emphasized both the psychological and
   the structural importance of this dual readership; see Sale 1–21; Carpenter
   1–2; Knoepflmacher 499–500; Shavit 63–66.

WORKS CITED

Ariès, Philippe. *Centuries of Childhood: A Social History of Family Life*. Trans.
Robert Baldick. New York: Knopf, 1962.
Beer, J. B. *Coleridge the Visionary*. New York: Collier, 1962.

Blake, William. *The Illuminated Blake.* Ed. David V. Erdman. Garden City: Doubleday Anchor, 1974.

Carpenter, Humphrey. *Secret Gardens: A Study of the Golden Age of Children's Literature.* Boston: Houghton, 1985.

Coleridge, Samuel Taylor. *Collected Letters of Samuel Taylor Coleridge.* Ed. Earl Leslie Griggs. 6 vols. Oxford: Clarendon, 1956–71.

———. *The Poems of Samuel Taylor Coleridge.* Ed. Ernest Hartley Coleridge. London: Oxford UP, 1912.

Coveney, Peter. *Poor Monkey: The Child in Literature.* London: Rockliff, 1957.

Holmes, Richard. *Shelley: The Pursuit.* New York: Dutton, 1975.

Knight, G. W. "Coleridge's Divine Comedy." *The Starlit Dome.* London: Methuen, 1941. 83–97. Rpt. in *English Romantic Poets: Modern Essays in Criticism.* Ed. M. H. Abrams. 2nd ed. London: Oxford UP, 1975. 202–13.

Knoepflmacher, U. C. "The Balancing of Child and Adult: An Approach to Victorian Fantasies for Children," *Nineteenth-Century Fiction* 37 (1983): 497–530.

Lefebure, Molly. *The Bondage of Love: A Life of Mrs. Samuel Taylor Coleridge.* London: Gollancz, 1986.

Moorman, Mary. *William Wordsworth: A Biography.* Vol. 2, *The Later Years, 1803–1850.* London: Oxford UP, 1965.

Pattison, Robert. *The Child Figure in English Literature.* Athens: U of Georgia P, 1978.

Perkins, David, ed. *English Romantic Writers.* New York: Harcourt, 1967.

Pickering, Samuel F., Jr. *John Locke and Children's Books in Eighteenth-Century England.* Knoxville: U of Tennessee P, 1981.

Sale, Roger. *Fairy Tales and After: From Snow White to E. B. White.* Cambridge: Harvard UP, 1978.

Shavit, Zohar. *Poetics of Children's Literature.* Athens: U of Georgia P, 1986.

Stone, Harry. *Dickens and the Invisible World: Fairy Tales, Fantasy, and Novel Making.* Bloomington: Indiana UP, 1979.

Stone, Lawrence. *The Family, Sex and Marriage in England, 1500–1800.* New York: Harper, 1977.

Summerfield, Geoffrey. *Fantasy and Reason: Children's Literature in the Eighteenth Century.* Athens: U of Georgia P, 1985.

Wordsworth, William. *The Prelude: 1799, 1805, 1850.* Ed. Jonathan Wordsworth, M. H. Abrams, and Stephen Gill. New York: Norton, 1979.

———. *Selected Poems and Prefaces.* Ed. Jack Stillinger. Boston: Houghton, 1965.

JEANIE WATSON

"The Raven: A Christmas Poem"

Coleridge and the Fairy Tale Controversy

he Other World of fairy tale was familiar ground for Samuel Taylor Coleridge throughout his life. The intense fascination surrounding his earliest childhood reading of *The Arabian Nights* (which he read in secret dread and delight) finds adult play in his most complex theological and philosophical writing. Despite the general strictures of the time against fairy tales, the genre is central to *Christabel* and also makes a strong contribution to Coleridge's other well-known poems of mystery, *The Rime of the Ancient Mariner* and *Kubla Khan*.[1] The touch of faery marks lesser-known poems as well. Coleridge uses elements of the genre, or elements of what he calls "Faery," in his poetry from beginning to end, a fact which helps make his work appealing to children as well as adults. In addition, his adherence to a belief in the importance of Faery makes him pivotal in what has been called the "battle" over fairy tales, or what might more accurately be described as the larger issue of the value to children, and grownups, of imaginative literature.

Coleridge's advocacy of fairy tales as appropriate children's reading matter was counter to the prevailing rationalistic atmosphere of the late eighteenth century. Moral tales, stories which were overtly didactic, overly simplistic, and—to Coleridge's mind—thoroughly unappealing, were the approved childhood reading for a "rational education" in the late eighteenth and early nineteenth centuries. For Coleridge, in contrast, fairy tales have value because they are capable of intensely engaging the imagination. Coleridge suggestively calls the "Land of Faery" a "mental space" (*Notebooks* 3: 4501); thus, Faery is a state of mind, a place of imagination, a condition of existence and awareness. Tales or parts of tales that give entrance to Faery—that are about that mental

14

space—are, to the extent and for the time they do so, tales of Faery. Further, through the action of the symbolic imagination, on the part of both the author and the reader, tales of Faery become for Coleridge symbolic tales; that is, they simultaneously show forth and partake of the world of Spirit.

Whatever doubts or psychological/emotional tensions existed for Coleridge in his conceptualization of the world, both physical and metaphysical, the one fundamental constant was his belief in the consubstantiality of being. Thus, the coherency for which he always strived in philosophical, political, educational, or critical theory-making found its nexus in the profoundly spiritual reality of a consubstantial world. This fact does not negate the very real influence on Coleridge of various arenas of societal and theoretical movements and endeavors—Coleridge was, after all, caught up in the active issues of his day; but it does place those historical events within an appropriate Coleridgean framework. As J. Robert Barth puts it: "The 'consubstantiality of all being' . . . is rarely discussed by Coleridge but is everywhere present by implication or indirection" (19). The consubstantial world is a symbolic world in which spirit manifests its being as the ongoing reconciliation of polarities in the things of this world, and the things of this world— whether the process and forms of nature or the human soul or the creative imagination—simultaneously represent and participate in the One Life that is Spirit. The realm of Faery becomes a symbolic metaphor for Spirit/God/the One Life, and the tale of Faery shows forth that Reality. Within this context, the tale of Faery may be more profoundly "moral" than the moral tale because it leads to the spiritual truths upon which morality is based. In this essay, then, I want first to trace some of the history of the fairy tale controversy which reached its peak during Coleridge's youth, as a context for discussing Coleridge's response to it and the rationale for his advocacy of fairy tales. Finally, I want to look in some detail not at one of the poems of mystery but at an occasional poem, "The Raven: A Christmas Tale," which serves as a tongue-in-cheek, yet serious, argument on Coleridge's side of the "debate."

Born in 1772, Coleridge grew up at a time when fairies and fairy stories in general were under suspicion. Although literary fairy tales, in the form of French tales, had begun entering the English market as early as 1699 and were extremely popular in the early and mid-eighteenth century,[2] these, as well as local superstitious tales of fairies and goblins, were increasingly thought to be, at the least, "prejudicial nonsense" (Kilner viii) or, at the worst—following the lead of John Locke's theories of human development and education—extremely harmful, especially to children. As Samuel Pickering explains, Locke, in the *Essay Concerning Human Understanding* and *Some Thoughts Concerning Education,*

> warned parents particularly against letting servants frighten children with "Notions of *Spirits* and *Goblings*" and "of *Raw-Head* and *Bloody Bones*," the matter of old wives' and fairy tales. Once such "*Bug-bear* Thoughts . . . got into the tender Minds of Children," he stated, they sank deep and fastened "themselves so as not easily, if ever, to be got out again." Not only did they "haunt" children with "Strange Visions," but they made them "afraid of their Shadows and Darkness all their Lives after." Even worse was the effect such stories had on religion. "Coming abroad into the World," young adults whose "tender Minds" had received "early Impressions of *Goblins, Spectres,* and *Apparitions*" and who had suffered "fearful Apprehensions, Weakness, and Superstition" as a result, often grew "weary and asham'd." In order to make "a thorough Cure, and ease themselves of a load, which has sate so heavy on them," Locke wrote, they threw "away the thoughts of all *Spirits* together" and ran "into the other but worse extream [*sic*]." (42–43)[3]

So influential were Locke's ideas that in 1803, Lucy Aikin could write in the preface to her *Poetry for Children* that fairy tales were no longer a danger to children, since the " 'wand of reason' had banished 'dragons and fairies, giants and witches' from the nursery."

Banishment of the fairies had been attempted long before the end of the eighteenth century and with as little ultimate success.[4] Geoffrey Chaucer's Wife of Bath said that in King Arthur's day, Britain was full of fairy folk, now driven away by the friars. The fairies, however, knew how to bide their time, live with country people, and wait for their re-emergence in the English Renaissance at the hands and in the lands of William Shakespeare's *A Midsummer Night's Dream,* Edmund Spenser's *Faerie Queene,* Michael Drayton's *Nymphidia,* and a host of other, lesser works.[5] The Renaissance world of fairies was a crowded one, filled with "bull beggars, spirits, witches, urchens, elves, hags, fairies, satyrs, pans, fauns, sylens, pit with the cansticke, tritons, centaurs, dwarfes, giants, imps, calcars, conjurors, nymphs, changlings, incubus, Robin good-fellowe, the spoorne, the mare, the man in the oke, the hell waine, the fierdrake, the puckle, Tom Thombe, hob goblin, Tom tumbler, boneless, and other such bugs," to give only Reginald Scot's list of creatures used at the time to frighten children and to people superstitious stories (152–53). This motley tribe originated as part of the oral tradition, and lived partly in legend and romance (Christian, Arthurian, or otherwise), partly in prose, partly in ballad; it fed on simple superstition and existed in common faith and communal story; it inhabited the imaginative world of the fabulous. It was never truly banished; instead, in the rationalistic seventeenth and eighteenth centuries, it stepped sideways, out of the mainstream of legitimate, suitable moral literature and into the "Other World" of the chapbook, in the process becoming universally available.

Chapbook literature encompassed everything. It was, as F. J. Harvey Darton says, a "pedlar's pack": "In short, the chapbook, from 1700 to 1840 or thereabouts, contained all the popular literature of four centuries in a reduced and degenerate form: most of it in a form rudely adapted for use by children and poorly educated country folk" (81–82). It should be noted that included as major components of this extremely popular chapbook literature were the fairy tales—both native English tales like *Jack the Giant-Killer* and the French tales like *Beauty and the Beast*, medieval and Arthurian romance, and Bunyan's *Pilgrim's Progress*.

Vital and flourishing as the chapbook tradition was—with its strong component of fairy and other imaginative stories—it was, nonetheless, outside the mainstream of acceptable children's literature. One of the most vocal and influential proponents of Locke's views concerning the danger to children of imaginative literature in general, and fairy tales in particular, was Sarah Trimmer. Born in 1741 and herself the successful author of many books, including *An Easy Introduction to the Knowledge of Nature* and *Reading the Holy Scriptures: Adapted to the Capacities of Children* (1780), *Fabulous Histories; or, The Robins* (1786), and treatises on education, Mrs. Trimmer established a review, *The Guardian of Education* (1802–6). With *The Guardian* as her forum, she wrote articles, reviewed children's books, and answered correspondence from readers—all in an attempt to preserve the innocence and promote the morals of youthful readers. The philosophical basis of the late eighteenth century's distrust of imaginative literature can be seen in Mrs. Trimmer's review of *Bible Stories, memorable Acts of the Ancient Patriarchs, Judges, and Kings, extracted from their original Historians, for the Use of Children,* by William Scolfield (*Guardian of Education* 1: 244–64), a review which grows into a discussion of the highly dubious desirability of encouraging the faculty of imagination in children. Ironically, Mrs. Trimmer's extended quotations from Scolfield, which she evidently thought would bolster her own position, actually tend to function in a contrary way.

Scolfield's preface laments the fact that books for children are no longer written to engage the imagination of children. In contrast with the products of the present day, he says, the old books "did not stop at every turn to moralize in language which no child's understanding can comprehend, and no child's temper relish. The old books described the real temper and passions of human beings. Their scenes were supernatural and impossible, but their personages were of our own species"—at which point, Mrs. Trimmer asks: "Are giants, dragons, and fairies then of our own species?" "The modern books, on the other hand," continues Scolfield, "abound in real scenes, but impossible personages. They would not for the world astonish the child's mind with a giant, a dragon, or a fairy; but their young people are all so *good,* and their old people so *sober,* so *demure,* so *rational,* that no genuine interest can be felt for their adventures. . . . The modern improvers have left out of their system that most essential branch of human nature, the IMAGINATION." Then, in a manner that Coleridge would have approved and in language that anticipates William Wordsworth's denunciation of contemporary pedagogy in book 5 of *The Prelude,* Scolfield concludes:

> Our youth, according to the most recent systems of education, will be excellent geographers, natural historians, and mechanics; they will tell you from what part of the globe you receive every article of your furniture, and will explain the process in manufacturing a carpet, converting metals into the utensils of life, and clay into the cups of your tea-table, and the ornaments of your chimney; in a word, they are exactly informed about all those things, which, if a man or woman were to live and die without knowing, neither man or woman would be an atom the worse. Everything is studied and attended to, except those things, which *open the heart,* which insensibly initiate the learner, in the relations and generous offices of society, and enable him to put himself in *imagination* in the place of his neighbor, to *feel* his *feelings,* and to *wish* his *wishes* (1: 246–47).

Mrs. Trimmer summarily dismisses Scolfield's concerns, citing God as her authority: "How the heart is to be cultivated by the force of *imagination* only, is to us inconceivable?—We are told by GOD himself, that *the imagination of the heart of man is evil from his youth*, and we are persuaded that this will be fully exemplified in those who have been accustomed in their earliest days to be led by it" (1: 248). Further, she dismisses Scolfield's book as a "mutilation" and warns parents: "What ideas children will form from their *own imagination* of the *Patriarchs*, or of JEHOVAH their GOD, from these lessons we cannot conceive— but they must necessarily be very erroneous ones" (1: 259).

Given her frame of reference, Mrs. Trimmer's approbation and denunciation of specific books for children are predictable. Of *The Faithful Contrast, or Virtue and Vice accurately delineated in a Series of Moral and Instructive Tales*, Mrs. Trimmer approves: "It is both *improving* and *amusing*: and let us add, that *Satan* has found no entrance here!" (*Guardian* 4: 74). Her review of Elizabeth Sommerville's *Flora; or, The deserted Child* reads as follows:

> In this little volume, "the author's view, (as she informs the public in her preface) has been to recommend gratitude, humanity, and universal good will; to discourage pride, cruelty, and gluttony; and to exemplify, that there is no creature so mean, but it may become in the hand of Providence, the instrument to effect that the greatest and most powerful might in vain struggle to accomplish." Important lessons! which the tale of Flora is well calculated to teach; and we can venture to promise young readers great pleasure in the perusal of it, and improvement also, if they pay attention to the moral instruction it conveys. A few improbabilities will be excused, in a work of imagination, when there is nothing to lead the mind astray from the path of duty. (2: 182–83)

Unfortunately, other works are rife with harmful improbabilities.

Mrs. Trimmer's tone is almost regretful as she discusses *Mother Bunch's Fairy Tales*: "Partial as we confess ourselves to be, to most of the books of the old school, we cannot approve of those which are only fit to fill the heads of children with confused notions of wonderful and supernatural events, brought about by the agency of imaginary beings. Mother Bunch's Tales are of this description" (2: 185). In the next review of this same issue, on *Histories and Tales of Past Times, told by*

Mother Goose, the musing tone initiates the discussion, but the stance is firm by the end:

> Though we well remember the interest with which, in our childish days, when books of amusement for children were scarce, we read, or listened to the history of *"Little Red Riding Hood,"* and *"Blue Beard,"* &c. we do not wish to have such sensations awakened in the hearts of our grandchildren, by the same means; for the terrific images, which tales of this nature present to the imagination, usually make deep impressions, and injure the tender minds of children, by exciting unreasonable and groundless fears. Neither do the generality of tales of this kind supply any moral instruction level to the infantine capacity. (2: 185–86)

The regretful tone is gone entirely by 1804 when Mrs. Trimmer once again takes on fairy tales, this time published as *Nursery Tales, Cinderella, Blue Beard,* and *Little Red Riding Hood:*

> These tales are announced to the public as *new translations,* but in what respect this term applies we are at a loss to say, for, on the perusal of them we recognized the identical *Mother Goose's Tales,* with all their *vulgarities of expression,* which were in circulation when those who are now grandmothers, were themselves children, and we doubt not but that many besides ourselves can recollect, their horrors of imagination on reading that of Blue Beard, and the terrific impressions it left on their minds. *Cinderella* and *Little Red Riding Hood* are perhaps merely absurd. But it is not on account of their subjects and language only that these Tales, (Blue Beard at least) are exceptionable, another objection to them arises from the nature of their embellishments, consisting of coloured prints, in which the most striking incidents in the stories are placed before the eyes of the little readers in glaring colours, representations we believe of play-house scenes, (for the figures are in theatrical dresses). In Blue Beard for instance, the second plate represents the opening of the *forbidden closet,* in which appears, not what the story describes, (which surely is *terrific enough!*) "*a floor clotted with blood, in which the bodies of several women were lying (the wives whom Blue Beard had married and murdered,*") but *the Flames of Hell were Devils* in frightful shapes, threatening the unhappy lady who had given way to her curiosity! The concluding print is, *Blue Beard* holding his terrified wife by the hair, and lifting up his sabre to cut off her head. We expected in Little Red Riding Hood, to have found a picture of the wolf tearing the poor innocent dutiful child to pieces, but happily the

number of prints was complete without it. A moment's consideration will surely be sufficient to convince people of the least reflection, of the danger, as well as the impropriety, of putting such books as these into the hands of little children, whose minds are susceptible of every impression; and who from the liveliness of their imaginations are apt to convert into realities whatever forcibly strikes their fancy. (4: 74–75)

Fairy tales being such dangerous fare for children, the prescribed antidote was a flood of moral tales. Mrs. Trimmer herself writes a goodly number, for example, *Instructive Tales*, collected from the *Family Magazine*, which was reviewed by the *British Critic* (October 1810) as tales "intended to counteract the poison of those profane and immoral books, which were at that period industriously, and too successfully, circulated among the lower classes of people." A host of others also add their moral tale contributions: Lucy Peacock, Lucy Cameron, Mrs. Barbauld, Mrs. Pinchard, Mary Pilkington, and Mrs. Sherwood, to name only a few. However, some of these "profane and immoral books" were too thoroughly a part of the popular bloodstream to eradicate altogether, so the cure was effected by surgery instead. Two examples of earlier popular works which are later "revised" by the moralists are illustrative: James Ridley's *The Tales of the Genii* and Sarah Fielding's *The Governess*.

James Ridley's *The Tales of the Genii; or, The Delightful Lessons of Horam, the Son of Asmar*—a close kin of the extremely popular and influential *The Arabian Nights*—was first published in 1764 and reprinted again and again in the next century. The work is dedicated to George, prince of Wales, with the claim that "this Work is designed to promote the cause of morality." In 1800, Elizabeth Somerville takes it upon herself to insure the moral character of the work by publishing *The Tales of the Genii; or, Moral Lessons: Abridged and Adapted to Amusement and Instruction of Youth*. The advertisement reads: "Conscious of the boldness of an attempt to abridge the Tales of the Genii, the compiler has only to plead, that in their original state, however replete with beauties, they are in many parts improper for the perusal of children. All that relates to a love of duty, religion, humanity, truth, and honour, she has carefully preserved, as proper to excite emulation, omitting only such descriptions as tend rather to inflame than benefit the mind" (iii).

The Tales of the Genii are indeed abridged, omitting, for example, in the Second Adventure of Abudah in the Groves of Shadaski, the ten beauties who lead Abudah through the "fragrant avenues"; through the "grand hall," filled with statues of nymphs, "some representing the lovely wood nymphs; some the naked beauties of the flood; others pursuing lovers; others the coyly willing virgins; who seemed, even in the ivory in which they were carved, to shew a soft reluctance" (1: 70); omitting, too, the "inner apartment, adorned with the softest sofas, whose walls were one entire mirror, which reflected the ten beauties to the amorous *Abudah* ten thousand ways; while smiles and soft languishing looks darting from on all sides at once upon him, ravished his senses beyond the power of description" (1: 71). Elizabeth Somerville also chooses to omit Abudah's bath, during which "the ten put off their own superfluous garments" (1: 71), as well as the banquet given by the queen of pleasures. Ridley and Somerville both draw the moral lesson against the "vanities and intemperance of this filthy grove" (1: 77); but the readers of the original know in great and lavish detail the vanities they are to abjure; the readers of Somerville's tale are left to their own "imagination." Ridley ends with a vision of "pagan blindness" exchanged for "Christian verities" (2: 364), but the rich tales themselves are the reason for the telling. With Somerville, the final message is all.

The case of Sarah Fielding's *The Governess*, published in 1749, is more curious, since even a modern reader of *The Tales of the Genii* must admit that the tales sometime run to a sensuality inappropriate for children. The major culprit in Fielding's collection of linked stories told at Mrs. Teachum's school, however, would seem to be innocuous fairy tales. In 1820, Mrs. Sherwood—without mentioning Sarah Fielding on the title page and referring to her only as "a sister of the celebrated Fielding" in the Introduction—rewrites *The Governess*, keeping the same title but omitting Fielding's fairy tales. In her rationale, Mrs. Sherwood notes that *The Governess* "is remarkable as having been one of the first books of the kind prepared purposefully for children: and in this view it may, perhaps, be found not uninteresting to the present generation of children, since it not only contains an exact and lively picture of their Grandmothers and Great-grandmothers, but was probably the favorite companion of their youthful days." Mrs. Sherwood omits the fairy tales:

> Several Fairy-tales were incidentally introduced into the original
> work; and as it is not unlikely that such compositions formed, at that
> period, one of the chief amusements of the infant mind, a single tale

of this description is admitted into the present edition. But since fanciful productions of this sort can never be rendered generally useful, it has been thought proper to suppress the rest, substituting in their place such appropriate relations as seemed more likely to conduce to female edification.

While one hopes the fairy tales did not contribute too substantially to the moral degeneration of all those Grandmothers and Great-grandmothers, it is even more interesting to note that the stories Mrs. Sherwood writes to replace Sarah Fielding's fairy tales might themselves be classified as fairy tales.

Fortunately for Coleridge, and subsequently for all of us, the banishment of the fairies from his particular nursery did not take place until he had read and absorbed many a fairy tale. Of the years October 1775 to October 1778, he says: "These three years [ages three to six] I continued at the reading-school—because I was too little to be trusted among my Father's School-boys—. . . . I took no pleasure in boyish sports—but read incessantly." Coleridge's reading list includes the most popular chapbooks available—"all the gilt-covered little books that could be had at that time"—fairy tales, *The Arabian Nights, Robinson Crusoe,* and all the rest. These stories then became the subject of imaginative play for the young boy: "I used to lie by the wall, and *mope*—and my spirits used to come upon me suddenly, & in a flood—& then I was accustomed to run up and down the church-yard, and act over all I had been reading on the docks, the nettles, and the rank-grass." "One tale," he adds, "made so deep an impression" that he was "haunted by spectres" when he was in the dark, and his father finally burnt the books to keep him from reading them (*Collected Letters* 1: 179). The effect of the reading was obviously as imaginatively intense as Mrs. Trimmer had suspected it would be. In *The Friend,* Coleridge explains: "Among my earliest impressions I still distinctly remember that of my first entrance into the mansion of a neighboring Baronet, awfully known to me by the name of THE GREAT HOUSE, its exterior having been long connected in my childish imagination with the feeling and fancies stirred up in me by the perusal of the Arabian Nights' Entertainments." And in a note, Coleridge elaborates:

> As I had read one volume of these tales over and over again before my fifth birthday, it may be readily conjectured of what sort these fancies and feelings must have been. The book, I well remember, used to lie in a corner of the parlour window at my dear Father's

> Vicarage-house: and I can never forget with what a strange mixture of obscure dread and intense desire I used to look at the volume and *watch* it, till the morning sunshine had reached and nearly covered it, when, and not before, I felt the courage given me to seize the precious treasure and hurry off with it to some sunny corner in our playground. (1: 148)

The book becomes a "precious treasure" precisely because the child's emotional, imaginative response, a "mixture of obscure dread and intense desire," is so strong. And although the reading contains no strictures on the proper behavior of children, it is hardly lacking in moral or spiritual instruction. In fact, just the opposite was the case.

Of the two years from October 1779 to October 1781, Coleridge declares, "I read every book that came in my way without distinction"; but as he reflects on these years, he makes a precise connection between his reading of fairy tales and his ability to accept with delight, unmixed with "incredulity," the vastness of the story of the stars. On a winter's evening walk, the eight-year-old boy listens as his father talks about the planets and constellations: "I heard him with a profound delight & admiration; but without the least mixture of wonder or incredulity. For from my early reading of Faery Tales, & Genii &c &c—my mind had been habituated *to the Vast*—& I never regarded *my senses* in any way as the criteria of my belief. I regulated all my creeds by my conceptions not by my *sights*—even at that age." Then, going in the face of a century of Lockean philosophy and strictures against fairy tales, Coleridge confidently continues:

> Should children be permitted to read Romances, & Relations of Giants & Magicians, & Genii?—I know all that has been said against it; but I have formed my faith in the affirmative.—I know no other way of giving the mind a love of 'the Great', & 'the Whole'.— Those who have been led to the same truths step by step thro' the constant testimony of their senses, seem to me to want a sense which I possess—They contemplate nothing but *parts* and all *parts* are necessarily little—and the Universe to them is but a mass of *little things*.—It is true, that the mind *may* become credulous & prone to superstition by the former method—but are not the Experimentalists credulous even to madness in believing any absurdity, rather than believe the grandest truths, if they have not the testimony of their own senses in their favor?—I have known some who have been rationally educated, as it is styled. They were marked by a microscopic acuteness; but when they looked at great things, all became a blank & they saw nothing—and denied (very logically) that any

thing could be seen: and uniformly put the negation of a power for the possession of a power—& called the want of imagination Judgment, & the never being moved to Rapture Philosophy. (*Collected Letters* 1: 354).

Coleridge's sense of the unity of being, which formed his understanding of the relationship between physical and spiritual realities as a young boy, never leaves him. Seeming opposites are reconciled, and the human spirit, through the creative imagination, acknowledges its participation in Spirit. It is precisely this imaginative comprehension of " 'the Great', & 'the Whole' "—the comprehension of the world of Spirit—that consumes Coleridge's entire intellectual and practical life and that he tries to pass on to his children, using the same means that functioned so effectively for him: fairy tales.

Coleridge's son Hartley was reading or being read fairy tales by the age of six, as is evident from a letter to Coleridge from Charles Lamb who, with his sister Mary, had been selecting books for Hartley. Lamb was convinced that "wild tales" (a popular name for fairy tales and other imaginative stories), which encouraged the imagination, were better for children than the currently prolific moral tales, epitomized by the writing of Mrs. Barbauld, Mrs. Trimmer, *et al.* On October 23, 1802, Lamb writes to Coleridge, complaining:

> "Goody Two Shoes" is almost out of print. Mrs. Barbauld's stuff has banished all the old classics of the nursery; and the shopman at Newbery's hardly deigned to reach them off an old exploded corner of a shelf, when Mary asked for them. Mrs. B.'s and Mrs. Trimmer's nonsense lay in piles about. Knowledge insignificant and vapid as Mrs. B.'s books convey, it seems, must come to a child in the *shape of knowledge*, and his empty noddle must be turned with conceit of his own powers when he has learnt that a Horse is an animal, and Billy is better than a Horse, and such like; instead of that beautiful Interest in wild tales which made the child a man, while all the time he suspected himself to be no bigger than a child. Science has succeeded to Poetry no less in the little walks of children than with men. Is there no possibility of averting this sore evil? Think what you would have been now, if instead of being fed with Tales and old wives' fables in childhood, you had been crammed with geography and natural history?

Still fuming, Lamb concludes: "Damn them! I mean the cursed Barbauld Crew, those Blights and Blasts of all that is Human in man and child" (Lamb 1: 326).[6]

Coleridge's daughter, Sara Coleridge—who, as Carl Woodring comments, "on the eve of Christmas Eve, 1802, was born a child of nature and of faerie" (211)—also listened to the fairy tales of her father and others. Eventually, she wrote her own fairy tale for children, *Phantasmion*, published in 1837.[7] It is evident, however, that, even at that date, fairy tales had not gained unqualified acceptance. In a letter to Arabella Brooke of July 29, 1837, Sara writes: "In these days, to print a Fairy Tale is the very way to be *not read*, but shoved aside with contempt. I wish, however, I were only as sure that *my* fairy tale is worth printing, as I am that works of this class are wholesome food, by way of variety, for the childish mind. It is curious that on this point Sir Walter Scott and Charles Lamb, my father, My Uncle Southey, and Mr. Wordsworth were all agreed" (Sara Coleridge 1: 181–82).

Fairy tales are wholesome food for the child's spirit, and the effect that Coleridge identifies with a child's fairy tale experience—that of the imaginative comprehension of the wholeness and unity of Spirit— is evident in his daughter as well as himself. Coleridge's life occupation was that of "traveller through the heavenly country" (Sara Coleridge 2: 30), and Faery and fairy tale elements are important and integral parts of his travel stories.

Although Coleridge's use of Faery as symbolic metaphor is more metaphysically significant than for most other writers, there is also a real sense in which his choice is simply a natural reaction against the extreme rationalistic nature of the time, a choice which places him in good company with Scott, Lamb, Southey, and Wordsworth—as his daughter noted. Simultaneously, it is related to an emerging interest in oral literature—in verse and prose, ballad and tale—occurring in Britain and Germany, and to concomitant interests in common folk and their lives and story traditions. Mrs. Trimmer's voice, loud as it was, was not the only voice to be heard in the land; by the turn of the century, the voice of imagination could whisper in a child's ear.

Meanwhile, Coleridge's tongue-in-cheek, but nonetheless serious, "revenge" on Mrs. Barbauld and Crew and their moral tales comes in a small, now obscure, poem called "The Raven." "The Raven" was first published as a piece of nonsense in *The Morning Post*, March 10, 1798, without title or headnote. As such, the poem is a bit of a "doggerel," as Coleridge himself calls it, with a surprise twist at the end. The speaker is assumed to be an adult, stringing together chronological but unconnected events in an *ad hoc* sort of way. When the poem was included in the 1817 *Sibylline Leaves*, however, Coleridge made several additions which focused the impact of the poem and made it a satiric commentary on moral tales and "rational education." The 1817 poem follows:

The Raven

A CHRISTMAS TALE, TOLD BY A SCHOOL-BOY TO HIS LITTLE
    BROTHERS AND SISTERS

Underneath an old oak tree
There was of swine a huge company,
That grunted as they crunched the mast:
For that was ripe, and fell full fast.
Then they trotted away, for the wind grew high:
One acorn they left, and no more might you spy.
Next came a Raven, that liked not such folly:
He belonged, they did say, to the witch Melancholy!
Blacker was he than blackest jet,
Flew low in the rain, and his feathers not wet.
He picked up the acorn and buried it straight
By the side of a river both deep and great.
    Where then did the Raven go?
    He went high and low,
Over hill, over dale, did the black Raven go.
    Many Autumns, many Springs
    Travelled he with wandering wings:
    Many Summers, many Winters—
I can't tell half his adventures.
At length he came back, and with him a She,
And the acorn was grown to a tall oak tree.
They built them a nest in the topmost bough,
And young ones they had, and were happy enow.
But soon came a Woodman in leathern guise,
His brow, like a pent-house, hung over his eyes.
He'd an axe in his hand, not a word he spoke,
But with many a hem! and a sturdy stroke,
At length he brought down the poor Raven's own oak.
His young ones were killed; for they could not depart,
And their mother did die of a broken heart.

The boughs from the trunk the Woodman did sever;
And they floated it down on the course of the river.
They sawed it in planks, and its bark they did strip,

And with this tree and others they made a good ship.
The ship, it was launched; but in sight of the land
Such a storm there did rise as no ship could withstand.
It bulged on a rock, and the waves rush'd in fast;
Round and round flew the Raven, and cawed to the blast.
He heard the last shriek of the perishing souls—
See! see! o'er the topmast the mad water rolls!
   Right glad was the Raven, and off he went fleet,
And Death riding home on a cloud he did meet,
And he thank'd him again and again for this treat:
   They had taken his all, and REVENGE IT WAS SWEET!

The changes Coleridge makes are significant. First, he adds the title, "The Raven," naming the poem after the central character. The events, which to any objective observer seem random and unrelated, are thus now more clearly seen to be connected by the perspective of the Raven. The swine, as swine will do, eat the mast (the nuts accumulated on the ground and used as food for swine) and then run away. That they eat all the acorns save one is a fact that the Raven, who next happens on the scene, thinks "folly." He buries it beside a river and flies away. During the "many Autumns, many Springs" of the Raven's wanderings, the acorn grows into an oak tree to which—almost as though he has been waiting for it to mature—the Raven returns with a "She." They build a nest in what has now been claimed as the "Raven's own oak." The Woodman who comes, merely fulfilling his function as a woodman, is seen through the Raven's eyes as a malicious evildoer with a sinister, sloping brow. Ominously silent, he chops down the tree. Her young ones cruelly murdered by the Woodman, the Mother Raven dies of a broken heart, and the Raven watches as the Woodman and his "accomplices" saw the tree into planks, strip the bark, and build a ship. When the storm comes and the ship is wrecked, the Raven's caws of delight match the "last shriek of the perishing souls." The Raven has had his revenge.

As adult readers, we might comment, "But the Woodman was only doing his job and didn't see the nest at the top of the tree." Or "Those people didn't deserve to die; they didn't even *know* about the Raven." Similarly, the pigs were only being pigs when they ate the mast, and the Raven was simply fulfilling his natural role as a male raven when he and his mate built a nest in the oak tree. Clearly, it is the Raven and the poem's narrator who are interpreting the objective and value-free facts of the case. Even more to the point, there are other, more expected, interpretations available, if one is inclined to interpret at all. For example, shouldn't the poem—with its acorn growing into a tree which is then made into a ship—really be about growth and the process of life? Or shouldn't it be about the acceptance of life's tragic events or about forgiving those who have wronged you? The poem's narrative provides for several conventional—and anticipated—morals, and we expect an acceptable, didactic, moral ending. What we get instead is an utterly unrepentant Raven who is "right glad" about the death of all those souls and who again and again thanks Death for the wonderful "treat" of the drowning. There is no remorse in the last line: "REVENGE IT WAS SWEET!"

Coleridge has taken a standard, rather contrived and silly moral tale narrative and turned it inside out. To make the point even clearer, he adds the headnote telling us that this is "a Christmas Tale, Told by a School-boy to His Little Brothers and Sisters." Rather than having a parent or other adult figure telling the moral tale with the appropriate, expected ending, we have a child, a schoolboy, instructing his younger brothers and sisters. Here is our "rationally educated" child who, home from school during the season of love and forgiveness, provides the lesson that "revenge is sweet!" His moral education seems to have gone awry. The Raven can reasonably be seen as a projection of the schoolboy narrator himself who sees himself as the center of the universe, with all events being personally related to him—a distorted view, but one that is psychologically right as a child's perspective. In addition, Coleridge knows that no matter what moral injunctions about forgiveness a child is given, he or she *enjoys* getting revenge for the "injustices" that seem to abound in the world of childhood. At one level, through the story, the schoolboy is telling his siblings, "Don't mess with me, or you'll be sorry!"

Though the Raven's story is one of revenge, it *is* a story; and the act of telling it is an emotionally positive one for the schoolboy, a way of harmlessly externalizing emotional felt-realities, as well as "playing out" a desire for retribution. Since the Raven belongs to the witch Melancholy, he is "magical"—*his* feathers don't get wet in the rain! Further, the Raven exults that at his need, he can even command Death to ride in on a cloud to help him get even with those who have wronged him. The Raven and, by extension, the child feel personally invulnerable. The Raven and the boy have a right to their angry feelings over life's injustices. The feelings are natural, and the expression of them is healthy. The child's ability to conceive of himself as magical and to project his feelings of aggression and injustice into a story in which he can safely identify himself with the witch Melancholy and with Death gives him a psychologically constructive outlet for his feelings. As the schoolboy tells the story, he may even begin to recognize the egocentric extremism of the Raven's response. Thus, the story may serve as, in Lamb's words, a "wild" tale which makes "the child a man, while all the time he suspected himself to be no bigger than a child."

In the 1817 printing, two lines (which are later removed) are tacked onto the poem: "We must not think so; but forget and forgive, / And what Heaven gives life to, we'll still let it live." Coleridge's note to the two lines speaks for itself: "Added thro' cowardly fear of the Goody! What a Hollow, where the Heart of Faith ought to be, does it not betray? this alarm concerning Christian morality, that will not permit even a Raven to be a Raven, nor a Fox a Fox, but demands conventicular justice to be inflicted on their unchristian conduct, or at least an antidote to be annexed" (*Poetical Works* 171). Surely ravens and foxes— and even, sometimes, schoolboys—can be excused from omnipresent "Christian morality." Didactic morals have little sense of humor, and, worse, they betray a lack of faith in the essential goodness of human nature. The witch Melancholy; the personified Death, who rides the stormclouds; and, of course, the talking Raven all live in the world of Faery. Through story, they give substance to subjective reality and promote growth and maturity. Coleridge, through his schoolboy narrator, addresses the children in his audience as he acknowledges and validates their feelings.

Central to both Coleridge and his schoolboy narrator is the question of the role of anger and the desire for revenge. As a natural, inevitable human emotion, what place does anger have in the scheme of the One Life? How can judgment and justice be reconciled with love and forgiveness? Anya Taylor rightly points out that the voice of vengeance in "The Raven" echoes also, for example, in *The Rime* and "The Three Graves," written during the same time period. She notes that these voices reflect Coleridge's interest in "the invisible life of the spirit" and deal with the issue of whether or not the effuxes and effluences of " 'Attraction and Repulsion' " cause "men and women [to] lose and gain power by virtue of interchanges of forces that are invisibly working through the vibrations of 'animated nature' " (104–5). Of Coleridge's footnote to the moral, Taylor comments: "He criticizes his own lack of faith that must offset the energies of nature with pious phrasing, ironically acknowledging that he has feared the dangerous feelings set loose in the earlier words. He is surprised at his own moralisms, fearing the natural rage of elemental beings" (106). Perhaps the eventual removal of the moral tag indicates Coleridge's own coming to terms with his "fear," as well as a more comfortable tolerance for the schoolboy and the Raven's emotional interpretation of events.

As a simple narrative, the Raven's story is one that children can understand and with which they can identify. In addition, at a psychological level, it allows adults a moment of self-indulgent identification, too. Who, after all, doesn't have fleeting moments of desiring revenge? But the moment of identification for the adult is tempered with objectivity and a sense of fair play. Coleridge conveys the message to his adult audience that, both psychologically and spiritually, heavy-handed didacticism is unnecessary and probably counterproductive for children's moral and spiritual growth. A child allowed imaginative play will eventually become an emotionally balanced, responsible adult, one with a perspective broad enough to encompass the Wholeness of the Universe.

NOTES

A portion of this essay has been published as part of the Introduction to my book *Risking Enchantment: Coleridge's Symbolic World of Faery* (Lincoln: U of Nebraska P, 1990).

1. My articles "Coleridge's *Rime of the Ancient Mariner:* An Encounter With Faerie" (*Children's Literature Association Quarterly* 11.4 [Winter 1987]: 165–70) and "Coleridge's Mariner in the Perilous Land" (*Charles Lamb Bulletin* ns 64 [Oct. 1988]: 270–76) discuss Coleridge's use of the fairy tale genre in *The Rime.*
2. Madame d'Aulnoy's *Contes des fées* was published in 1698 and translated into English as *Tales of the Fairies* in 1699. A three-volume edition of her works was published in 1721–22, bringing into English "The White Cat," "Finetta the Cinder-Girl," and "The Yellow Dwarf." In 1727, Charles Perrault's *Histories ou Contes du temps passé: Avec des Moralitez* was published in Paris, and in 1729 Robert Samber translated it into English as *Histories; or, Tales of Past Times.* The eight tales of Perrault's collection were "Sleeping Beauty," "Little Red Riding Hood," "Bluebeard," "Puss in Boots," "Diamonds and Toads," "Cinderella," "Riquet à la Houpp," and "Hop o' my Thumb." In 1756, clearly influenced by Sarah Fielding's *The Governess; or, Little Female Academy*, Madame Leprince de Beaumont published *Magasin des enfans* in London. This was translated into

English in 1761 as *Young Misses Magazine*. It contained "Beauty and the Beast" and "The Three Wishes." The English attitude toward fairy tales as dangerous to the rational mind shifted abruptly with the publication in 1823 of the Grimm brothers' *German Popular Stories*. By the time Hans Christian Andersen's five collections of *Wonderful Stories for Children* appeared in 1846, the acceptability, and indeed desirability, of fairy tales was firmly established. But Grimm and Andersen and the new attitude toward fairy tales was a long time in the future when Coleridge was growing up and when *Christabel* was published in 1816, and Coleridge's poetry and theories of the creative imagination did much to prepare the way. For a more thorough account of the appearance of fairy tales into English, from which I have taken much of my information, see Iona and Peter Opie's *The Classic Fairy Tales*.

3. Pickering's quotations from Locke are taken from John Locke, *The Educational Writings of John Locke*, ed. James L. Axtell (London: Cambridge UP, 1968) 114, 242–44, 303, and John Locke, *An Essay Concerning Human Understanding*, ed. John W. Yolton (London: Dent, 1965) 1, 77–80, 338.

4. See Darton, Meigs, Muir, Pickering, and Thwaite for a fuller treatment of the subject.

5. See Wooden's essay.

6. Rod McGillis's essay, "that great writer in the English language," reminds us of some of the reasons, in addition to the philosophical ones, that neither Lamb nor Coleridge was fond of Mrs. Barbauld. It also reminds us that the "debate" over imaginative literature was certainly not a simplistic or clear-cut one (*Children's Literature Association Quarterly* 13.4 [Winter 1988]: 162–64).

7. Hartley Coleridge's fairy tale, *Adolph and Annette*, until recently only in manuscript, has now been published in *Children's Literature* 14 (1986): 151–61, edited by Judith Plotz. Plotz discusses the story in the same issue in "Childhood Lost, Childhood Regained: Hartley Coleridge's Fable of Defeat" (133–48).

WORKS CITED

Aikin, Lucy, ed. *Poetry for Children*. 2nd ed. London, 1803.

Barth, J. Robert. *Coleridge and Christian Doctrine*. Cambridge: Harvard UP, 1969.

Coleridge, Samuel Taylor. *Collected Letters of Samuel Taylor Coleridge*. Ed. Earl Leslie Griggs. 6 vols. Oxford: Clarendon, 1956–71.

——. *The Complete Poetical Works of Samuel Taylor Coleridge*. Ed. Ernest Hartley Coleridge. 2 vols. Oxford: Clarendon, 1912.

————. *The Notebooks of Samuel Taylor Coleridge.* Ed. Kathleen Coburn. 5 vols. to date. Princeton: Princeton UP, 1957–.

Coleridge, Sara. *Memoir and Letters of Sara Coleridge.* Ed. Edith Coleridge. 2 vols. London: H.S. King, 1873.

Darton, F. J. Harvey. *Children's Books in England: Five Centuries of Social Life.* 1932. 2d ed. Intro. Kathleen Lines. Cambridge: Cambridge UP, 1958.

Fielding, Sarah. *The Governess: or; Little Female Academy. A Facsimile Reproduction of the First Edition of 1749.* Introd. and biblio. Jill E. Grey. Juvenile Library. London: Oxford UP, 1968.

Kilner, Dorothy. *The Histories of More Children Than One.* London. 1783.

Lamb, Charles. *The Letters of Charles Lamb.* Ed. E. V. Lucas. 3 vols. London: Dent, 1935.

Meigs, Cornelia, et al. *A Critical History of Children's Literature.* New York: Macmillan, 1953.

Muir, Percy. *English Children's Books, 1600 to 1900.* 1954. New York: Praeger, 1969.

Opie, Iona, and Peter Opie. *The Classic Fairy Tales.* New York: Oxford UP, 1974.

Pickering, Samuel F., Jr. *John Locke and Children's Books in Eighteenth-Century England.* Knoxville: U of Tennessee P, 1981.

Ridley, James. *The Tales of the Genii.* 2nd ed. London: printed for J. Wilkie, 1764.

Scot, Reginald. *The Discoverie of Witchcraft.* London: W. Brome, 1584.

Sherwood, M. M. *The Governess; or, The Little Female Academy.* Wellington: Houlston, 1820.

Somerville, Elizabeth. *The Tales of the Genii; Or, Moral Lessons, Abridged and Adapted to Amusement and Instruction of Youth.* London: Sampson Low, 1800.

Taylor, Anya. *Coleridge's Defense of the Human.* Columbus: Ohio State UP, 1986.

Thwaite, Mary F. *From Primer to Pleasure in Reading: An Introduction to the History of Children's Books in England From the Invention of Printing to 1914 with an Outline of Some Developments in Other Countries.* 1963. Rev. ed. Boston: Horn Book, 1972.

Trimmer, Sarah. *The Guardian of Education.* 5 vols. London: Hatchard, 1802–6.

Wooden, Warren W. "A Child's Garden of Sprites: English Renaissance Fairy Poetry." *Bulletin of the West Virginia Association of College English Teachers* 6 (1981): 37–54. Rpt. in *Children's Literature of the English Renaissance.* Ed. Jeanie Watson. Lexington: U of Kentucky P, 1986. 97–120.

Woodring, Carl. "Sara *fille:* Fairy Child." *Reading Coleridge: Approaches and Applications.* Ed. Walter B. Crawford. Ithaca: Cornell UP, 1979. 211–22.

ALAN RICHARDSON

Wordsworth, Fairy Tales, and the Politics

of Children's Reading

n his *Miscellanies* (1696) John Aubrey records a late sighting of an English fairy: "Anno 1670, not far from Cyrencester, was an Apparition: Being demanded, whether a good Spirit, or a bad? returned no answer, but disappeared with a curious Perfume and a melodious Twang. Mr. W. Lily believes it was a Fairie" (50). With this decorous exit, the fairies seem to have left England both in person and, largely, by reputation, thanks in part (as Aubrey elsewhere records) to the growth of literacy among the lower classes:

> Before Printing, Old-wives tales were ingeniose: and since Printing came in fashion, till a little before the civil-Warres, the ordinary sort of People were not taught to read: now-a-dayes Bookes are common, and most of the poor people understand letters: and the many good Bookes, and variety of Turnes of Affaires, have put all the old Fables out of dores: and the divine art of Printing, and Gunpowder have frighted away Robin-good-fellow and the Fayries. (290)

By the time antiquarians like Bishop Percy and Sir Walter Scott began collecting oral traditions in earnest, the "authentic" folk tale, in contrast to the popular ballad, was relatively scarce in England (Thompson 19). In its place, however, and among a sophisticated, upper-class and predominantly adult audience, a vogue had developed for imported, modernized, and often moralized fairy tales translated from French collections—Madame d'Aulnoy in 1699, Charles Perrault in 1729, Madame Leprince de Beaumont in 1761 (Pickering 40)—and from Antoine Galland's French version of the Arabic *Thousand and One Nights* first published in 1706 (Ali 11). If a newly literate "ordinary folk" had banished Robin Goodfellow and his like from their hearths, Cinderella and Scheherazade had found a place in the libraries of their betters.

34

The traditional fairy tale did not readily find a place, however, in the new literature for children that emerged in the latter half of the eighteenth century. Instead, fairy tales especially and fantasy literature in general came under attack from two sides: the rationalist school of education drawing on John Locke (Pickering 40–69) and Jean-Jacques Rousseau (Patterson), and (though significantly less so) the Christian moralist critique of children's fiction which found exponents in writers like Sarah Trimmer and M. M. Sherwood. Locke's *Some Thoughts Concerning Education* (1693) set the tone for over a century in its harsh dismissal of supernatural fictions: "I would not have children troubled whilst young with Notions of *Spirits* . . . I think it inconvenient, that their yet tender Minds should receive early impressions of *Goblins, Spectres,* and *Apparitions,* wherewith their Maids, and those about them, are apt to fright them into compliance with their orders" (302–3). For Locke, Aesop's *Fables* (a work tailored for children's reading well before the development of a children's literature proper) was "the only Book almost that I know fit for children" (298).

Sharing Locke's rational and genetic approach to education but going well beyond him to criticize a pervasively irrational, "unnatural" society, Rousseau did not consider "Fables, not even those of La Fontaine" fit for Emile's education (112); on the contrary, "reading is the plague of childhood" (116) and fables "contain nothing intelligible or useful for children" (113). The rationalist tradition in education theory represented by such figures as Richard and Maria Edgeworth, John and Lucy Aikin, Anna Letitia Barbauld, and Mary Wollstonecraft followed Locke and Rousseau in rejecting any form of fantastic or supernatural reading (often including too early an exposure to Christian notions of the soul and afterlife). In his preface to his daughter's *The Parent's Assistant* (1796) Richard Edgeworth, for example, takes Samuel Johnson to task for condescending to children's fairy tales: "Why should the mind be filled with fantastic visions, instead of useful knowledge? . . . It is to be hoped that the magic of Dr. Johnson's name will not have power to restore the reign of fairies" (xii).

The objections posed by Christian moralists were on the whole gentler but ultimately no less dismissive. Although Sarah Trimmer found her own childhood reading of Perrault relatively "harmless" (1: 63), she nevertheless rejected fairy tales as "only fit to fill the heads of children with confused notions of wonderful and supernatural events, brought about by the agency of imaginary beings" (2: 185). While Trimmer dismissed Sarah Fielding's *The Governess* for its inclusion of fairy tales,

Mrs. Sherwood revised them out of it (but inserted one of her own devising to give her version a period flavor): "Since fanciful productions of this sort can never be rendered generally useful, it has been thought proper to suppress the rest, substituting in their place such appropriate relations as seemed more likely to conduce to juvenile edification" (iv).

Edgeworth's emphasis on "useful knowledge" over the "fantastic," or Sherwood's on "edification" over the "fanciful," suggests the dualistic model—didacticism and imagination, instruction and delight, reason and fantasy—underlying most accounts of the development of children's literature. The latter term in each opposition is, of course, invariably privileged at the expense of the former. F. J. Harvey Darton, for whom children's literature forms a perpetual field of conflict between "instruction and amusement" (vii), nevertheless finds in the "return" of the fairy tale with such collections as Benjamin Tabart's *Popular Fairy Tales* (1818) and Edgar Taylor's translations of Grimm (1823–26) the transition to a more humane children's library dominated by delight (214–18). Samuel Pickering, who provides a detailed and fairly sympathetic account of the rationalist tradition, still celebrates the wiser Victorian age when "fairy tales would be welcomed with a more open imagination" (69). The triumph of the fairy tale over a didactic tradition perpetrated by a "monstrous regiment" (Muir 82) of women writers plays a similarly pivotal role in the progressive narrative informing most accounts of English children's literature.[1]

Within this pervasive schema, the first-generation Romantic poets garner praise for their defense, in the name of the imagination, of the popular fairy tale (e.g. Kotzin 12–14), although this "defense" admittedly took place more in private—through letters and unpublished manuscripts—than in public. Charles Lamb, who wrote with his sister Mary a didactic children's book (*Mrs. Leicester's School*) in the tradition of Fielding and Wollstonecraft, is celebrated for his attack on Barbauld and Trimmer in a letter to Samuel Taylor Coleridge (23 October 1802): "Is there no possibility of averting this sore evil? Think what you would have been now, if instead of being fed with Tales and old wives fables in childhood, you had been crammed with Geography & Natural History? *Damn them.* I mean the cursed Barbauld crew" (Lamb, *Letters* 2: 82). Coleridge had already written to Thomas Poole (16 October 1797) of his own "early reading of Faery Tales" in the same vein: "Should children be permitted to read Romances, & Relations of Giants & Magicians & Genii?—I know all that has been said against it; but I have formed my faith in the affirmative.—I know no other way of giving the mind a love of 'the Great,' & 'the Whole' " (*Collected Letters* 1: 354). According to Geoffrey Summerfield, whose study *Fantasy and Reason* constitutes the most recent refinement of the dichotomized, progressive history of children's literature codified by Darton, both Lamb and Coleridge pale beside William Wordsworth's "uniquely powerful defence of freedom and of fantasy in the lives of children" in book 5 of *The Prelude* (xvii). The author of the period's "most coherent and radical critique of 'moral' literature" (200), Wordsworth serves Summerfield's study of eighteenth-century children's literature as its hero, the Romantic champion of fantasy and fairy tale.

Such accounts, although they begin to seem inevitable, still remain attractive, appealing as they do to our own notions of the importance of fantasy in the lives and books of children. However, when placed in its historical context, a period when the rapid and unforeseen growth of popular literacy, the mass distribution of radical political pamphlets, and the reaction of established interests in the form of censorship and mass propaganda of their own produced what Richard Altick has called the literacy "crisis" of the 1790s (67–77), Wordsworth's patronage of fairy tales may be interpreted as something other than disinterested libertarianism. Moreover, when read critically, Wordsworth's valorization of the fairy tale can be shown to rely on a conservative, traditionalist conception of "oral literature" which, despite its presence behind most current studies of the fairy tale as children's literature, has long been discredited. Before addressing either of these problems, however, the stock opposition of fantasy and reason, imaginative and didactic literature should itself be questioned. Especially in regard to the fairy tale, it is not always clear where the moral tale leaves off and the fantasy begins.

If one concentrates on children's literature itself rather than the ongoing polemic in reviews and prefaces, the relation of didactic writers to the fairy tale might better be described as one of appropriation than one of censorship. Fairy tales were regularly appropriated for didactic purposes in at least four ways. Children's familiarity with fairy tale personages and trappings could be exploited most simply by borrowing them for the titles, prefatory matter, and packaging of otherwise didactic works, a fairy coating over the moral pill. Eleanor Fenn, author of *The Rational Dame*, entitled one of her thoroughly didactic works *The Fairy Spectator;* John Newberry's playful but decidedly Lockean *A*

Little Pretty Pocket-Book (1744) appeals to its child readers through two letters ("to little Master Tommy" and "to Pretty Miss Polly") written by Jack the Giant-Killer, returned from fairyland as an enlightened moralist. Pickering notes several such appropriations, including the disappointingly anticlimactic title *The Prettiest Book for Children; Being the History of the Enchanted Castle; Situated in one of the Fortunate Isles; and Governed by the Giant Instruction* (47). Even the "Purple Jar" of Maria Edgeworth's most celebrated moral tale has been described as "a property from a stage fairy-land" (Darton 141).

More elaborately, the didactic writer could borrow fairy tale motifs, types, and settings to construct moral fairy tales of her or his own. Rousseau himself wrote (though more for adults than for children) "La Reine Fantasque," a literary fairy tale featuring "la Fée Discrètte"; Samuel Johnson's fairy tale "The Fountains" illustrates the vanity of even magic wishes, and many of the "Oriental tales" in *The Idler* and *The Rambler* moralize the conventions of *The Arabian Nights*. Some of the most popular didactic story books included such moral fairy tales: "The Story of the Cruel Giant Barbarico" and "The Princess Hebe: A Fairy Tale" (an Oriental tale after Johnson) in Sarah Fielding's *Governess;* "The Transmigrations of Indur" and "Order and Disorder, A Fairy Tale" in Aikin's and Barbauld's *Evenings at Home;* "The History of Princess Rosalinda" in Sherwood's revision of Fielding, a surprisingly energetic tale which is, if anything, more imaginative than the one it replaces. Pickering describes several book-length didactic fairy tales, including a moralized Robin Goodfellow (62–69).

A didactic writer could also silently adapt fairy tale plots or patterns into the empirical world of the rational tale. The hero of Thomas Day's "The Good-Natured Little Boy" in *The History of Sandford and Merton* helps out a dog, a horse, a blind man, and a crippled sailor, who fortuitously reappear to save him from danger as night comes on; his pendant in "The Ill-Natured Little Boy" spurns a similar series of potential helpers and is later punished by them. The two tales together illustrate an extremely common fairy tale motif, the test which separates the kindly hero or heroine from unkindly (and usually older) siblings or other rivals (Propp 39–43). Day's *History of Little Jack* recounts the life of a boy abandoned in infancy and suckled by a goat (cf. AT 535, "The Boy Adopted by Tigers [Animals]").[2] The Cinderella story (AT 510) was moralized as *The Renowned History of Primrose Prettyface, Who By Her Sweetness of Temper and Love of Learning, Was Raised from Being the*

Daughter of a Poor Cottager, to Great Riches and the Dignity of Lady of the Manor (Avery, *Childhood's Pattern* 17); and Goody Two-Shoes, despite her own warning against "tales of *Ghosts, Witches* and *Fairies*" as "the Frolics of a distempered Brain" (56), herself rises from poverty to a bourgeois establishment in Cinderella fashion (Pickering 49).

Finally, traditional fairy tales were themselves moralized by their redactors, translators, and editors. The early fairy tale collections designed for middle-class children were cleaned up and often given didactic applications. An early (1798) children's version of *The Thousand and One Nights,* by a Rev'd. Mr. Cooper, was entitled *The Oriental Moralist* (Muir 28); Tabart's *Popular Fairy Tales,* the first such English collection, had a "decidedly moral slant" and was designed to meet the approval, in Tabart's words, of "every tender mother, and every intelligent tutor" (Avery, *Childhood's Pattern* 43–44). As John Ellis has shown, even the Brothers Grimm, despite their claims to unvarnished folk authenticity, censored some tales, selected the most acceptable version of others, and further refined the tales both in transcribing them and in revising them for later editions; Maria Tatar has more recently argued that most of these revisions were made specifically with the burgeoning children's book market in mind (3–38). Edgar Taylor's English translations of the Grimms' tales in the 1820s, which have been described as a "point of no return" in the victory of the fairies over didacticism (Summerfield xvi), were marked by a still greater degree of what Jack Zipes has termed the "bourgeoisification" of the folk tale (*Breaking* 29). Taylor assured his adult purchasers that a number of the Grimms' tales, despite their "great merit," had been passed over in deference to "the scrupulous fastidiousness of modern taste especially in works likely to attract the attention of youth" (1: xi). Those Taylor selected were further sanitized in the interests of middle-class morality. In Giambattista Basile's seventeenth-century Italian version, Cinderella is a determined young woman who murders her first stepmother by breaking her neck; in the Grimms' version, "Aschenputtel" is much more child-like and docile, although she does allow her attendant ravens to peck out her stepsisters' envious eyes at her wedding.[3] In Taylor's translation, the stepsisters are spared, the better to support her character throughout as a pattern child, "always good and kind to all about her" (2: 34).

Contrary to what might be called the Whig version of the history of English children's reading, the opposition between moral didacticism and the imaginative fairy tale is hardly absolute. Although the fairy tales remembered by Coleridge, Lamb, and Wordsworth would have been in chapbook versions rather than the blatantly moralized collections of the early nineteenth century, the Romantic sponsorship of fairy tales can nevertheless be described as a special instance of fairy tale appropriation for moral ends; it may be less ironic than is usually supposed that Lamb begins his fulminations against the cursed Barbauld crew with a lament for the passing of *Goody Two-Shoes*, "the very foundation," as Darton writes, "of the Moral Tale" (129). And we should not ignore entirely that, at a time when debates on children's literature were highly politicized, the Barbauld "crew" was dominated by liberal and radical figures like the Aikins, the Edgeworths, Joseph Priestley, Thomas Beddoes, Mary Wollstonecraft, and William Godwin (who produced a charming if sometimes awkward *Fables* designed to answer Rousseau's critique). The Romantic advocates of fairyland, on the other hand, had already turned from Godwin and their youthful radicalism toward the conservative social and political stances that would mark their later careers.

Aubrey, writing in the late seventeenth century, felt that the rise of literacy among the "ordinary sort of People" had driven away the fairies, but some folktales and literary fairy tales did find their way into the chapbooks that formed much of this group's reading (Neuberg 102–11). Although its production and distribution were almost wholly uncontrolled, the chapbook did not represent a threat to established interests. While chapbooks could be populist in tone and critical of the upper classes, Olivia Smith has argued against overestimating the political significance of Robin Hood or Jack the Giant Killer: "While the [lower-class] audience read chap-books and ballads, it was considered to have a distinct and subordinate province. Although such material might express ideas about political events, it was not regarded as an attempt to participate in public life" (ix). Not so the new political literature, written in a vernacular intellectual style and distributed in pamphlet form at low prices, that emerged in the late eighteenth century and found its apotheosis in Thomas Paine's vastly popular *Rights of Man* (1791–92). As T. J. Mathias noted in *Pursuits of Literature* (1794), the mass distribution of Paine's two-part tract effected a revolution in English reading habits: "We no longer look for learned authors in the usual places, in the retreats of academic erudition, and in the seats of religion. Our peasantry now read the *Rights of Man* on mountains, and on moors, and by the wayside" (qtd. in Smith 58–59).

Although the earlier eighteenth century apparently saw a decline in popular literacy, its sudden and unlooked-for resurgence in the 1780s and 1790s, brought out so vividly by the unprecedented sales of *The Rights of Man*, was perceived as a serious and immediate threat by the established political and religious interests (Altick 70–75). As Lawrence Stone has pointed out, the "notion that literacy is somehow good in itself, one of the natural rights of man" dates back only a hundred years or so (89), and Claude Levi-Strauss argues that literacy as a social institution has on the contrary generally "favoured the exploitation of human beings rather than their enlightenment" (337). But in order to facilitate social control, literacy and the distribution of literature must be carefully managed by those in power. The new mass readership of the 1790s had come about almost spontaneously through a highly unregulated, disorganized, private, and largely unprofessional patchwork of educational institutions: village schools, Sunday schools supported by various (often competing) denominations, Charity schools, "dame" schools, evening and Sunday classes held by clerks or artisans. The radical writers Thomas Spence and William Cobbett were taught to read at home by their fathers (Smith 97, 234), as were many others (Altick 240–59).

The English establishment's answer to the literacy crisis was to call for increased systematization and superintendence of the schools, lest they remain, as the Bishop of Rochester characterized them in 1800, "schools of Jacobinical rebellion" (Stone 86), and to hegemonize the writing and distribution of popular reading matter. Radical tracts were prohibited in 1795 and 1798 (Smith 89), but something was needed to fill their place. As William Hazlitt pointed out in retrospect, "when it was impossible to prevent our reading something," "the fear of the progress of knowledge and a *Reading Public* . . . made the Church and State anxious to provide us with that sort of food for our stomachs, which they thought best" (Altick 73).

In a period when reading designed for the working classes and for children was grouped together as "class-literature," which Charlotte Yonge (writing in 1869) defined as "books . . . for children or the poor" (229), children's literature was critically affected by the ruling interests' program for hegemonizing popular reading through such institutions as Hannah More's Cheap Repository Tracts, the Religious Tract Society, the Society for Promoting Christian Knowledge, and the early Association for Preserving Liberty and Property against Republicans and Levellers (Altick 100, Smith 68). This program included the deliberate appropriation by conservative writers of existing popular modes and styles. More, for example, who wrote fifty Cheap Repository Tracts and published one hundred between 1795 and 1797 (Smith 91), two million copies of which had been distributed by 1796 (Altick 74–75), had "made her own collection of chapbooks so that she could learn the secret of their popularity" (Neuberg 256). More and other tract writers developed an "anti-intellectual" approach meant to counteract not only the message of radical pamphlets but the popular engagement with political thought which they had fostered as well (Smith 72). For such purposes a return to the chapbook mode helped both to insure the tracts' popularity and to restore the simpler, apolitical discursive mode temporarily displaced by Paine's intellectual vernacular. As a result, "throughout the *Cheap Repository* the characters and narrative devices of traditional chapbooks were turned to moral purposes" (Pickering 129).

From a historicist perspective it becomes evident that, like the chapbook tradition of which they made a part, fairy tales could represent a harmless, pacifying alternative to radical intellectualism rather than a threat to moral seriousness. And in the early nineteenth century fairyland found unexpected allies in writers who found in fantasy a happy escape from more direct assaults on conventional morality and conservative politics. If not always edifying, the fairy tale was at least, when compared with the "master pamphlets of the day" (*Prelude* [1850] 9.97), harmless. A reviewer for the *Christian Observer* (censuring, of all things, Dr. Bowdler's *Family Shakespeare*) commended fairyland for its very distance from controversial issues: "Had the creative fancy of the poets merely summoned into being elves, fairies, and other denizens of their ideal world, not the most marble-hearted moralist would have interdicted the perusal of the drama. Oberon, Puck, Titania, Cobweb and Peachblossom [*sic*], as far as our recollection goes, are very innoxious characters" (328). *The London Magazine* in 1820 praised the "moral tendency" of Tabart's *Popular Fairy Tales,* while deploring the "corrupting" and "contaminating" "licentiousness" of the current vogue for social satire in children's poetry, a dangerous form undoubtedly produced by political hacks: "They are most probably the same who bring out the political caricatures, and personal lampoons of the day . . . They are evidently done by men ready to do anything" (480–81).

The *London Magazine*'s reviewer was further exercised by the imposition of "modern criticism" on "the solemn traditions of a people": "The nursery songs and stories, to have their proper effects, should be permitted, like the common law, to depend solely on tradition" (482). Here the appeal to "solemn traditions," the privileging of oral over written discourse, and the analogy with English common law signal the reviewer's conceptual adherence to the Burkean conservatism which, as James Chandler has shown, had so decisive an influence on the development of Wordsworth's thought in the later 1790s. Chandler traces the increasing emphasis in Wordsworth's writing on custom, on rural traditions, and on oral tales to Burke's valorization of habit and tradition, which together constitute what Chandler terms a "second nature" (66–67) for both writers. Wordsworth's Pedlar in "The Ruined Cottage" exemplifies an education guided by "second nature" rather than the suspect rational approach associated with Godwin and the Edgeworths:

> Small need had he of books; for many a tale
> Traditionary round the mountains hung,
> And many a legend peopling the dark woods
> Nourished Imagination in her growth.
> (lines 167–70, *Poetical Works* 5: 383).

Although Chandler does not consider the role of fairy tales in Wordsworth's attack on rational education in book 5 of *The Prelude*, his discussion of Wordsworth's "tales traditionary" and of the "ideological purport of writing that aspires to the condition of speech" (144) helps situate the early Romantics' defense of fairy tales in terms of the contemporary politics of literacy.

Wordsworth argues in *The Prelude* for a kind of "negative education" which might seem to ally him with Rousseau. Yet his criticisms of innovatory educational schemes in book 5 are in fact directed against the rational school of educators and writers for children in a direct line of descent from *Emile*. Wordsworth opposes the literature of this movement, with its emphasis on utilitarian knowledge and rational explanations—writings fit for a "dwarf man" (*Prelude* [1805] 5.295) rather than a child—preferring the fairy tales and legends of his own childhood:

> Oh, give us once again the wishing-cap
> Of Fortunatus, and the invisible coat
> Of Jack the Giant-killer, Robin Hood,
> And Sabra in the forest with St George.
> (5.364–67)

In contrast to the Satanic architecture of the rationalists—

> These mighty workmen of our later age
> Who with a broad highway have overbridged
> The froward chaos of futurity
>
> (5.370–72)

—the traditional tales are presented as a literal "second nature," a landscape through which Wordsworth and Coleridge freely wandered as children:

> wandering as we did
> Through heights and hollows and bye-spots of tales
> Rich with indigenous produce, open ground
> Of fancy, happy pastures ranged at will.
>
> (5.234–37)

The organic "produce" of the tales is further equated with the traditionary teachings of the poet's mother, "Fetching her goodness . . . from times past" (5.267), a "parent hen amid her brood" (5.246) whose maxims are as natural as the "innocent milk" of "mothers' breasts" (5.272). The popular ballads of children and peasants are no less natural: "Wren-like warblings made / For cottagers and spinners of the wheel . . . / Food for the hungry ears of little ones" (5.208–12). And his childhood "slender abstract of the *Arabian Tales*" (5.484) makes part of a textual landscape, "a block / Hewn from a mighty quarry" (5.487–88). Because of their rootedness in tradition, their oral perpetuation among the folk, the "tales that charm away the wakeful night / In Araby" (5.520–21) gain the permanence and inevitability of rocks, and stones, and trees: "These spread like day, and something of the shape / Of these will live till man should be no more" (5.528–29).

Although the organicized text is a common trope throughout Wordsworth's poetry and criticism, his particular insistence on naturalizing fairy tales through metaphor and his Burkean emphasis on an oral tradition equivalent in its permanence to nature suggest a subtly conservative impetus behind the Romantic defense of fantasy. Wordsworth in *The Prelude* is hardly advocating increases in literacy and political awareness among the rural laboring classes. By 1805, he had firmly rejected the "master pamphlets of the day," maintaining that their effect upon him had been disastrous and barely reparable. In a letter dated a few years later, writing of the "objectionable" contents of "penny and two-penny histories," Wordsworth expressed his wish to supplant them with "indigenous produce" of his own: "I have so much felt the influence of these straggling papers, that I have many a time wished that I had talents to produce songs, poems, and little histories, that might circulate among other good things in this way, supplanting partly the bad; flowers and useful herbs to take place of weeds" (letter to Francis Wrangham, 5 June 1808 [*Letters: Middle Years*, 1: 248]). Wordsworth's advocacy of fairy tales as "innocent" food for rural folk and children— readers of "class-literature"—can be seen, like More's use of the chapbook, as yet another appropriation of the popular tale in the interests of returning the new mass readership to an apolitical, class-specific discourse.

Wordsworth's defense of fairy tales in *The Prelude* is usually viewed from a very different perspective, as growing out of his deep suspicion of new educational modes seeking to limit, indoctrinate, and trap the child in a "pinfold of his own conceit," constantly superintended by "some busy helper" ([1805] 5.356–58). Here fairy tales might be seen as providing an ideologically neutral "open ground" between the radical pamphlet and the reactionary tract, both symptomatic of the politicization of education in "these too industrious times" (5.293). There is still much to be said for such a perspective, although it should be placed within a more fully developed account of contemporary theories of education than one based on Wordsworth's simple opposition of rationalist jailers and undisturbed natural fosterage. Wordsworth's own involvement in the educational debates of the early nineteenth century, for example, suggests a more complicated story. Within a decade of composing the 1805 *Prelude*, Wordsworth (along with Coleridge and Robert Southey) had become an advocate of Andrew Bell's "Madras system," designed initially to facilitate the socialization of the half-Indian children of English colonial officers, and brought to England in order to provide efficient, minimal schooling, through a system of teachers and student "monitors" for poor children (Byatt 186–94). In his own account of the Madras system, Bell opposed his method's inculcation of "habits of industry, morality and religion" to those "Utopian schemes for the universal diffusion of knowledge" which would "confound that distinction of ranks and classes of society, on which the general welfare hinges" (13, 90). Wordsworth shared Bell's distaste for the new institutions designed to provide substantial and continuing education for English laborers, like the Mechanics' Institutes, eventually characterizing them as "unnatural" schemes whose "means do not pay respect to the order of things," hotbeds of "discontented spirits and insubordinate and presumptuous workmen," (letter to Hugh James Rose, late January 1829 [*Letters: Later Years* 2: 23–24]).[4]

Wordsworth's depiction of the fairy tale as a natural rather than a cultural product demands critical scrutiny not simply for its contemporary political implications. In assigning the fairy tale an absolute origin, and in thus claiming for it a transcendent status beyond criticism, the early Romantics set the tone for many of the literary studies of fairy tales to follow. Claims to a pure traditional status and oral, folk origins of the fairy tale inform the work of critics as diverse as Roger Sale, Bruno Bettelheim, and Jack Zipes—three of the most widely influential writers on children's literature at the present time. And yet their work relies on Romantic theories of the fairy tale which have been widely discredited by folklorists and social historians alike.

W. H. Auden's "Afterward" to George MacDonald's *The Golden Key* typifies the persistence of the Romantic idealization of fairy tales: "Most fairy tales and myths have come down to us from a prehistoric past, anonymous stories which cannot be attributed to the conscious invention of any individual author" (83). Such an appeal to an ahistorical, communal, and necessarily oral origin underlies the approaches of the humanist Roger Sale (24–26), the psychoanalyst Bruno Bettelheim (150), and the Marxist Jack Zipes (*Breaking* 4, 20; *Fairy Tales* 3, 8), although the latter does specify a feudal, "pre-capitalist folk" origin. The Romantic myth of origin is maintained in support of the claim, in Sale and Bettelheim, that fairy tales are universal (and unassailable) expressions of human experience and, in Zipes, that European fairy tales express a utopian and thus inherently "subversive" collective folk consciousness.

There is no reason, however, to believe that most traditional fairy tales are particularly ancient, orally (or collectively) composed, or of a folk origin. As the folklorist Alan Dundes has recently pointed out, "the reality of far too much of what passes for fairy tale scholarship . . . is that [unadulterated, oral] fairy tale texts are not considered" ("Fairy Tales" 260). Folklorists agree that many tales in the standard repertory are not properly oral folktales at all. Stith Thompson, for example, states: "That many of our European and Asiatic folktales go back to a literary source is as clear as any fact in scholarship can be made" (126). Max Lüthi rejects a folk origin for fairy tales altogether: "Fairy tales certainly do not originate among simple folk but with great poets, perhaps the so-called 'initiated' or religious poets" (*Once Upon a Time* 142); and Lüthi questions the antiquity of the tales in general: "Students of the folktale have not been able to agree whether the tales still current today are many thousands of years old or only a few hundred" (*European Folktale* 2). Iona and Peter Opie find that far from degenerating from "whole and perfect" oral originals, the "classic" fairy tales have as often gained value through literary retellings: "They are as likely to have acquired significance, or to have acquired fresh significance, as they passed through sophisticated communities, as to have lost it" (21). And the Opies (like Ellis) point out the irony of the Grimms transcribing tales from supposedly untainted oral sources later traced to their originals in Andersen or Perrault (74, 102).

Another quarrel raised by folklorists and historians with the Romantic view of fairy tales concerns the importance of context in the telling or writing of a tale. As Dundes argues in "Textures, Text, and Context," a tale cannot be accurately interpreted apart from its specific tellings, through which its message can vary considerably with the teller's audience and purpose. Robert Darnton has shown that the significance of a tale like "Little Red Riding Hood" depends on whether it is told with a cautionary or merely amusing purpose (9–13), and Ruth Bottigheimer has recently demonstrated how fairy tale heroines in the Grimms' tales are "silenced" in accordance with the dominant ideology: "To the extent that these tales corroborated and codified the values of a society in which they appeared, they reinforced them powerfully, symbolizing and codifying the status quo and serving as paradigms for powerlessness" ("Silenced Women" 130). A tale can as likely be told (or published) for a repressive as for an imaginatively liberating effect. Humanists commonly complained that nurses and other paid caretakers used supernatural tales to terrify their charges into submission, a complaint we have already seen made by Locke. The folklorist Rudolf Schenda, after dismissing the "orality of fairy tales" and their "folk or lower-class origins," cites as early evidence that such tales were indeed told to children the author of a 1726 German dissertation who "writes about nursemaids and old women who frighten little girls in order to force their spirit and their common sense under the yoke of blind obedience" (78, 87).

For Schenda, the "idolatry" informing the Romantic and current literary approaches to fairy tales is not only incorrect but misguided as well, "a denial of what the folk really recounted and what the actual psycho-social requirements of the members of the lower class were" (79). It seems ironic that a Marxist critic like Zipes, whose approach is anything but unsophisticated, should nevertheless adapt the Romantic myth of a pure origin in order to support a "subversive" reading of fairy tales as projections of the utopian strivings of an underclass. Folklorists and social historians, on the contrary, view the folk tale as a predominantly conservative form. Lüthi (whom Zipes frequently cites) cautions against reading fairy tales as expressions of wish-fulfillment in general, and as "the literature of the poverty-stricken" in particular (*European Folktale* 87). The Opies similarly note that "the lowly are seldom made noble. . . . Fairy tales are unlike popular romances in that they are seldom the enactments of dream wishes" (14). Darnton explicitly rejects a "subversive" reading of fairy tales: "It would be in vain to search in such fantasies for the germ of republicanism. To dream of confounding a king by marrying a princess was hardly to challenge the moral basis of the Old Regime." Far from embodying "latent . . . radicalism," the folktale trickster validates the system by successfully exploiting its loopholes (59).

Whether we view the fairy tale as a safety valve for lower class aspirations, as politically neutral entertainment, or as a particularly subtle instrument of socialization, it would be naive uncritically to celebrate Wordsworth and his literary circle for liberating children's literature. When the Romantic brief for the fairy tale is set against contemporary debates on literacy and education, and when the traditionalist, conservative discourse of Wordsworth's defense has been traced to its Burkean matrix, it becomes more difficult to distance the Romantics from the common practice of fairy tale appropriation. Unlike the Grimms or the English ballad collectors, the Romantics were not motivated by the rediscovery of a national folk culture or by local antiquarianism, since the tales they mention most often and most fondly derive from a Persian literary collection by way of an Arabic recension and French translation. The "revival" of the fairy tale does fit remarkably well, however, with the call for a harmless "food" for the new mass readership recalled by Hazlitt, with the conscious attempts of More and others to reestablish the apolitical discourse of the chapbooks, and with Burke's influential valorization, in response to revolution in France and radicalism in England, of custom and tradition.

Unlike William Blake, whose *Songs of Innocence*—particularly "The

Lamb," "The Chimney Sweeper," and "The Little Black Boy"—expose and deconstruct the disciplinary strategies informing contemporary children's literature, schooling, and religious instruction alike, Wordsworth responds to the politicization of childhood in the 1790s by idealizing the child and attributing to it an "ideology-proof, organic sensibility" naturally resistant to radical and conservative indoctrination alike (Richardson 861). In place of Blake's subversive songs with their poetics of resistance, Wordsworth chose to advocate instead an "innocent," traditional children's reading that implicitly supported the reaction against an informed and politically engaged lower-class readership—"discontented spirits" and "presumptuous workmen."

Such a conclusion will seem harsh, and is admittedly polemical. It is meant, however, as a step toward rethinking the role of childhood in late eighteenth- and early nineteenth-century culture, a project which requires a profound revaluation of Romantic attitudes toward education and children's reading. Rather than maintain a simplistic opposition between didacticism and fantasy, indoctrination and a negative "natural" education—a model inherited from the Romantics themselves—critical studies might profitably develop more complex approaches attuned to the intricate politics of literacy and education in the Romantic period. A new history of children's literature in England, for example, could take into account such sympathetic reappraisals of didactic writers as Marilyn Butler's work on Maria Edgeworth and Mitzi Myers's on Mary Wollstonecraft, as well as the critique of fairy tales posed by feminist critics like Marcia Lieberman and Karen Rowe. The study of Romantic attitudes toward education could take greater cognizance of the Romantics' own involvement in debates on educational policy, the links between rationalist education schemes and radical politics, the conservative reaction against education for the poor, and Michel Foucault's suggestive juxtaposition of the discourses of the prison, the factory, and the school in *Discipline and Punish*. And studies of nineteenth-century childhood generally could profit from greater attention to Jacqueline Rose's analysis of the special "contradictions and difficulties" involved in addressing "how our culture constitutes and reproduces its image of the child" (112). Such revaluations demand, however, that we first assess our own investment in the Romantic idealization of childhood and its fairy tales.

25

NOTES

1. For a recent textbook statement of the pivotal return of the fairy tale, compare John Rowe Townsend, *Written for Children:* "In the early nineteenth century . . . imagination emerged from the long imprisonment it had suffered in the name of reason; and the old fairy tales, which had circulated mainly by word of mouth and in the humbler forms of print, began to find their place in the 'approved' children's literature . . . they were joined by the modern fairy tale and fantasy" (90).

2. Tale type (AT) numbers are taken from Antti A. Aarne, *The Types of the Folktale.*

3. Translations of the Basile and Grimm versions can be found in Dundes, *Cinderella* (3–13, 22–29).

4. Compare Coleridge in *The Statesman's Manual* (1816): "The humblest and least educated of our countrymen must have wilfully neglected the inestimable privileges, secured to all alike, if he has not himself found . . . the sufficiency of the Scriptures in all knowledge requisite for a right performance of his duty as a man and a christian. Of the labouring classes . . . more than this is not demanded, more than this is not perhaps generally desirable—'They are not sought for in public counsel, nor need they be found where politic sentences are spoken.—It is enough if every one is wise in the working of his own craft: so best will they maintain the state of the world' " (*Lay Sermons* 7).

WORKS CITED

Aarne, Antti A. *The Types of the Folktale: A Classification and Bibliography.* Trans. and rev. Stith Thompson. 2nd rev. ed. Folklore Fellows Communications 184. Helsinki: Suomalainen Tiedeakatemia, 1961.

Aikin, John, and Anna Letitia Barbauld. *Evenings at Home; Or, The Juvenile Budget Opened.* 12th ed. 6 vols. London: Baldwin, Cradock and Joy, 1819.

Ali, Muhsin Jassim. *Scheherazade in England: A Study of Nineteenth-Century English Criticism of the Arabian Nights.* Washington: Three Continents, 1981.

Altick, Richard D. *The English Common Reader: A Social History of the Mass Reading Public, 1800–1900.* Chicago: U of Chicago P, 1957.

Aubrey, John. *Three Prose Works: Miscellanies, Remaines of Gentilisme, Observations.* Ed. John Buchanan-Brown. Carbondale: Southern Illinois UP, 1972.

Auden, W. H. Afterword. *The Golden Key.* By George MacDonald. New York: Farrar, Straus and Giroux, 1967. 81–85.

Avery, Gillian. *Childhood's Pattern: A Study of the Heroes and Heroines of Children's Fiction, 1770–1950*. London: Hodder and Stoughton, 1975.

———. *Nineteenth Century Children: English Children's Stories, 1780–1900*. London: Hodder and Stoughton, 1965.

Bell, Andrew. *An Analysis of the Experiment in Education, Made at Egmore, near Madras*. 3rd ed. London: Cadell and Davies, 1807.

Bettelheim, Bruno. *The Uses of Enchantment: The Meaning and Importance of Fairy Tales*. New York: Vintage, 1977.

Bottigheimer, Ruth B., ed. *Fairy Tales and Society: Illusion, Allusion and Paradigm*. Philadelphia: U of Pennsylvania P, 1986.

———. "Silenced Women in the Grimms' Tales: The 'Fit' Between Fairy Tales and Society in Their Historical Context." Bottigheimer, *Fairy Tales* 115–132.

Butler, Marilyn. *Maria Edgeworth: A Literary Biography*. Oxford: Clarendon, 1972.

Byatt, A. S. *Wordsworth and Coleridge in Their Time*. London: Nelson, 1970.

Chandler, James K. *Wordsworth's Second Nature: A Study of the Poetry and Politics*. Chicago: U of Chicago P, 1984.

Coleridge, Samuel Taylor. *Collected Letters of Samuel Taylor Coleridge*. Ed. Earl Leslie Griggs. 6 vols. Oxford: Clarendon, 1956–71.

———. *Lay Sermons*. Ed. R. J. White. *The Collected Works of Samuel Taylor Coleridge*. Vol. 6. Princeton: Princeton UP, 1972.

Darnton, Robert. "Peasants Tell Tales: The Meaning of Mother Goose." *The Great Cat Massacre and Other Episodes in French Cultural History*. New York: Vintage, 1984. 9–74.

Darton, F. J. Harvey. *Children's Books in England: Five Centuries of Social Life*. 1932. 3rd ed. Rev. Brian Alderson. Cambridge: Cambridge UP, 1982.

Day, Thomas. "The History of Little Jack." *The Children's Miscellany*. London: John Stockdale, 1788.

———. *The History of Sandford and Merton*. New York: Derby and Jackson, 1857.

Dundes, Alan. *Cinderella: A Folklore Casebook*. New York: Garland, 1982.

———. "Fairy Tales from a Folkloristic Perspective." Bottigheimer, *Fairy Tales* 259–70.

———. "Texture, Text, and Context." *Interpreting Folklore*. Ed. Alan Dundes. Bloomington: Indiana UP, 1980. 20–32.

Edgeworth, Richard Lovell. Preface. *The Parent's Assistant; or, Stories for Children*. By Maria Edgeworth. Rev. ed. London: Longman, 1858. v–xii.

Ellis, John M. *One Fairy Story Too Many: The Brothers Grimm and Their Tales*. Chicago: U of Chicago P, 1983.

Rev. of *The Family Shakespeare*, by Thomas Bowdler. *Christian Observer* 7 (1808): 326–34.

Fielding, Sarah. *The Governess; or, Little Female Academy. A Facsimile Reproduction of the First Edition of 1749.* Introd. and biblio. Jill E. Grey. Juvenile
Library. London: Oxford UP, 1968.

Foucault, Michel. *Discipline and Punish: The Birth of the Prison.* Trans. Alan
Sheridan. New York: Vintage, 1979.

The History of Little Goody Two-Shoes. London: J. Newbery, 1765.

Johnson, Samuel. "The Fountains: A Fairy Tale." *Children's Literature*
6 (1977): 42–53.

Kotzin, Michael C. *Dickens and the Fairy Tale.* Bowling Green: Popular, 1972.

Lamb, Charles, and Mary Lamb. *The Letters of Charles and Mary Lamb.* Ed.
Edwin A. Marrs, Jr. 3 vols. to date. Ithaca: Cornell UP, 1975–.

Levi-Strauss, Claude. *Tristes Tropiques.* Trans. John and Doreen Weightman.
New York: Washington Square, 1977.

Lieberman, Marcia. " 'Some Day My Prince Will Come': Female Acculturation through the Fairy Tale." *College English* 34 (1972): 383–95.

"The Literature of the Nursery." Rev. of *Popular Tales*, by Benjamin Tabart.
The London Magazine 2 (1820): 477–83.

Locke, John. *The Educational Writings of John Locke: A Critical Edition
With Introduction and Notes.* Ed. James L. Axtell. Cambridge: Cambridge
UP, 1968.

Lüthi, Max. *The European Folktale: Form and Nature.* Trans. John D. Niles.
Philadelphia: Institute for the Study of Human Issues, 1982.

———. *Once Upon a Time: On the Nature of Fairy Tales.* Trans. Lee Cha-
deayne and Paul Gottwald. Bloomington: Indiana UP, 1976.

Muir, Percy. *English Children's Books, 1600–1900.* London: Batsford, 1954.

Myers, Mitzi. "Impeccable Governesses, Rational Dames, and Moral Mothers:
Mary Wollstonecraft and the Female Tradition in Georgian Children's
Books." *Children's Literature* 14 (1986): 31–59.

Neuberg, Victor E. *Popular Literature: A History and Guide.* London: Penguin, 1977.

Newbery, John. *A Little Pretty Pocket-Book.* Ed. M. F. Thwaite. London:
Oxford UP, 1966.

Opie, Iona, and Peter Opie. *The Classic Fairy Tales.* New York: Oxford
UP, 1974.

Patterson, Sylvia W. *Rousseau's Emile and Early Children's Literature.* Metuchen: Scarecrow, 1971.

Pickering, Samuel F., Jr. *John Locke and Children's Books in Eighteenth-
Century England.* Knoxville: U of Tennessee P, 1981.

Propp, Vladimir. *Morphology of the Folktale.* 2nd ed. Trans. Laurence Scott
and Louis A. Wagner. Austin: U of Texas P, 1968.

Richardson, Alan. "The Politics of Childhood: Wordsworth, Blake, and Cate-
chistic Method." *ELH* 56 (1989): 853–68.

Rose, Jacqueline. *The Case of Peter Pan or The Impossibility of Children's Fiction*. London: Macmillan, 1984.

Rousseau, Jean-Jacques. *Emile; or, On Education*. Trans. Allan Bloom. New York: Basic, 1979.

———. "La Reine Fantasque." *Oeuvres Complètes*. 4 vols. Paris: Gallimard, 1959–69. 1179–92.

Rowe, Karen E. "Feminism and Fairy Tales." *Women's Studies* 6 (1979): 237–57.

Sale, Roger. *Fairy Tales and After: From Snow White to E. B. White*. Cambridge: Harvard UP, 1978.

Schenda, Rudolf. "Telling Tales—Spreading Tales: Change in the Communicative Forms of a Popular Genre." Bottigheimer, *Fairy Tales* 75–94.

Sherwood, M. M. *The Governess; or, The Little Female Academy*. Wellington: Houlston and Sons, 1820.

Smith, Olivia. *The Politics of Language 1791–1819*. Oxford: Clarendon, 1984.

Stone, Lawrence. "Literacy and Education in England 1640–1900." *Past and Present* 42 (1969): 69–139.

Summerfield, Geoffrey. *Fantasy and Reason: Children's Literature in the Eighteenth Century*. Athens: U of Georgia P, 1984.

Tatar, Maria. *The Hard Facts of the Grimms' Fairy Tales*. Princeton: Princeton UP, 1987.

Taylor, Edgar. *Grimms' Fairy Tales*. 2 vols. London: Scolar, 1977.

Thompson, Stith. *The Folktale*. 1946. Berkeley: U of California P, 1977.

Townsend, John Rowe. *Written for Children: An Outline of English-language Children's Literature*. 2nd rev. ed. New York: Lippincott, 1983.

Trimmer, Sarah. *The Guardian of Education*. 5 vols. London: Hatchard, 1802–6.

Wordsworth, William. *The Poetical Works of William Wordsworth*. Ed. Ernest De Selincourt and Helen Darbishire. 2nd ed. 5 vols. Oxford: Clarendon, 1952–59.

———. *The Prelude: 1799, 1805, 1850*. Ed. Jonathan Wordsworth, M. H. Abrams, and Stephen Gill. New York: Norton, 1979.

Wordsworth, William, and Dorothy Wordsworth. *The Letters of William and Dorothy Wordsworth*. Ed. Ernest de Selincourt. 2nd ed. *The Middle Years*, Part 1, 1806–11. Ed. Mary Moorman. *The Later Years*, Part 2, 1829–34. Ed. Alan G. Hill. Oxford: Clarendon, 1969, 1979.

Yonge, Charlotte. "Children's Literature of the Last Century." *MacMillan's Magazine* 20 (1869): 229–37, 302–10, 448–56.

Zipes, Jack. *Breaking the Magic Spell: Radical Theories of Folk and Fairy Tales*. Austin: U of Texas P, 1979.

———. *Fairy Tales and the Art of Subversion: The Classical Genre For Children and the Process of Civilization*. New York: Wildman, 1983.

JAMES HOLT MCGAVRAN, JR.

Catechist and Visionary

Watts and Wordsworth in "We Are Seven"

and the "Anecdote for Fathers"

In *The Living Temple*, Stanley Fish ingeniously accounts "for the simultaneous presence in [George] Herbert's poetry of order and surprise" (25), security and instability, by arguing that Herbert is catechizing his reader, subtly leading him by a series of implicit questions to discover, or recover, the Christian faith which Herbert as Anglican poet-priest already holds secure. According to Fish, Herbert's catechetical strategy steers a middle course between the mindless rote instruction used by many contemporary ecclesiastics, which Herbert himself likened to "parrats" (20), and the brilliant but godless intellectualism of the Socratic dialogues (22); like Socrates he draws out the mind of his reader-pupil, but he can only lead him so far with his linked questions, since "the law he teaches—the law of faith—is unavailable to merely natural capacities; it must be revealed" (22). Over a century and a half later, influenced by the Puritan Isaac Watts as well as the Anglican tradition, William Wordsworth also used catechetical method in his poetry, in both its classical mode of intellectual debate and its Judeo-Christian mode of spiritual instruction. Two of his best-known *Lyrical Ballads*, "We Are Seven" and the "Anecdote for Fathers," cast adult narrators in the role of priests catechizing children and ministering to the reader (Sheats 196). But in a reversal of Watts characteristic of the Romantic who later called the child "father of the Man," the adults involved in the exchanges—both narrator and reader—are offered an opportunity to learn from "a little cottage Girl" (line 5, in *Selected Poems* 49) and "a boy of five years old" (line 1, in *Selected Poems* 51) of the interaction of human consciousness with the natural world, and of a spirit that pervades and transcends both. In Paul Sheats's words, "The narrator himself becomes an object of criticism and a butt of irony, and the reader is invited to rise above him" (196). And increasing the reader's awareness of paradox, these children teach that knowledge of the spirit cannot be formally taught at all, or even fully spoken, and that the logical structures of debate—of question and answer—and the imagistic and formal structures of verse, when put to the test, stand to fail both adult and child.

Beginning with Samuel Taylor Coleridge in the *Biographia Literaria*, readers have discovered mystery and indeterminacy coexisting with matter-of-factness and morality in Wordsworth's poetry. Earlier considerations of Wordsworthian mysticism have given way in the present critical generation to concern with the poet's views regarding the relationship of experience, language, and consciousness;[1] much recent commentary on the *Lyrical Ballads* reflects this shift of interest.[2] Stephen Parrish praises the "Anecdote for Fathers" and "We Are Seven" for their "magisterial frolicsomeness" (185), that is, the combination of playfulness and instruction in the dramatic dialogues of child and adult. Carl Woodring, however, emphasizes the magisterial, calling them examples of "didactic anecdote" (37) and noting the "hymnal . . . measure of their stanzas" (39). He further comments, "These poems present pedagogical situations, with the adult in the unexpected role of learner" (39), but he finds no significant authorial distance between Wordsworth as poet and his adult speaker, suggesting the poems be studied as "didactic anecdote spoken in the poet's own person" (37). Implicitly opposing Woodring, Susan Wolfson analyzes the "exchanges of question and response" (*Questioning* 42) and notes "occasions when no satisfactory answer is forthcoming, the response often eluding the terms in which the question has been posed" (43). Extending Parrish's argument, she asserts: "by exploiting the discontinuity between question and response, . . . [Wordsworth] compels his reader to turn to the disparate utterances themselves as the sole possible register of meaning. In each instance, the speaker as questioner . . . becomes a dramatic participant in the action and situation of the poem" ("Speaker" 548).[3] But Mary Jacobus closes again at least some of the distance Wolfson opens between speaker and poet, asserting that "We

Are Seven" and the "Anecdote for Fathers" are "jokes at . . . [Words-worth's] own expense," and that "both undermine the complacent and bullying morality offered to eighteenth-century children by those who wanted to improve them" (101).

Chief among these improvers, Jacobus suggests, was Isaac Watts (1674–1748), whose hymns for children Wordsworth both honored and parodied in the *Lyrical Ballads;* "for all their threatening morality," she states, Watts's *Divine Songs Attempted in Easy Language for the Use of Children (1715)* "played an important part in creating a popu-lar devotional idiom" (92). Jacobus here parallels earlier defenses of Watts which emphasize his enormous popularity with children and adults alike throughout the eighteenth and most of the nineteenth cen-turies: though both a relentless moralist and a social snob who de-spised the lower classes, Watts communicated more apparent concern for children's lives and souls, in the simple, gentle language of his songs and catechisms, than all of his fire-breathing Puritan ancestors com-bined, notably John Bunyan and James Janeway (Darton 108–9; Watts, *Divine Songs* 8–12, 38, 46). More recently, Samuel Pickering, Jr., terms "speculative" the question of a direct influence of Watts on Words-worth but points out that both were heirs of John Locke's empirical theory of the understanding, and that both used natural theology to teach the truths of the human spirit (160).

They differed totally, however, in their approaches to these truths. Guided by a Calvinistic dualism, Watts demands—however gentle the language—that children make either-or choices between flesh and spirit, and thus between evil and good, in order to be saved. For Wordsworth, however, the matter became far more complex (Coveney 3–9). Locke's *tabula rasa* was first augmented by David Hartley's asso-ciationist concept of child development through sensory perception—still essentially a mechanistic concept—and then almost inverted by Jean-Jacques Rousseau's impassioned defense of childhood as the time of natural innocence uncorrupted by society. Arthur Beatty exhaus-tively documented Wordsworth's debt to Hartley many years ago; and Dorothy Wordsworth provides evidence of Rousseau's influence on her brother in a well-known letter of March 1797, written at Racedown, Dorset, where since 1795 she and William had been taking care of young Basil Montagu. She revealingly says, "our system respecting Basil . . . is a very simple one, so simple that in this age of systems you will hardly be likely to follow it" (*Early Letters* 164). Like Rousseau, the Wordsworths thought relatively little of knowledge gained through reading and less of severe punishments (164–65), but unlike the creator of *Emile*, Wordsworth came to disapprove generally of pedagogic schemes and plans, even those designed to further or reinforce experiential learning itself. Moreover, in spite of the seminal description of the sky-child "trailing clouds of glory" in his "Ode: Intimations of Immortality," Wordsworth never fully accepted Rousseau's claim for the Edenic innocence of children (Coveney 36). In a letter of 1796 he remarked of Basil that "he lies like a little devil" (*Early Letters* 154); the child-self he reconstructs in the "spots of time" in *The Prelude* ([1799] 1.288) is frequently guilty of a trespass or transgression, for instance stealing a rowboat ([1799] 1.81–129); and he allows the children in "We Are Seven" and the "Anecdote for Fathers" to be interpreted by their interrogators—and doubtless some of their readers—not as innocent and spiritual but as stupid and mendacious. As with many of his other opinions, Wordsworth's view of childhood is finally paradoxical. On the one hand, he can exclaim idealistically:

> O heavens, how awful is the might of souls,
> And what they do within themselves while yet
> The yoke of earth is new to them, the world
> Nothing but a wild field where they were sown.
> 　　　　　　　　　(*Prelude* [1805] 3.179–82)

But he can also reminisce about his Hawkshead classmates thus:

> A race of real children, not too wise,
> Too learned, or too good, but wanton, fresh,
> And bandied up and down by love and hate;
> Fierce, moody, patient, venturous, modest, shy.
> 　　　　　　　　　(*Prelude* [1805] 5.436–39)

It seems impossible, as Pickering implies, to find any direct written record linking Watts and Wordsworth. But Watts's rhythms, language, and imagery appear in the *Lyrical Ballads* often and clearly enough to suggest the possibility of direct, deliberate echoes on Wordsworth's part of his Puritan predecessor. The very title of one of the best-known *Divine Songs*, "Against Idleness and Mischief," will serve as an example, since it might well have both inspired and goaded Wordsworth to the articulation of an opposing viewpoint in "To My Sister." Watts's song, later parodied by Lewis Carroll, begins:

> How doth the little busy Bee
>   Improve each shining Hour,
> And gathers Honey all the day
>   From every opening Flower!
>
> (Watts, Divine Songs 93; Carroll 38)

Emphasizing rationally but simplistically that busy is good and idle is evil, Watts moralizes in the third stanza:

> In Works of Labour or of Skill,
>   I would be busy too,
> For *Satan* finds some Mischief still
>   For idle Hands to do.
>
> (Watts, Divine Songs 177)

Almost greedy in his zeal to snatch their souls from the devil, Watts cared little for the perceptions or feelings of his young readers and apparently thought them safer from sin if constantly employed in routine tasks. In what seems a total reversal of Watts, Wordsworth encourages his grown-up sister Dorothy in an act of childish truancy on "the first mild day of March": "Make haste, your morning task resign; / Come forth and feel the sun" ("To My Sister" 1, 11–12, in *Selected Poems* 47). Unlike Watts, Wordsworth has learned that being too busy with work or study can actually hinder one's personal awareness of what he calls the "blessing in the air" (line 5), "the blessed power that rolls / About, below, above" (lines 33–34). Then, almost as if he thought Watts were overhearing them, and daring him to object, Wordsworth urges his sister: "Put on with speed your woodland dress; / And bring no book: for this one day / We'll give to idleness" (lines 38–40). But Wordsworth is not perversely praising idleness merely because Watts had condemned it; he is speaking instead of the open readiness of the mind to experience which in "Expostulation and Reply" he called a "wise passiveness" (line 24, in *Selected Poems* 106).

If Wordsworth recalled any of Watts's *Songs* during the writing of *Lyrical Ballads*, he would have found catechetical method in several. For example, "Against Pride in Clothes" begins:

> Why should our Garments (made to hide
> Our Parents Shame) provoke our Pride?
> The Art of Dress did ne'er begin,
> Till *Eve* our Mother learnt to sin.
>
> (Watts, Divine Songs 179)

Both here and in "The Child's Complaint" the concerned child is in fact made to catechize himself:

> Why should I love my Sport so well,
>   So constant at my Play?
> And lose the Thoughts of Heaven and Hell,
>   And then forget to pray?
>
> (Watts, *Divine Songs* 182)

As we have seen, Wordsworth saw in children's sport not natural depravity but natural energy, a thirst for experience, and a potential for spirituality; he would have rejected Watts's rhyming opposition between "play" and "pray," his tidy polarization of the child's indulgent enjoyments of life in this world and the sobering "Thoughts of Heaven and Hell." For the children in Wordsworth's ballads—especially "We Are Seven" and the "Anecdote for Fathers"—and for their readers, these contraries are blended in moments of imaginative power, of "wise passiveness," when the spiritual becomes manifest in the physical through the simultaneous development of opposed perspectives, the catechizing adult's and the visionary child's.

Wordsworth's few direct remarks about catechetical instruction (Moorman 2–4) both confirm and extend the complex view of childhood and education outlined earlier. He recalls in one of the *Ecclesiastical Sonnets*, written in 1821, that as a boy he had to study the Anglican catechism found in the 1662 *Book of Common Prayer*. Unlike the dissenting Protestant catechisms, even Watts's simplified ones— where the questions and answers tended to be rather intricately linked, and where original sin, the power of the devil, and the horrors of damnation are heavily emphasized (Watts, *Divine Songs* 6, 56–57)—the Anglican text uses the catechetical form simply as a framework for rote learning of the Apostles' Creed, the Ten Commandments, and the Lord's Prayer, and for a simple understanding of the two sacraments of baptism and the Lord's Supper. Nevertheless, there are indications that even in the absence of dissenters' hell-fire, and however distant and altered by time, Wordsworth's memory of catechetical instruction was not a very happy one. In his sonnet he recalls, "We stood, a trembling, earnest Company!" "Around the Pastor," apparently at Easter (lines 1–2, in *Poetical Works* 3:395, 571): "With low soft murmur, like a distant bee, / Some spake, by thought-perplexing fears betrayed; / And some a bold unerring answer made" (lines 5–7). Wordsworth's chief pleasure in the recollection results neither from his mock-epic treatment of the catechizing process itself nor from his deprecating portrayal of the rote learners as buzzing bees too busy memorizing to understand. Instead, he suddenly has a vision of his mother, his first and best teacher, lost to him in time since her death before his eighth birthday:

> Beloved Mother! Thou whose happy hand
> Had bound the flowers I wore, with faithful tie:
> Sweet flowers! at whose inaudible command
> Her countenance, phantom-like, doth reappear.

(lines 9–12)

Several passages in *The Prelude* confirm the primacy and benevolence for Wordsworth of his mother's integrated vision of nature, family, and God. "Blessed the infant babe," Wordsworth begins a key passage in the second book, "Nursed in his mother's arms":

> No outcast he, bewildered and depressed:
> Along his infant veins are interfused
> The gravitation and the filial bond
> Of Nature that connect him with the world.

([1799] 2.267, 270, 291–94)

Through his mother's love, the child finds himself a part of nature, society, and God, becoming "An inmate of this *active* universe" (296). Having seen his young world whole through the love in his mother's eyes, Wordsworth feels no need of manipulative approaches to child development or learning; preferring experiential knowledge, he tends to resent the more formal instructional methods of all those who, perhaps influenced by Hartley or Rousseau, may have believed more than Watts in the validity of children's own perceptions of their world but relentlessly continued to strive for control of their minds (Pickering 8–10; Leader 22ff., esp. 27).

In book 5, written several years later, Wordsworth emphasizes even more strongly that he prefers his mother's approach to child-rearing to those of some unnamed contemporaries—possibly William Godwin and the Wedgwoods (Glen 242), or possibly Mary Wollstonecraft, Thomas Day, and Benjamin Heath Malkin (Leader 178–80). Using the homely metaphor of "the parent hen amid her brood" (*Prelude* [1805] 5.246), he illustrates her sympathizing, caring presence, not her abstract reasoning or moralizing: "Yet doth she little more / Than move with them in tenderness and love, / A centre of the circle which they make" (250–52). Contrasting with this maternal geometry of love—simple yet profound in its implicit reconciliation of self and other, of motion and stillness—are the designs of those whom Wordsworth sarcastically calls "These mighty workmen of our later age" (370):

> Sages, who in their prescience would controul
> All accidents, and to the very road
> Which they have fashioned would confine us down
> Like engines . . .
>
> (380–83)

And the "child, no child, / But a dwarf man" (294–95) these sages produce, though he can answer any question put to him, is a soulless automaton, devoid of imagination and feeling, who learns compulsively, quantitatively, not naturally through experience:

> He sifts, he weighs;
> Takes nothing upon trust. . . .
> All things are put to question; he must live
> Knowing that he grows wiser every day,
> Or else not live at all, and seeing too
> Each little drop of wisdom as it falls
> Into the dimpling cistern of his heart.
>
> (337–38, 341–45)

He is, Wordsworth concludes in the 1850 text, like a tree that, instead of simply growing to fullness, is flattened by a gardener against a wall so that each separate branch is carefully, perfectly, but unnaturally articulated (328–29).

Not only, then, does Wordsworth come to express disapproval of the sort of instruction that emphasizes learning by question and answer—whether about Christianity or the things of this world; he may well have had a particular distaste for certain statements in the catechism itself. Wordsworth, who helped to bring about the democratization of literature, thought himself blessed since youth in the relative freedom of his remote native region:

> It was my fortune scarcely to have seen
>
> . . . .
> The face of one, who, whether boy or man,
> Was vested with attention or respect
> Through claims of wealth or blood.
>
> (*Prelude* [1805] 9.218–22)

But Wordsworth's spirit of "mountain liberty" (line 242) directly con-
tradicts the part of the Anglican catechism that glosses the Ten Commandments, especially the following answer:

> My duty towards my Neighbour is to love him as myself. . . . To love,
> honour, and succour my father and mother: to honour and obey the
> King, and all that are put in authority under him: To submit myself
> to all my governors, teachers, spiritual pastors and masters: To order
> myself lowly and reverently to all my betters: but to learn and labour
> truly to get mine own living, and to do my duty in that state of life,
> unto which it shall please God to call me. (*Book of Common Prayer*
> 292–93)

Clearly the purposes of the catechism included not only the priest's
control of the child's mind, but the control by the upper classes of society over the lower. Watts used similar phrasing in his "Second Catechism: Of the Principles of Religion": "Q. How must you show your
love to your neighbor? A. By honoring and obeying those that are set
over me." (7).[4]

Nevertheless, it seems likely that however Wordsworth in the late
1790s may have disagreed with some of the political or sociological implications of these interpretations of the Decalogue, it was the method
itself that he found the most troublesome—the reductive insistence on
analysis and classification that violates the mysteries of faith in the very
act of trying to teach them. Typical is the Anglican definition of sacraments: "*Question:* How many parts are there in a Sacrament? *Answer:*
Two: the outward visible sign, and the inward spiritual grace" (294).
The outward sign of the Lord's Supper, the prayer-book continues, is
the bread and wine; the inward part, the Body and Blood of Christ
(295). To Wordsworth, for whom outward and inward, like play and
prayer, were so often interfused in his "spots of time," such distinctions
as the catechists insisted upon must have seemed almost the antithesis
of education.[5]

Returning to "We Are Seven" and the "Anecdote for Fathers," we
shall see that Wordsworth works through his adult narrators to deplore
the bullying tone implicit in both the moralizing content of Watts's
Divine Songs and their rationalizing method. In "We Are Seven" he
further implies that the adult's increasingly exasperated insistence on
death as subtraction, as difference, results not only from his reliance
on empirical logic but also from some accompanying consciousness of
sexual and social difference.[6] The resulting tension feeds the adult's

desire to dominate the child—to lead her, in the terms of the Anglican catechism, to submit herself to her betters. His condescending intro-duction suggests he is attempting to repress the powerful effect she has had on him:

> ————A simple Child,
> That lightly draws its breath,
> And feels its life in every limb,
> What should it know of death?
>
> (lines 1–4, in *Selected Poems* 49)

To this question the speaker has obviously received from the child no answer he considers satisfactory. But ironically, in one of the more chill-ing of the *Divine Songs*, "Solemn Thoughts of God and Death," Watts provides just the knowledge of death that Wordsworth's adult speaker would find suitable for the girl on this occasion:

> There is an Hour when I must die,
> Nor do I know how soon 'twill come;
> A thousand Children young as I
> Are call'd by Death to hear their Doom.
>
> Let me improve the Hours I have
> Before the Day of Grace is fled;
> There's no Repentance in the Grave,
> Nor Pardons offer'd to the Dead.
>
> (163–64)

In Watts's poem the morbid awareness of the power of time and mor-tality—actually an adult's knowledge, not a child's—emphasizes the irrevocability of the moment of death as a one-time, one-way bound-ary crossing. But as Frances Ferguson has written, "No answer in . . . [the man's] subtraction will account for the girl's loss—and retention—of her siblings, because she knows better than he the ambiguities of the boundaries between life and death" (25; see also Ferry 84; Wood-man 7; Swingle 122). To judge from the story Wordsworth's speaker goes on to tell in "We Are Seven," the girl freely crosses and recrosses the boundary in her mind, thus coming to know death more intimately than he, and far too well to mourn her sister and brother; she sees them as part of her own ongoing life, not as apart from her, so she is tranquil in the churchyard, not depressed or fearful. Indeed her vital energy considerably disturbs the speaker. He admires her thick, curly hair, and he cannot help confessing that "Her beauty made me glad" (line 12), almost as if he desired her, but simultaneously he seems compelled to deny this attraction, and so he patronizingly calls her "a little cottage Girl" (line 5) or "my little Maid" (line 33), noting her uncouth, "rustic, woodland air" (line 9) and her "wildly clad" appearance (line 10). First, he catechizes her: "How many are you, then . . . / If they two are in heaven?" (lines 61–62). Then he remonstrates with her: "But they are dead; those two are dead!" (line 65).[7] The speaker's final comment, " 'Twas throwing words away" (line 67), can be applied to the girl's speeches as well as his own; neither seems really to hear the other. Sheats believes that the adult retreats before the child's vision, which cannot distinguish between the physical and the spiritual (line 197); however, both the catechist's and the child's viewpoints remain intact at the end of the poem for the reader, who is left to ponder which is obsessed with death and which possesses the priestly access to life in the midst of death.

Although there may be an undercurrent of Oedipal conflict (Bialotosky 113–14), the "Anecdote for Fathers" lacks the tensions caused in "We Are Seven" by the co-presence of sexual and social difference— and of course by death itself. The child, in real life young Basil Montagu, is not being coerced into acknowledging anything so grim and final as the loss of siblings, or even the limits of societal or gender-based roles, but only to choose between two settings, "here at Liswyn farm" and "Kilve's smooth shore, by the green sea" (lines 31–32, in *Selected Poems* 52), both of which seem beautiful, hospitable places. Yet this absence of enriching but complicating factors puts into even starker relief the main issue, the adult's protracted insistence on a reasoned analysis which leads not to enlightenment but to confusion. As the poem begins, the speaker, subtler than his more forthright counterpart in "We Are Seven," sounds innocent and loving, but it soon becomes clear how self-indulgently he likes to examine his own moods, measure his emotions, and then rationalize that manipulation:

> A day it was when I could bear
> Some fond regrets to entertain;
> With so much happiness to spare,
> I could not feel a pain.
>
> (lines 13–16)[8]

Wordsworth's adult speaker feels the harmony of past and present, of Kilve and Liswyn, of lambs and birds and earth and sunshine, but he experiences it like Milton's Satan in Paradise, who "saw undelighted all delight" (*Paradise Lost* 4.286 in *Complete Poems* 285; see Wood-man 3–5). So he turns to the child who embodies this harmony and, like the less sophisticated narrator of "We Are Seven," cannot resist the temptation to violate the child's innocent imagination with a question:

> My boy beside me tripped, so slim
> And graceful in his rustic dress!
> And, as we talked, I questioned him,
> In very idleness.
>
> (lines 25–28)

This is not the surface idleness, the result of a heightened inner aware-ness, that Wordsworth praises in "To My Sister," but is closer, ironically, to the sloth Watts warns against in his poem on the busy bee. Similarly, the boy's answer, "At Kilve I'd rather be / Than here at Liswyn farm" (lines 35–36), is spoken "in careless mood" (line 33), as if he could not take the question seriously. But having elicited this response from the boy, the adult begins to insist on knowing his reason. Does he inter-pret the child's preference for the other place as a rejection of him? If so, it is his own feelings of inferiority that he transfers to the boy, who "blushed with shame, nor made reply" (line 46) to his thrice-repeated demand. In its original version, this poem carried the sarcastic subtitle, "Shewing How the Art of Lying May Be Taught," and in several subse-quent editions a Latin motto from Eusebius which translates, "Restrain that force of yours, for I shall tell lies if you drive me to it" (*Selected Poems* 506). Since the letter of 1796 where he wrote that Basil "lies like a little devil," Wordsworth has realized that adults sometimes force children into lies.[9] It is not clear, however, which of the boy's replies is a lie—the preference for Kilve or the presence of the weathercock at Liswyn; whether both are lies; or whether it is rather the man who lies, first with his own feelings, and then by asking his questions. Moreover, the boy's distaste for the weathercock may be intended by Wordsworth as a desperate or outrageous lie; but it could also truthfully and clev-erly symbolize the child's resentment of both the man's vanity and his insistence on rational answers: by defining the energy of the breeze, the vane with its two-dimensional Chauntecleer inevitably trivializes it. Even more than in "We Are Seven," both child and adult here seem to be "throwing words away"; language has led through conflict not to resolution but only to increased uncertainty—at least when it is tied so relentlessly to the quest for rational answers. In "Against Lying" Watts has his own way of dealing with this sort of complexity, accurate as far as it goes:

> But Lyars we can never trust,
> Tho' they should speak the thing that's true,
> And he that does one fault at first,
> And lyes to hide it, makes it two.
>
> (*Divine Songs* 170)

In fact both characters in the "Anecdote" can be accused of these compounded lies, but such a view is itself simplistic and lacking in depth, refusing to allow for the innumerable ambiguities that arise both in experience and in attempts to articulate it. Wordsworth's poem, no mere "anecdote," thus affords a deeper view into the complex relationship between subject and object, and between experience and language, providing finally not a definite meaning but instead the possibility of meaning (McGillis 51–52)—if the reader can find one between the chattiness of the speaker and the poet's silence (Swingle 91). As a final demonstration of this complexity, the speaker's conclusion implies a strong Wordsworthian refutation of Isaac Watts, but does this with a suspect glibness:

> O dearest, dearest boy! my heart
> For better lore would seldom yearn,
> Could I but teach the hundredth part
> Of what from thee I learn.
>
> (lines 57–60, in *Selected Poems* 52)

Paradoxically, and by no means altogether convincingly, the speaker claims to have derived both understanding and joy from the encounter with the child. Is this another lie, a smug anecdotal reduction? Or is it as much of the truth as he can put into words in his weak attempt to teach? But if this is so, then why would he even "seldom yearn" "for better lore"? Has the adult learned anything at all? And has the child?

It will be more helpful finally to ponder what Wordsworth himself has learned from the writing of these poems, and what he is trying to teach. While he reverses the traditional catechetical relationship of teacher and student and mocks its form in his general hostility toward pedagogy, Wordsworth does not simply reject Isaac Watts or ridicule the intellectual, moral, and religious dilemmas of his songs and catechisms. Instead, along with his sympathy for the child, Wordsworth accurately presents the restless, death-driven need of the adult, bereft of the child's unreflecting sense of unity with nature and spirit, for order and security in his life and language; "all things are put to question" because, finally, they must be, even at the risk of "throwing words away." This is a need with which children, too, must come to terms, both in order to get along with adults every day and to prepare for their own future in the adult world. And the poetry itself offers the best evidence of the value of adult struggles to question and to know. Unlike William Blake's *Songs of Innocence and of Experience*, the *Lyrical Ballads* were not written for both child and adult readers; nevertheless the Wordsworthian tension between adult and child speakers prefigures the ambivalent "balancing of child and adult" readership in Carroll's *Alice* books and other Victorian children's fiction (Knoepflmacher 497; Shavit 63).[10] And the moral indeterminacy anticipates both the aesthetic and ethical development of twentieth-century fiction as it moved from closed to open form (Friedman, introduction). Wordsworth has proved that "There is knowledge to be gained from living with uncertainties" (McGillis 60). As Fish suggests in his study of Herbert, Wordsworth implies that if his readers can synthesize reason and faith, become both catechist and visionary, they may find their own love of the world and its inhabitants strangely enhanced.

NOTES

I am grateful to Robin Brabham and his staff in the Mary and Harry Dalton Rare Book and Manuscript Reading Room of the Atkins Library, at the University of North Carolina at Charlotte, for help with their collection of eighteenth-century children's literature and catechisms. To Frederik N. Smith, Chair, and the Department of English, UNC Charlotte, I am indebted for released time needed to complete this essay.

1. At the turn of the twentieth century A. C. Bradley spoke of Wordsworth's "hostility to 'sense'" (130) and of his this-worldly mysticism, whereby the poet could penetrate to something beyond the world of sense yet approachable only through the senses (132). Writing near the beginning of the great recent wave of critical interest in Wordsworth, David Ferry saw this Wordsworthian paradox as the result of a long-continued struggle between what he calls the sacramental and the mystical imaginations, the former uniting man and nature in harmony, the latter sensing chaos in both subject and object and yearning for direct contact with the eternal (160–73, esp. 169). The role of language itself, either mediating between

man and nature or questing beyond, concerns Frank McConnell (175), who believes that Wordsworth attempted in *The Prelude* "Edenic words," "a language . . . which recreates the lost Eden of Man's innocence within the successful narrative of each man's private life" (10). Focusing on the unstable juxtaposition of consciousness and language for both Wordsworth and his readers, Frances Ferguson suggests that "neither human incarnation nor linguistic incarnation is a fixed form which can be arrived at and sustained. The life of language in poetry, like the life of the individual, is radically implicated with death" (xvi). Still, Ferguson concludes that language "can communicate at all between an unknown poet and an anonymous reader" simply because we all tend "to take another's words or world at more than face value" (250; see also McGavran 48–49).

2. Thus John Jordan speaks of Wordsworth's belief "that when people were under the influence of strong emotions they had difficulty in organizing their ideas and in expressing themselves" (179). Jordan also emphasizes the underlying universality of the feelings and situations Wordsworth portrayed in the *Ballads* (178–79), while Stephen Parrish has placed a complementary emphasis on the complexities of Wordsworthian form, referring to the ballads as Wordsworth's "experiments in dramatic form, in characterization, and in narrative technique" (83).

3. Gene Bernstein restates Wolfson's concept of "disparate utterances" in structuralist terms derived from Ferdinand de Saussure and Claude Levi-Strauss: "the nature-culture opposition—represented in both poems by the conflict between child and adult respectively—is mediated within the structure of juxtaposed words, images, phrases and verb tenses, and thus makes meaning possible" (339).

4. For a different reading of the political importance of Wordsworth's catechetical poetry, see Alan Richardson's "The Politics of Childhood: Wordsworth, Blake, and Catechetical Method," esp. 857–61.

5. Even Watts had hesitated before subjecting his young followers to some of the finer points of church history and doctrine. In a footnote to his historical catechism on the Old Testament, Watts confessed: "The laws of the Jews which relate to their behaviour as men, to their religion as a church, and to their government as a nation, are all intermingled in such a manner, that it is hard to say under which head some of them must be ranked" (19n). And he all but falls into self-parody in this apologetic aside: "The doctrine of the priesthood and sacrifices had a larger room in this Catechism, but I was constrained to cut this matter short, as well as many others, lest it should be thought tedious to children" (20n). Surely it was not children alone, but their parents and ministers as well, who were relieved of some tedium by Watts's sense of constraint.

6. Don Bialotosky's suggestion of a parallel with Creon and Antigone (114–18) is thus an apt one.

7. Thus another of Watts's *Songs*, "Love Between Brothers and Sisters," becomes relevant here, again as a negative example:

> The Devil tempts one Mother's Son
> To rage against another;
> So wicked Cain was hurried on
> Till he had kill'd his Brother.
>
> (173)

Of course Cain was already full grown when he murdered Abel: what Wordsworth implies, whether or not he had Watts's Cain in mind, is that in desiring to violate the child's imagination, the adult is also in a sense attempting murder since he would destroy the still-living vision she has of her dead siblings.

8. Heather Glen has commented similarly on these lines: "The verse does not analyse or dwell upon these habits of his: its quiet regularity asks the reader to accept them as inevitable. And it is therefore the more devastating when their real nature is revealed in his conversation with the child, . . . [which] becomes an increasingly aggressive attempt to get the boy to "reason and compare" in the same way as himself" (242).

9. Watts, like Wordsworth, was "Against Lying," as another of the *Songs* makes clear, although Wordsworth might have questioned Watts's insistence on a Hell for liars: "every Lyar / Must have his Portion in the Lake / That burns with Brimstone and with Fire" (171).

10. U. C. Knoepflmacher states, "By the last third of the nineteenth century . . . authors . . . [were] self-consciously admitting their own role as mediators between the states of childhood and maturity" (498); he adds, "Torn between the opposing demands of innocence and experience, the author who resorts to the wishful, magical thinking of the child nonetheless feels compelled, in varying degrees, to hold on to the grown-up's circumscribed notions about reality" (499). And Zohar Shavit applies a structuralist analysis to "the simultaneous (often contradictory) need to appeal to both the child and the adult" (63).

WORKS CITED

Beatty, Arthur. *William Wordsworth: His Doctrine and Art in Their Historical Relations.* Madison: U of Wisconsin P, 1927, 1962.

Bernstein, Gene M. "A Structuralist Reading of 'Anecdote for Fathers' and 'We Are Seven.'" *WC* 10 (1979): 339–43.

Bialotosky, Don H. *Making Tales: The Poetics of Wordsworth's Narrative Experiments.* Chicago: U of Chicago P, 1984.

The Book of Common Prayer . . . of the Church of England. Cambridge: Cambridge UP, 1968.

Bradley, A. C. "Wordsworth." *Oxford Lectures on Poetry.* London: Macmillan, 1909, 1959. 100–47.

Carroll, Lewis. *The Annotated Alice: Alice's Adventures in Wonderland and Through the Looking Glass.* Ed. Martin Gardner. New York: Potter, 1960.

Coveney, Peter. *Poor Monkey: The Child in Literature.* London: Rockliff, 1957.

Darton, F. J. Harvey. *Children's Books in England: Five Centuries of Social Life.* 1932. 3rd ed. Rev. Brian Alderson. Cambridge: Cambridge UP, 1982.

Ferguson, Frances. *Wordsworth: Language as Counter-Spirit.* New Haven: Yale UP, 1977.

Ferry, David. *The Limits of Mortality: An Essay on Wordsworth's Major Poems.* Middletown: Wesleyan UP, 1959.

Fish, Stanley. *The Living Temple: George Herbert and Catechizing.* Berkeley: U of California P, 1978.

Friedman, Alan. *The Turn of the Novel.* New York: Oxford UP, 1966.

Glen, Heather. *Vision and Disenchantment: Blake's Songs and Wordsworth's Lyrical Ballads.* Cambridge: Cambridge UP, 1983.

Jacobus, Mary. *Tradition and Experiment in Wordsworth's "Lyrical Ballads" (1798).* Oxford: Clarendon, 1976.

Jordan, John E. *Why the "Lyrical Ballads"?* Berkeley: U of California P, 1976.

Knoepflmacher, U. C. "The Balancing of Child and Adult: An Approach to Victorian Fantasies for Children." *NCF* 37 (1983): 497–530.

Leader, Zachary. *Reading Blake's Songs.* London: Routledge and Kegan Paul, 1981.

McConnell, Frank D. *The Confessional Imagination: A Reading of Wordsworth's "Prelude".* Baltimore: Johns Hopkins UP, 1974.

McGavran, James Holt, Jr., "The 'Creative' Soul of *The Prelude* and the 'Sad Incompetence of Human Speech.' " *SiR* 16 (1977), 35–49.

McGillis, Roderick. " 'He Lies like a Little Devil': Wordsworth's 'Anecdote for Fathers,' 1798 to 1845." *English Studies in Canada* 10 (March 1984): 50–61.

Milton, John. *Complete Poems and Major Prose.* Ed. Merritt Y. Hughes. New York: Odyssey, 1957.

Moorman, Mary. *William Wordsworth: A Biography. Vol. 1, The Early Years 1770–1803.* Oxford: Oxford UP, 1968.

Parrish, Stephen Maxfield. *The Art of the Lyrical Ballads.* Cambridge: Harvard UP, 1973.

Pickering, Samuel F., Jr. *John Locke and Children's Books in Eighteenth-Century England.* Knoxville: U of Tennessee P, 1981.

Richardson, Alan. "The Politics of Childhood: Wordsworth, Blake, and Catechetical Method." *ELH* 56 (1989): 853–68.

Shavit, Zohar. *Poetics of Children's Literature.* Athens: U of Georgia P, 1986.

Sheats, Paul D. *The Making of Wordsworth's Poetry, 1785–98.* Cambridge: Harvard UP, 1973.

Swingle, L. J. *The Obstinate Questionings of English Romanticism.* Baton Rouge: Louisiana State UP, 1987.

Watts, Isaac. *Divine Songs Attempted in Easy Language for the Use of Children.* Ed. J. H. P. Pafford. London: Oxford UP, 1971. Facsimile reproductions of the 1st edition of 1715 and an illustrated edition of circa 1840.

————. *Dr. Watts' Plain and Easy Catechisms for Children.* Hartford, CT: Cooke, 1820.

Wolfson, Susan J. *The Questioning Presence: Wordsworth, Keats, and the Interrogative Mode in Romantic Poetry.* Ithaca: Cornell UP, 1986.

————. "The Speaker as Questioner in Lyrical Ballads." *JEGP* 77 (1978): 546–68.

Woodman, Ross. "Milton's Satan in Wordsworth's 'Vale of Soul-Making.'" *SiR* 23 (1984): 3–30.

Woodring, Carl. *Wordsworth.* Cambridge: Harvard UP, 1968.

Wordsworth, William. *The Poetical Works of William Wordsworth.* Ed. Ernest De Selincourt and Helen Darbishire. 2nd ed. 5 vols. Oxford: Clarendon, 1952–59.

————. *The Prelude: 1799, 1805, 1850.* Ed. Jonathan Wordsworth, M. H. Abrams, and Stephen Gill. New York: Norton, 1979.

————. *Selected Poems and Prefaces.* Ed. Jack Stillinger. Boston: Houghton, 1965.

Wordsworth, William, and Dorothy Wordsworth. *The Early Letters of William and Dorothy Wordsworth, 1787–1805.* Ed. Ernest De Selincourt. Oxford: Clarendon, 1935.

ROSS WOODMAN

The Idiot Boy as Healer

*I*n his gradual withdrawal from his youthful conversion to the French Revolution, a conversion in which, "look[ing] for something that [he] could not find," he initially "affect[ed] more emotion than [he] felt" (*Prelude* [1850] 9.72–73),[1] William Wordsworth, despite his insistence upon "juvenile errors" (*Prelude* 11.54) as his theme, realized that the psychic damage was immense. His imaginative identification with France as "a country in romance" (11.112) constituted in his withdrawal from it "a sense, / Death-like, of treacherous desertion, felt / In the last place of refuge—my own soul" (10.413–15). He suffered a profound moral and emotional collapse that endured "through months, through years, long after the last beat / Of those atrocities" (10.399–400). The product of that collapse, far more diligently forged and therefore far more deeply grounded than his youthful conversion to the revolution, was an inner revolution that changed the course of English literature even as the French Revolution changed the course of history.[2] In deciding, with his sister's help, "to seek beneath" the name of poet, "and that alone, [his] office upon earth" (11.346–47), Wordsworth set out to complete within himself the revolution that had failed in France.

The "country in romance," reason "making of herself / A prime enchantress" (11.112–15), was no longer the France of the revolution. It was his own childhood. The psychic projection onto the French Revolution that led to "treacherous desertion" was relocated onto himself; the "myself" that was Wordsworth at the age of twenty-eight became in his metaphor of childhood what he calls in *The Prelude* "some other Being" (2.32–33). The "vacancy" (2.29) between the historical "myself" and the mythical "other Being," a "vacancy" that was in part the result of his moral and emotional collapse, his engulfment "in the ravenous sea" (9.4), was a trauma that had to be healed. That healing lay for Wordsworth in the creation of the *puer aeternus*, the divine child, who, nourished at the breast of the Great Mother, feeds upon "honey-dew" and drinks "the milk of Paradise" ("Kubla Khan" 53–54, in Coleridge, *Poems* 298).[3]

Wordsworth, of course, had no interest in identifying the child-hero of his "country in romance" with "a history only of departed things, / Or a mere fiction of what never was" (*Recluse* 50–51, in *Poetical Works*, ed. Hutchinson, 590); he wished, on the contrary, to locate or find him in the "simple produce of the common day" (55). He wished, that is, to naturalize the world of romance, having witnessed in France the terrors to which the failure to naturalize can lead. Instead of the knight fighting in the name of the Queen of Heaven, he would ground his poetry in the babe "who with his soul / Drinks in the feelings of his Mother's eye" (*Prelude* 2.236–37). And in that child he would locate the healer who would restore him as poet to the moral and spiritual health which the revolution in France had destroyed. That child, the living icon of "the first / Poetic spirit of our human life" (2.260–61), becomes in its bonding with the mother Wordsworth's healing archetype. Nowhere does he more boldly celebrate it than in "The Idiot Boy," which becomes, in the context of Wordsworth's inner revolution correcting the errors of the French one, perhaps his most genuinely revolutionary poem. In what follows an attempt will be made to explore the poem as Wordsworth's most joyous account of "a country in romance," a healing nature bathed in maternal love under the rule of an eternal child that constitutes Wordsworth's naturalized world of faery, the proper domain of children's literature.

A dominant trope of that "country in romance" is the "vernal wood" ("The Tables Turned" 21, in *Poetical Works*, ed. Hutchinson, 377) into which the idiot boy, spontaneously led by the uncorrupted instinct that is Johnny upon his pony, settles as a presiding or containing presence. There "from eight o'clock till five" (line 446, in *Poetical Works*, ed. Hutchinson, 104), he "sits upright on a feeding horse" (line 351) in a state of blissful unconsciousness ("As careless as if nothing were" [line 350]): seeing, not seeing, the moon reflected in the water; hearing, not hearing, the hooting owls and the "waterfall, / Which thunders down with headlong force" (lines 347–48). The healing power of his presence, at once physical and psychic, is enacted in the magical cure of Susan Gale, who rises from her bed to take to the wood to find him. This mythos of the omnipresent child fed by impulses from a vernal wood, which (like William Blake's lost and found children in *Songs of*

Innocence and of Experience) the adult world has lost and must again find, constitutes a recurrent motif of children's literature, to which in this essential sense "The Idiot Boy," like many others of the *Lyrical Ballads,* belongs.

The adult's search for the lost child is a search for a lost innocence. In "The Idiot Boy" the search of Betty Foy and Susan Gale for the lost Johnny enacts in Wordsworth's confessed designs upon his reader a healing recovery of a lost innocence, through a radical reevaluation of that disordered or artificial taste which Wordsworth believed was predisposed to reject the poem on the grounds that it was "so materially different from those upon which general approbation is at present bestowed" (1800 Preface, in *Poetical Works,* ed. Hutchinson, 734). If not actually rejected, it was accepted for the wrong reasons, which Samuel Taylor Coleridge described as "the gilded side" of "SIMPLICITY," Wordsworth becoming in the eyes of "some affected admirers . . . a *sweet, simple poet!* and *so* natural, that little master Charles, and his younger sister, are *so* charmed with them, that they play at 'Goody Blake,' or at 'Johnny and Betty Foy!' " (*Biographia Literaria* 2: 158–59). The correction of disordered taste by restoring it to a true perception of Johnny is, for Wordsworth, an inner revolution in which he hopes to engage the reader. "The Idiot Boy," in short, is a children's tale for educated adults who "in these tutored days" could no longer view Johnny and his mother "with undisordered sight" (*Prelude* 3.156–57). Wordsworth's avowed purpose is to correct that adult disorder to which he himself first fell prey at Cambridge. In the healing of it lay for Wordsworth the real revolution, overthrowing the corrupted taste of an *ancien régime* and replacing it with a true republic of the soul presided over by a divine child. In his "Ode: Intimations of Immortality" Wordsworth celebrates this achievement by crowning himself—"My head hath its coronal" (40, in *Poetical Works,* ed. Hutchinson, 460)—at a May Day festival presided over by shepherd boys. The demonic parody of that crowning was for Wordsworth epitomized by the failure of the French Revolution,

> when, finally to close
> And rivet down all the gains of France, a Pope
> Is summoned in, to crown an Emperor.
>
> (*Prelude* 11.357–59)

Unlike the crowning of the poet who celebrates the *puer aeternus*, the crowning of Napoleon is the last sinking of

> a people,
> That once looked up in faith, as if to Heaven
> For manna, take a lesson from the dog
> Returning to his vomit.
>
> (11.360–63)

Viewed in this context, the crowning of Johnny in "The Idiot Boy" becomes Wordsworth's answer to the crowning of Napoleon described in *The Prelude*. Courting or inviting parody in a manner that Coleridge will explore in his criticism of the poem in the *Biographia Literaria*, Wordsworth manages boldly to affirm Johnny. He affirms as a kind of divine madness an irrational mode of behavior that incorporates his own early vision of the Revolution, a vision betrayed in the outward, political attempt to realize it. "The Idiot Boy" thus generates within its own creative dynamics that same system of ironies which in his "Immortality" ode allows the outward to belie the inward, the "six years' Darling of a pigmy size" (line 86) being also in its "Soul's immensity," and to Coleridge's bewilderment, a "Mighty Prophet! Seer blest!" (line 114). The "Soul's immensity," Wordsworth will argue in *The Prelude*, does not show itself in the "banners," "trophies," and "spoils" of Napoleon. On the contrary, it remains hidden in its own "beatitude" (6.609–13). Beatitude belongs to Johnny, not Napoleon. To recognize it there is to encounter a healing power that Wordsworth compares in *The Prelude* to "the mighty flood of Nile / Poured from his fount of Abyssinian clouds / To fertilise the whole Egyptian plain" (6.614–16).

"The Idiot Boy" belongs in that same domain of "jubilee" and "festival" that is the May Day rite of childhood celebrated in the "Immortality" ode. Johnny belongs among those "blessed Creatures" with whom the heavens join in laughter. The poem enacts a childhood game of lost and found, hide and seek. Johnny is Wordsworth's supreme "Child of Joy" (line 34). To respect the poem's mythic conventions, which are like those of a fairy tale or children's game, is to respect conventions which Wordsworth considered proper to the lyrical ballad. To betray them, as the revolutionaries in France (including Wordsworth) betrayed them, is to turn tropes into literal events which destroy their "life and efficiency" (Coleridge, *Biographia Literaria* 1: 82) as tropes.

The success of "The Idiot Boy" resides in Wordsworth's obvious celebration of the poetic conventions that contain it, conventions which helped him to relocate his powers after their French betrayal in the metaphorical world to which as a poet he believed they properly belonged. Not surprisingly, it was composed, as Wordsworth confessed, "almost extempore" and with "much glee" (*Poetical Works*, ed. De Selincourt and Darbishire, 2: 478).[4]

Coleridge's word for "glee" is "giddiness" (see James McGavran's introduction to this volume). In "a world of sin," Coleridge writes as a conclusion to the second part of "Christabel" (after the aged Sir Leoline, "turning from his own sweet maid, / . . . Led forth the lady Geraldine!" [lines 653–55]), "Such giddiness of heart and brain / Comes seldom, save from rage and pain" (lines 673–77, in *Poems* 235–36). The innocence of Christabel is seldom unattended. She appears in the shadow-presence of the "led forth" Geraldine. Wordsworth's Johnny is protected by idiocy from that shadow presence. He moves, lives, and has his being in an autonomous world of innocence. Critical of that autonomy, while remaining in awe of it, Coleridge called upon Wordsworth to defend his "faery" vision against accusations of "SIMPLICITY"—"vulgarity of style, subject, and conception," as he was to call it in *Biographia Literaria* (2: 158)—by composing, in accordance with Coleridge's own prescription, "the FIRST GENUINE PHILOSOPHIC POEM" (2: 156). Addressing himself to the "godlike" state attributed to his own son, Hartley, in Wordsworth's "Immortality" ode, Coleridge asks: "at what time were we dipt in the Lethe, which has produced such utter oblivion of a state so godlike?" (2: 138–39). The question, as Plato earlier acknowledged, requires a mythological rather than a philosophical answer. Wordsworth would make the tragic mistake of attempting to answer Coleridge on his own ground, a ground which Coleridge himself admitted had crushed his own poetic spirit (he finally, in more than one sense, abandoned "Christabel"). Unable on moral grounds to inhabit for long a mythopoeic world, Coleridge was driven, when philosophy failed him, to turn to theology where the guilt-ridden poet finally offered himself upon the altar of the "infinite I AM" (*Biographia Literaria* 1: 304), who appears in some subliminal way as Coleridge's "aged knight, Sir Leoline." Wordsworth's idiot boy, free as it were of Coleridge, wanders for a brief span, "from eight o'clock till five" (line 446), in the tigerless woods of his own enchantment. Their shadow form, from which Wordsworth was in his "glee" blessedly, if momentarily—"almost extempore"—released, no longer haunts the Johnny in himself as it had once haunted the Wordsworth for whom the streets of Paris following the September massacres, though "hushed and silent . . . , / Appeared unfit for the repose of night, / Defenceless as a wood where tigers roam" (*Prelude* 10.91–93). Mythically perceived, Wordsworth's Johnny acts as a Shaman exorcising a demon.

The "glee" experienced by Wordsworth in his "almost extempore" composition of "The Idiot Boy" resides in the apparent abandoning of himself, during what he calls "those happy moments," to the "glad animal movements," "aching joys," and "dizzy raptures" of an earlier period of his life that, as he points out in "Tintern Abbey," are "now no more" (lines 74–85, in *Poetical Works*, ed. Hutchinson, 164). Johnny setting off on his pony is not unlike Wordsworth's image of himself as a boy bounding

> like a roe
> . . . o'er the mountains, by the sides
> Of the deep rivers, and the lonely streams,
> Wherever nature led.
>> ("Tintern Abbey," lines 67–70)

"His heart it was so full of glee," Wordsworth writes of Johnny, that he quite forgot "all his skill in horsemanship" (lines 82–85), allowing his pony to follow its own instinctual path "wherever nature led." In giving himself over to "sensations sweet, / Felt in the blood, and felt along the heart" ("Tintern Abbey" 27–28, in *Poetical Works*, ed. Hutchinson 164), Wordsworth was not only binding his days together, after the catastrophic severing which constitutes the "independent intellect" (*Prelude* 11.244) and which was enacted as a crime by Oswald in *The Borderers*,[5] but, in that binding, performing upon himself (and by extension upon the reader) a healing action. While in "Tintern Abbey" and the "Immortality" ode Wordsworth remains remote from the childhood he invokes, so that both poems are permeated with an elegiac tone, in "The Idiot Boy" he abandons himself completely to that world, as if defiantly celebrating in the idiocy of his hero a madness which "may in these tutored days no more be seen / With undisordered sight" (*Prelude*, 3.156–57).

What to the outward eye appeared to be "madness" (3.149) was,

Wordsworth in *The Prelude* writes of his own childhood, the unconscious operations of "an unrelenting agency" of vision which "spake perpetual logic to [his] soul" (3.167–68). That "perpetual logic" issuing in prophecy, and known by "poets in old time and higher up / By the first men, earth's first inhabitants" (3.154–55),[6] is the logic that governs the actions of Johnny. Wordsworth therefore rejected Coleridge's published criticism of the poem as "an impersonation of an instinct abandoned by judgement" in which "the idiocy of the *boy* is so evenly balanced by the folly of the *mother*, as to present to the general reader rather a laughable burlesque on the blindness of anile dotage, than an analytic display of maternal affection in its ordinary workings" (*Biographia Literaria* 2: 48–49). To liberate the poem from that kind of judgment which he knew in advance the "general reader" in these "tutored days" would impose was the purpose of Wordsworth's long letter to John Wilson.

Writing first to Wordsworth, John Wilson levelled the same criticism against the poem that Coleridge would later publish. Indeed, his letter, judging from Wordsworth's response, raised many of the issues that arose between Coleridge and Wordsworth in the publication of the *Lyrical Ballads*. The letter to John Wilson, who was only seventeen at the time and a stranger to Wordsworth, may therefore have been prompted by Wordsworth's growing awareness that between himself and Coleridge a schism was developing that neither he nor Coleridge wished to address directly.

Whatever his motives, Wordsworth seemed clearly surprised by his own behavior. Partly "from some constitutional infirmities, and partly from certain habits of mind," he told Wilson, he did not write any letters "unless on business, not even to [his] dearest friends." Indeed, he continues, "except during absence from my own family I have not written five letters of friendship during the last five years" (*Letters* 293). He then refers to the advice of a friend that voiced Wilson's criticism, advice that Wordsworth followed only to have the poem reject it. The friend may indeed have been Coleridge:

> A friend of mine knowing that some persons had a dislike to the poem, such as you have expressed, advised me to add a stanza describing the person of the Boy [so as] entirely to separate him in the imaginations of my readers from that class of idiots who are disgusting in their persons; but the narration in the poem is so rapid

and impassioned, that I could not find a place in which to insert the
stanza without checking the progress of the poem and [so leaving] a
deadness upon the feeling. (298)

Wordsworth in his letter to John Wilson is defending the wildness of
his idiot boy and his mother against the overly refined taste of a certain
class of readers associated in his mind with the silk stockings and pow-
dered hair adopted by the Cumberland schoolboy at Cambridge. He
found himself in the composition of the poem tapping into the "eagerness of infantine desire" (*Prelude* 2.26) to the point, rarely achieved,
of being directly united with it. He had, that is, tapped "the hiding"—
and healing—"places of man's power" (12.279). Far from taking into
consideration the disgust of what he calls in his letter "people in our
rank"—"Gentlemen, persons of fortune, professional men, ladies, persons who can afford to buy, or can easily procure, books of a half-guinea
price, hot-pressed, and printed upon superfine paper" (295)—he would
confront them aggressively with their disgust. By the sheer force of the
poem itself, which he compares to a "deluge," he would overpower
"every feeble sensation of disgust and aversion." He hoped, that is, to
awaken in his readers what he had often witnessed in "the lower classes
of society:" "the conduct of fathers and mothers . . . towards Idiots."
That conduct, epitomized by Betty Foy, he calls "the great triumph of
the human heart." "It is there," Wordsworth continues, "that we see
the strength, disinterestedness, and grandeur of love" (297). Having
himself witnessed such love, Wordsworth describes himself as "hal-
lowed" by it, an experience which he would like "people in our rank"
to experience. "[It] is not enough for me as a Poet," he writes, "to delin-
eate merely such feelings as all men *do* sympathise with; but it is also
highly desirable to add to these others, such as all men *may* sympathise
with, and such as there is reason to believe they would be better and
more moral beings if they did sympathise with" (298). His purpose,
in short, is to heal the reader even as the idiot boy heals Susan Gale,
who, forgetting her own sick condition, turns her mind to the idiot boy
and his mother: "I'll to the wood," she cries. "The word scarce said,"
the poem continues, "Did Susan rise up from her bed, / As if by magic
cured" (lines 424–26). Wordsworth's hope is that the same magic will
work upon the reader, that the reader will rise up from his/her bed
and take to the wood, "one impulse" from which "May teach you more

of man, / Of moral evil and of good, / Than all the sages can" ("The Tables Turned" 21–24, in *Poetical Works*, ed. Hutchinson, 377).

      Part of the "glee" which Wordsworth experienced in the "spontaneous overflow of powerful feelings" that constitutes "The Idiot Boy" lay also in the release it afforded from the burden imposed upon him by Coleridge's estimation of his genius. "Dumb yearnings, hidden appetites, are ours," Wordsworth insists in *The Prelude*, "And they *must have their food*" (5.506–7). Wordsworth images the feeding of these yearnings and appetites in their primal ("dumb" and "hidden") form as the infant feeding at the breast of the mother. That image, in turn, becomes Wordsworth's reigning trope of "the first / Poetic spirit of our human life" which is, he writes, "in most, abated or suppressed," remaining in the poet "through every change of growth and of decay, / Pre-eminent till death" (2.260–65). As trope, then, the infant in the arms or on the lap of the mother is, much to Coleridge's disapproval, a "Mighty Prophet" seated "upon a throne / That hath more power than all the elements" (5.508–9). The idiot boy, whose "dumb yearnings" and "hidden appetites" are fed by the "torrent's force" (line 374) of Betty Foy's love, is seated upon just such a throne. And even as a "torrent's force" issues from Betty Foy, "so she, receiving from her idiot child what she so recklessly gives, "quaffs" from him "a drunken pleasure" (line 380). Conceived in epic terms, this becomes in *The Prelude* "the mighty flood of Nile / Poured forth from his fount of Abyssinian clouds / To fertilise the whole Egyptian plain" (6.614–16). The ecstatic pleasure which they give to each other—"Her limbs are all alive with joy," while "Johnny burrs, and laughs aloud" (lines 377–91)—becomes in the early books of *The Prelude*, and particularly in the 1798–99 two-part version, what Wordsworth describes as "unconscious intercourse with beauty / Old as creation," the ten-year-old boy "drinking in a pure / Organic pleasure from the silver wreaths / Of curling mist" (1.562–65). The idiot boy is Wordsworth's portrait of the poet as an infant, a portrait from which Coleridge struggled to wean him.

    What, of course, distinguishes "The Idiot Boy" from the accounts of childhood in "Tintern Abbey," the "Immortality" ode, and *The Prelude* is the relative absence of "a remoter charm, / By thought supplied" ("Tintern Abbey" 81–82, in *Poetical Works*, ed. Hutchinson, 164). What is felt in the blood of Johnny and in the heart of his mother is not filtered through the "purer mind" ("Tintern Abbey" 29) of the poet to the reader. It is, rather, fed to the reader directly as if the mind of the reader were in these "tutored days" cut off from "dumb yearnings" and "hidden appetites" as from the source itself of life and power. Present in the joy of "The Idiot Boy" is the horror of the "independent intellect" described by Coleridge in his "Dejection: An Ode." The "natural man" (line 90, in *Poems* 367) in him is dead, he suggests, sucked dry by "abstruse research" (line 89), which acts upon the mind as an infection. Contrasting himself with Wordsworth, he says in "To William Wordsworth" that everything opened up to him by Wordsworth's chanting aloud of *The Prelude* was "but flowers / Strewed on my corse, and borne upon my bier / In the same coffin, for the self-same grave!" (lines 73–75, in *Poems* 407).

Wordsworth chanting *The Prelude* thus becomes not a poet bringing life but a priest conducting a funeral. More desperate remedies, it would appear, were necessary, though, as Wordsworth realized to his sorrow, those like Coleridge, who needed them most, could not absorb them. "The poem has, I know, frequently produced the same effect as it did upon you and your friends," he wrote to John Wilson, "but there are many also to whom it affords exquisite delight, and who, indeed, prefer it to any other of my poems" (*Letters* 298). Among this latter group Wordsworth included himself, separating himself thereby from the Coleridge now urging him in another direction that would in *The Prelude* transform infant joy into an elegy for a dead child—a memorial, that is, in which to enshrine him. In *The Excursion* that followed, the controlling image of the first book is a mother who abandons her children to her despair, leaving the poet, "in the impotence of grief" (1.924, in *Poetical Works*, ed. Hutchinson, 602) to bestow upon her a Christian blessing that allows him finally to turn away and walk along another road in another kind of happiness. Describing the poet reduced by the poverty of modern taste to a condition unknown in former times, Wordsworth in *The Excursion* writes:

> —An irksome drugery seems it to plod on,
> Through hot and dusty ways, or pelting storm,
> A vagrant Merchant under a heavy load
> Bent as he moves, and needing frequent rest;
> Yet do such travellers find their own delight;
> And their hard service, deemed debasing now,
> Gained merited respect in simpler times;

> When squire, and priest, and they who round them dwelt
> In rustic sequestration—all dependent
> Upon the PEDLAR'S toil—supplied their wants,
> Or pleased their fancies, with the wares he brought.
>   (1.322–32, in *Poetical Works*, ed. Hutchinson, 595)

"The Idiot Boy," composed "almost extempore," is the antithesis of *The Excursion*, which reflects "the PEDLAR'S toil."

In "The Idiot Boy," as in "The Thorn" and "Goody Blake and Harry Gill," Wordsworth is interested in the ways in which superstition acts upon the mind as well as the conditions that render the mind prone to accept it. He is not interested in religion; rather, like Blake and Percy Shelley, he tends to equate religion with the organization of superstition into a system, which, as Blake points out in *The Marriage of Heaven and Hell*, turns "poetic tales" into "forms of worship" (Blake 37). This hardening of "poetic tales" into a religious system, of superstition into religious belief rather than a "suspension of disbelief," occurs, Blake and Shelley argue, when "the mind in creation" (Shelley, *Defence of Poetry*, 503–4) withdraws from its own activity and attributes what is created not to the imagination but to gods whose pronouncements, Blake points out in *The Marriage of Heaven and Hell*, "ordered such things" (37). Precisely in this withdrawal of mind from its own activity Blake, like Shelley, locates the origin of priesthood, which, Blake writes, enslaves "the vulgar by attempting to realize or abstract the mental deities from their objects" (37).

When Wordsworth in *The Recluse* declares that he will in his post-Miltonic epic pass unalarmed "Jehovah—with his thunder, and the choir / Of shouting Angels, and the empyreal thrones" (lines 33–34, in *Poetical Works*, ed. Hutchinson, 590), he is, by rejecting Milton's "system," restoring it to what Blake calls "the human breast," where it survives as "poetic tales" (37), the origins of which reside in the putting forth of "all strength" and "all terror" in "personal form" (*The Recluse* 31–32). That putting forth largely governs for Wordsworth the child who unknowingly is the god-like creator of the world he inhabits. "Unknown, unthought of, yet I was most rich—," Wordsworth writes of his first seventeen years, "I had a world about me—'twas my own; / I made it, for it only lived to me, / And to the God who sees into the heart" (*Prelude* 3.143–46). In the making of that world, which in *The*

Recluse he calls "the creation," no "lower name" (69, in *Poetical Works*, ed. Hutchinson, 590) being suitable, Wordsworth found the "heroic argument" (*Prelude* 3.184) that surpassed Milton's because it restored to the mind what Milton as a Christian attributed to God. "Of genius, power, / Creation and divinity itself / I have been speaking," he writes in *The Prelude* (3.173–75), having retraced his life "up to an eminence" (3.171),

> for my theme has been
> What passed within me. Not of outward things
> Done visibly for other minds, words, signs,
> Symbols or actions, but of my own heart
> Have I been speaking, and my youthful mind.
>
> (3.175–79)

Wordsworth's concern is to preserve Milton's sublimity without making that sublimity a form of worship. He wishes, that is, to preserve it within the limits of a poetic tale "Of matters which not falsely may be called / The glory of my youth" (3.172–73). More than that, however, he wishes to confine it to what he calls in *The Recluse* the "simple produce of the common day" (line 55, in *Poetical Works*, ed. Hutchinson, 590). What Milton attributed to Jehovah's thunder, "the choir / Of shouting Angels, and the empyreal thrones" (34), Wordsworth in the *Lyrical Ballads* will attribute to a thorn tree. The poem, he pointed out in a note dictated to Isabella Fenwick in 1843, "arose out of my observing, on the ridge of Quantock Hill, on a stormy day, a thorn which I had often passed in calm and bright weather without noticing it. I said to myself, 'Cannot I by some invention do as much to make this Thorn permanently an impressive object as the storm has made it to my eyes at this moment?' " (*Poetical Works* 2: 511).

The "invention" ("*inventio*") that renders the thorn "permanently an impressive object" is not the poet's repetition of its creation in the "infinite I AM" (Coleridge, *Biographia Literaria* 1: 304); it is, rather, the poet's repetition of its creation in the mind of a superstitious mariner not unlike Coleridge's mariner. The invention, that is, exhibits what Wordsworth in his note appended to the 1800 edition of the *Lyrical Ballads* calls "the general laws by which superstition acts upon the mind" (*Poetical Works*, ed. Hutchinson, 701), rather than, as in Coleridge's definition of the imagination, the general laws by which the "infinite I AM" acts upon it. Sublimity, in short, resides in superstition rather than

spiritual law, spiritual law having far more to do with priesthood than
with poetry. Though in the composition of "Tintern Abbey" Wordsworth is moving toward priesthood, identifying "poetic numbers" with
the "priestly robe" of "a renovated spirit singled out, / . . . for holy
services" (*Prelude* 1.51–54), that movement is alien to the spirit of the
ballads as Wordsworth originally conceived them. "Tintern Abbey,"
that is, reveals Wordsworth moving in the spiritual direction Coleridge
assigned him, a direction that would become the very basis of their
impending schism.

Betty Foy is superstitious rather than religious. When stirred by terror at Johnny's failure to return, she does not pray. Rather, she puts
forth her terror in personal form, which is to say in the form of her
own child-like mind. Johnny, as Wordsworth imagines her fears, may
have climbed into an oak to stay there until he dies, or been misled by
the wandering gypsy-folk and joined their band, or been carried by his
pony to the dark cave, the goblin's hall, or gone to the castle in pursuit
of ghosts. As her fears grow even sharper, she imagines that Johnny
has climbed to the peak of the cliffs to lay his hands upon a star, pocket
it and bring it home, or turned himself around facing his pony's tail
to become like a horseman-ghost, or turned himself into a devil with
head and heels on fire.

In this putting forth of her terror, Wordsworth suggests, the soul
reveals a power greater "than all the elements" (*Prelude* 5.509). Un-
willing to guess, as he will in his "Immortality" ode, "what this tells
of Being past, / Nor what it augurs of the life to come" (5.510–11),
Wordsworth sees in it a refusal to live

> In reconcilement with our stinted powers,
> To endure this state of meagre vassalage;
> Unwilling to forego, confess, submit,
> Uneasy and unsettled, yoke-fellows
> To custom, mettlesome, and not yet tamed
> .And humbled down.
>
> (5.517–22)

Precisely in this "dubious hour, / That twilight when we first begin to
see / This dawning earth, to recognise, expect" (5.512–14), the fears of
Betty Foy for the fate of her idiot child become essential to the pres-
ervation of the soul from its fading "into the light of common day."
It is also essential to its creative freedom, protecting it from the en-

slavement to which "priesthood" would reduce what Blake calls "the vulgar." "Oh! then we feel, we feel," Wordsworth writes,

> We know where we have friends. Ye dreamers, then,
> Forgers of daring tales! we bless you then,
> Imposters, drivellers, dotards, as the ape
> Philosophy will call you: *then* we feel
> With what, and how great might ye are in league,
> Who make our wish our power, our thought a deed,
> An empire, a possession.
>
> (Prelude 5.522–29)

"The Idiot Boy" is Wordsworth's attempt to restore "wish" to the condition of "power," "thought" to the form of "deed," to make the world of the soul "an empire, a possession" that, sustained at the level of a "poetic tale," still remains free of "priesthood," which is to say, a system of belief such as *Paradise Lost* tended to assert. The greatness of "The Idiot Boy" resided for Wordsworth in its blessed freedom from the assertions and justifications of religious belief, a freedom that for Milton would constitute a debasement of true liberty into license. Susan Gale, that is, is healed by "magic," not by miracle. She is healed, as the characters of William Shakespeare's *As You Like It* or *A Midsummer Night's Dream* are healed. She takes to the woods, which in "The Idiot Boy" are presided over, not by Oberon and Titania or Puck, but by Betty Foy's Johnny, who bears a certain resemblance to Puck. As to precisely what Johnny has been doing in the woods from eight till five, Johnny is unprepared to answer with anything like a dogmatic or didactic assertion: "The cocks did crow to-whoo, to-whoo, / And the sun did shine so cold!" (lines 450–51, in *Poetical Works*, ed. Hutchinson, 104). No Zen master could describe it better!

   In *Alastor*, Shelley, responding to *The Excursion*, suggests that the death of Wordsworth as a visionary poet lay in the sacrifice of "dumb yearnings, hidden appetites" to Christian faith. Defeated in his attempt to unveil the "inmost sanctuary" (line 38, in Shelley 71) of "our great Mother" (line 2) by making through the union of "strange tears" and "breathless kisses" such "magic" as would compel "the charmed night / To render up thy charge" (lines 34–37)—"the tale / Of what we are" (lines 28–29)—he settled for what Shelley considered in *The Excursion* the "pale despair" of the Solitary and the "cold tranquillity" (line 718, in Shelley 87) of the Pedlar. While there is no external evidence to suggest that Shelley had poems like "The Idiot Boy" in mind, the "charmed night" which Betty Foy superstitiously invokes does render up its charge in the discovery of her Johnny close to a waterfall watching the reflection of the moon upon the water. The union of "strange tears" and "breathless kisses" is suggested in Wordsworth's description of Betty Foy's "bliss" at the discovery of her son "almost stifled" by "a few sad tears" (lines 385–86).

But what most clearly relates Shelley's account of the Wordsworthian narrator to poems like "The Idiot Boy" is the focus upon the poet as magician and on poetry itself as incantation or spell whose source is the "eagerness of infantine desire" (*Prelude* 2.26). Nowhere does Shelley better capture the essence of the animistic Wordsworth than in his imaging of the poet's quest as the infant's union with the mother, who is nature itself "put forth in personal form" (*Recluse* 52, in *Poetical Works*, ed. Hutchinson, 590). The sudden "vacancy" that overcomes the Visionary in *Alastor* as the veiled maid folds him "in her dissolving arms" (187, in Shelley 75) constitutes for Shelley the repression of Wordsworth's "hidden appetite" understood as "the first / Poetic spirit of our human life" (*Prelude* 2: 260–61). That "first Poetic spirit" strives in *The Prelude* toward an incestuous "Union that cannot be" (2.24). Wordsworth in *The Excursion* abandoned that striving. He assumed what would in the fullness of time be recognized as a more Victorian stance in which the realm of faery is answerable to moral imperatives. He joined, that is, the "most" in whom the "first Poetic spirit" is, in the name of morality, though not without misgivings, "abated or suppressed" (2: 263). In his "Immortality" ode, Wordsworth could, Shelley suggests, genuinely grieve the loss of that spirit. Shelley alone, however, could deplore it.

The initiation described in *The Prelude* as the initiation of a poet's mind resides in the recovered ability to tap "appetites" that are in Wordsworth's view "far hidden from the reach of words" (3.187); "Burr, burr, burr" is the "far hidden," oft repeated, animistic cry of Johnny. Those appetites, Wordsworth further suggests, are also "far hidden" from the reach of religious orthodoxy. The gradual superimposition of that orthodoxy—already evident in both the 1805 and 1850 versions of *The Prelude* (more particularly in the latter)—reveals a sealing off, partly under Coleridge's influence, of what Wordsworth calls "the hiding-places of man's power" (*Prelude* 12.279). Initially open to him, they are in the extensions that constitute the 1804, 1805, and 1850 versions increasingly inaccessible. And the more inaccessible they become, the more "dumb yearnings" and "hidden appetites" are replaced by the Coleridgean "philosophic mind" ("Immortality" ode, 190). Bowing down before the Coleridgean mind that was alien to his "first Poetic spirit," Wordsworth submitted to it as his "lord and master" (12.222), oppressively declaring it to be "a thousand times more beautiful than the earth / On which . . . [the poet] dwells" (14.451–52). The "fabric more divine" (14.456), which he recognized in the mind of Coleridge, Coleridge projected back onto him, thereafter abandoning Wordsworth to a task he could not successfully perform.

The image of the poet more identified with hidden appetites that must be fed than with the "philosophic mind," an image undermined by Wordsworth's 1800 Preface, brings the reader of the *Lyrical Ballads* closer to the kind of primitivism that Wordsworth is celebrating, a primitivism that tends to be lost when, under Coleridge's influence, Wordsworth attempts consciously to explain his choice of what he calls in the Preface "humble and rustic life" (*Poetical Works*, ed. Hutchinson, 734). When he suggests that the rustic's language "is a more permanent, and a far more philosophical language, than that which is frequently substituted for it by Poets" (735), he lays himself open to the kind of criticism Coleridge levelled against him. And precisely here, in his attempt to understand Coleridge rather than consult his own experience in the composition of poems like "The Thorn" and "The Idiot Boy," Wordsworth badly misrepresented his own astonishing achievement in the ballad genre. In defending himself against the attacks of readers drawn from his own social class, he inadvertently identified himself with their prejudices, making the overcoming of them a matter of moral responsibility. Far from defending "dumb yearnings, hidden appetites" in and for themselves, he located them in a Coleridgean hierarchy of faculties in which they became subordinated to the fully conscious mind affirming a divinity for itself that transcended the earth on which it dwells. Viewed in this Coleridgean context, "The Idiot Boy" comes dangerously close to being read as a mock-heroic poem, a kind of Wordsworthian *Dunciad*. Coleridge himself recognized this danger when he described the poem's effect upon the "general reader" as "a laughable burlesque" (*Biographia Literaria* 2: 48).

Instead of falling prey to this temptation, one should, I suggest, read the poem as the radical affirmation of a revolutionary poet. The author of "The Idiot Boy" is an English convert to the French Revolution. The spirit informing that radical political act is the spirit informing "The Idiot Boy." In Johnny's joyous night wanderings through the woods accompanied at every turn not by Coleridge but by the hooting of the owls and the shining of the moon, Wordsworth is celebrating the kind of education that, he argues, stands out in marked contrast to what is offered in the great public schools and in the universities. Thinking perhaps of Coleridge "reared / In the great city, 'mid far other scenes" (*Prelude* 2.451–52) from the age of nine, Wordsworth asks:

> Oh! where had been the Man, the Poet where,
> Where had we been, we two, beloved Friend!
> If in the season of unperilous choice,
> In lieu of wandering, as we did, through vales
> Rich with indigenous produce, open ground
> Of Fancy, happy pastures ranged at will,
> We had been followed, hourly watched, and noosed,
> Each in his several melancholy walk
> Stringed like a poor man's heifer at its feed,
> Led through the lanes in forlorn solitude;
> Or rather like a stallèd ox debarred
> From touch of growing grass, that may not taste
> A flower till it have yielded up its sweets
> A prelibation to the mower's scythe.
>
> (*Prelude* 5.232–45)

In the "melancholy walk / Stringed like a poor man's heifer at its feed," Wordsworth images the "tutored" education which he rejects, an education devoted to the disordering of the sight. In the image of that "poor man's heifer," however, he also finds his metaphor of the tyranny of the *ancien régime* that converted him to the French Revolution. "And when we chanced / One day to meet a hunger-bitten girl," Wordsworth writes of his conversion under the influence of Michael Beaupuy,

> Who crept along fitting her languid gait
> Unto a heifer's motion, by a cord
> Tied to her arm, and picking thus from the lane
> Its sustenance, while the girl with pallid hands
> Was busy knitting in a heartless mood
> Of solitude, and at the sight my friend
> In agitation said, ' 'Tis against *that*
> That we are fighting,' I with him believed

That a benignant spirit was abroad
Which might not be withstood, that poverty
Abject as this would in a little time
Be found no more, that we should see the earth
Unthwarted in her wish to recompense
The meek, the lowly, patient child of toil.
All institutes for ever blotted out
That legalised exclusion, empty pomp
Abolished, sensual state and cruel power,
Whether by edict of the one or few;
And finally, as sum and crown of all,
Should see the people having a strong hand
In framing their own laws; whence better days
To all mankind.

(*Prelude* 9.509–32)

Of course, Wordsworth does not suggest that Johnny, shaking his holly-bough in his hand as he rides off on his pony too excited to hold the bridle, is Jerusalem leading the people; nevertheless, some such vision of him is half-present to his mother:

And he must post without delay
Across the bridge and through the dale,
And by the church, and o'er the down,
To bring a Doctor from the town,
Or she will die, old Susan Gale.

(lines 42–46, in *Poetical Works*, ed. Hutchinson, 100)

The idiot boy is in Wordsworth's presentation a "benignant spirit . . . / Which might not be withstood." In his communication with the moon and the hooting owls as well as his unbridled pony, the earth stands "unthwarted in her wish to recompense / The meek." As for Wordsworth's more conscious intent, he makes it clear in his letter to John Wilson that in drawing the reader's sympathy toward the idiot boy he hoped to blot out forever all institutes "that legalised exclusion" and, at the same time, abolish "empty pomp." He wished, that is, to make the crowning of Napoleon a ludicrous event, an act of political insanity. "The Idiot Boy" is, in short, Wordsworth's most revolutionary poem, one that transcends any desire for the framing of laws by focusing directly upon the hallowing presence of what he calls in the letter to Wilson "the grandeur of love." That "grandeur" viewed at its source is maternal. By locating it there in its most primitive form, Wordsworth is celebrating what he calls "the great triumph of the human heart," a "triumph" that in the announcement of his epic theme finds its proper image in the descent of the New Jerusalem adorned as a bride to meet the bridegroom. "The Idiot Boy," devoid as it is of "banners militant," "trophies," "spoils," and "prowess" (*Prelude* 6.609–11), strong rather in a "beatitude / That hides [the soul]" (6.613–14), must be numbered among Wordsworth's "spousal verse / Of this great consummation" (*Recluse* 57–58, in *Poetical Works*, ed. Hutchinson, 590).

As a celebration of the healing power of innocence grounded in a profound knowledge of the world of experience, "The Idiot Boy" should perhaps finally be included not among the classics of children's literature but among those texts which work upon the adult mind the way children's literature works upon the child. Wordsworth, that is, wished to arouse and engage what he considered the authentic "powers of manhood" by invoking and capturing "the feelings of childhood" (Coleridge, *Biographia Literaria* 1: 80–81). He addresses that true "manhood" which he believed is fathered by the child. As an "active partisan" (*Prelude* 11.153) of radical innocence, Wordsworth's avowed intention was to cast off the "oppression" which a lifeless "Antiquity" grants to "error" (11.160–62). In casting off this "oppression," he was aware that poetically as well as politically the release "must be work / As well of License as of Liberty" (11.162–63). Wordsworth's essential "glee" as a poet lay, it may be argued, more in the "License" which he took than in the "Liberty" traditionally granted to the poet. Affirming that socially opposed "License" with reference to his youthful political partisanship, Wordsworth describes himself in *The Prelude* as "Not caring if the wind did now and then / Blow keen upon an eminence that gave / Prospect so large into futurity" (11.165–67). The keen wind of "License" extending beyond the traditional scope of "Liberty" was simply his attempt ultimately to enlarge that scope, to diffuse

> those affections wider
> That from the cradle had grown up with me,
> And losing, in no other way than light
> Is lost in light, the weak in the more strong.
>
> (11.169–72)

The "infantine eagerness" of the ballad narrative, the gratification of the soul's "dumb yearnings" and "hidden appetites"—which must be, and in "The Idiot Boy" are, at once licensed and fed—affirm and demonstrate Wordsworth's radical notion that the poetic sensibility has its origin in the infant at the breast of the mother; and for the licensed poet, as opposed to those others in whom it is "abated or suppressed," there it remains "pre-eminent till death." In the relations between Johnny and his mother, Wordsworth, as in a Henry Moore sculpture or the frontispiece to Blake's *Songs of Innocence*, constructs "a throne / That hath more power than all the elements" (*Prelude* 5.508–9). In its religious context, this throne assumes the stature of the madonna and child in a Gothic church dedicated to Our Lady. That Wordsworth was unable to relocate Johnny and his mother in some such Gothic setting perhaps best describes the integrity of "The Idiot Boy." Its power over Wordsworth, initially in its composition a power within the poet, may indeed have prevented Wordsworth from completing the Gothic struc-ture which he describes in his preface to *The Excursion*. It may have worked against it, reducing it to a ruin, when Johnny and his mother refused to abide there.

The poem's success, I suggest, lies finally in the license which re-leases it from the controlled liberty of an imposed meaning. Words-worth's muses will not and need not explain—"And can ye thus un-friended leave me" (344), Wordsworth cries in mock despair—because, "unknown, unthought of" (*Prelude* 3.143), the reader is fed even as a child is fed. By the end of the poem the reader has a world about him, not unlike the one the Wordsworthian child unconsciously creates for itself. Wordsworth, that is, could say of this poem what he said in *The Prelude* of his life at Cambridge: "I had a world about me—'twas my own; / I made it, for it only lived to me, / And to the God who sees into the heart" (3.144–46). That God, I suggest, was, like Wordsworth's Johnny, far more primitive that Coleridge's "infinite I Am" or the pre-siding deity of Wordsworth's doomed Gothic church. "I have often applied to idiots, in my own mind, that sublime expression of Scripture that, *their life is hidden with God*" (*Letters* 297), he wrote to John Wil-son. In Johnny's "hidden appetites" resided the God of Wordsworth's "first Poetic spirit" which Coleridge, without fully intending, taught him to suppress as the way to a final transcendence.

NOTES

1. All quotations from *The Prelude*, unless otherwise noted, are taken from the 1850 text found in the Norton Critical Edition.

2. The date, duration, and significance of Wordsworth's mental and moral crisis remains unsettled. G. W. Meyer went so far as to deny its actual (as distinct from poetical) existence (177). For a sensitive reading of Wordsworth's enactment of his own rejected experience of the Revolution, see Thorslev 103).

3. The best Freudian reading of *The Prelude* focusing upon the trauma of the death of Wordsworth's mother when Wordsworth was eight, a trauma that found "abundant recompense" in his denial of loss in the projection of the mother imago onto nature immediately following her death, is to be found in Richard J. Onorato's reading of the epic. That the absent mother achieves a hallucinogenic presence in nature is one possible reading of the healing spell constellated by the idiot boy in his trance-like state beneath the moon "From eight o'clock till five." Johnny's instinctual bonding with a maternal nature enacts Wordsworth's myth of the "infant Babe" (*Prelude* 2.232) in the arms of the Great Mother. Archetypally perceived, not only is the Babe "an innmate of this active universe" (2.254) whose "infant veins are interfused" with "the filial bond / Of nature" (2.242–44); he is also "an agent of the [Coleridgean] one great Mind" (2.257), a "creator and receiver both, / Working but in alliance with the works / Which it beholds" (2.258–60).

4. For a very different account of writing, one indicated in his reference to "some constitutional affirmities" (293) in his letter to John Wilson, see Wordsworth's letter to Thomas De Quincey, in which he confesses: "I have a kind of derangement in my stomach and digestive organs which makes writing painful to me, and indeed almost prevents me from holding correspondence with any body: and this (I mean to say the unpleasant feeling which I have connected with the act of holding a Pen) has been the chief cause of my long silence" (368). Dorothy, who did hold his pen, becomes not only his amanuensis but the "healing" of the broken bond with the mother that is at the same time a creative regression to his primal creation myth essential to the breaking of silence. In the idiot boy's binding to his mother, Wordsworth is enacting that primal myth of the God who inhabits "dumb yearnings, hidden appetites" (*Prelude* 5.506) in the fairy tale context of the lost and found child.

5. Wordsworth's diagnosis of his moral and spiritual collapse as the intellect rendered independent of the heart and the blood (the feelings and the instinct) constitutes a nightmarish condition, a reign of inner terror culminating in a symbolic guillotining. Dorothy's act of restoration lay in maintaining for him what Wordsworth calls "a saving intercourse / With my true self" (11.341–42). She, Wordsworth explains, "led me back through opening day / To those sweet counsels between head and heart / Whence grew that genuine knowledge, fraught with peace" (11.351–53).

The restoration of "those sweet counsels" (reuniting the head and the heart) suggests the relationship of Isis to her brother-husband, Osiris, a relationship hauntingly suggested in Wordsworth's account of the secret healing that in him took place through the "beatitude" of Dorothy's ministrations. His overflowing soul, restored by his sister to its youthful fecundity, poured "like the mighty flood of Nile" from "his fount of Abyssinian clouds" (Dorothy as Wordsworth's "Abyssinian maid") "To fertilise the whole Egyptian plain" (6.613–16). In the Egyptian myth, Osiris is dismembered to be re-membered by Isis, his sister-wife. Gathering the scattered members of his body, she miraculously brings him back to life. The form of this miraculous recovery lies in "the mighty flood of Nile" which each year brings fertility to "the whole Egyptian plain," Osiris being a fertility god associated with the Nile.

The dismembering–re-membering rite that provides the governing trope of Wordsworth's account in *The Prelude* of the revolution and its aftermath constitutes not only an act of healing but, more significantly, a Shamanistic initiation (see Woodman) which both brings the healed person into direct contact with the spirit world and, through that contact, confers upon him healing powers. When Wordsworth says that his sister "preserved me still / A Poet, made me seek beneath that name, / And that alone, my office upon earth" (11.345–47), he is first identifying himself as poet with Dorothy's healing and preserving power (Isis also preserves Osiris by swathing him in mummy wrappings as a sign of his imperishability). Beyond that, however, he is affirming the healing power granted to him behind the "fount of Abyssinian cloud." He becomes, that is, the Prophet of Nature, "sanctified" and "blest," performing a work of "deliverance, surely yet to come" (14.445–48).

This mythological dimension is never, I suggest, fully present to Wordsworth's consciousness. It remains as a "beatitude" hidden from the "myself" of *The Prelude*, even as to some extent the "some other Being" remains hidden. In "The Idiot Boy," Wordsworth, I believe, confronts this "beatitude" not as Osiris but as the idiot boy whose life "*is hidden with God*" and is, "probably from a feeling of this sort," worshipped "in several parts of the East" (*Letters* 297). Osiris's mother, by the way, was the sky-goddess, Nut.

6. Alan Bewell argues that "the poem can be seen as a devastating burlesque of the 'high seriousness' with which idiocy entered into the philosophical debates of the eighteenth century." In "an illiterate mother's urgent questioning of her idiotic son," he suggests, "an age of interrogations of idiocy aimed at recovering the 'truth' of human nature would seem to come to its parodic end" (325). However, Bewell continues, Wordsworth had a genuine philosophic interest in the debates because he was himself struggling in formulating his plan for *The Recluse* "to establish a general theory of

the transition from nature to society" based upon empirical evidence. The search for that evidence "placed the idiot at the center of his thought" (326). He therefore concludes that "The Idiot Boy" cannot be read "simply as a parody of the eighteenth-century speculative use of idiots, but also requires us to see it as an ambiguous narrative in which Wordsworth is tempted, and partly succumbs to the temptation, to contribute his own philosophical discourse on idiots, a seriousness concealed, self-consciously, by comedy" (326).

This reading substitutes the philosophical Wordsworth for the mythopoeic poet who grounded the poetic spirit in the infant babe at its mother's breast. *The Recluse*, I suggest, was Coleridge's idea, not Wordsworth's. In accepting Coleridge's reading of his genius, Wordsworth imposed an intolerable burden upon himself from which in poems like "The Idiot Boy" he found at least momentary release. In precisely that release his true genius lay. In his celebration of the idiot, he is, against Coleridge's objection, affirming his own power.

A more productive approach to Wordsworth's interest in the idiot boy, closely connected to his interest in the transition from nature to society and the philosophical debate surrounding it, is to be found in Jacques Derrida's treatment of Jean-Jacques Rousseau in *Of Grammatology*, particularly the notion of a hypothetical or natural language "common to all" which is prior to writing and approximates the pure sound of music. This "full speech" (8), as Derrida describes it, is perhaps best exemplified by the "mock apparel" with which Hartley Coleridge at the age of six "fittest to unutterable thought / The breeze-like motion and the self-born carol" ("To H.C." 2–4, in *Poetical Works*, ed. Hutchinson, 70). "The Idiot Boy," I suggest, is Wordsworth's attempt at a "self-born carol" moving with "a breeze-like motion" into a realm of "unutterable thought," the truth of which remains "*hidden with God.*" His hero, Johnny, is Wordsworth's image of "the first men, earth's first inhabitants" (*Prelude* 3.155).

In "Cogito and the History of Madness," Derrida describes writing as a "structure of deferral" in which the "absolute excess" that constitutes the hypothetical original state of man is tranquillized into a rational structure in order to exclude madness. Derrida describes this rational structure as a betrayal. "I philosophize," Derrida writes, "only in *terror*, but in the *confessed* terror of going mad" (62). The madness of Johnny is Wordsworth's own attempt to penetrate the philosophical mind oppressively imposed upon him by Coleridge in order to recover what Derrida calls the "fabulous scene" which is effaced by metaphysics ("White Mythology," 11).

WORKS CITED

Blake, William. *The Complete Poetical Works of William Blake.* Ed. David Erdman. Berkeley: U of California P, 1982.

Bewell, Alan J. "Wordsworth's Primal Scene: Retrospective Tales of Idiots, Wild Children, and Savages." *English Literary History* 5 (1983): 321–46.

Coleridge, Samuel Taylor. *Biographia Literaria.* 2 vols., in 1. Ed. James Engell and W. Jackson Bate. Princeton: Princeton UP, 1984.

———. *The Poems of Samuel Taylor Coleridge.* Ed. Ernest Hartley Coleridge. London: Oxford UP, 1912.

Derrida, Jacques. "Cogito and the History of Madness." *Writing and Difference.* Trans. Alan Bass. Chicago: U of Chicago P, 1978.

———. *Of Grammatology.* Trans. Gayatri Chakravorty Spivak. Baltimore: Johns Hopkins UP, 1976.

———. "White Mythology." Trans. F. C. T. Moore. *New Literary History* 6 (1974): 7–77.

Meyer, G. W. *Wordsworth's Formative Years.* Ann Arbor: U of Michigan P, 1943.

Onorato, Richard J. *The Character of the Poet: Wordsworth in "The Prelude."* Princeton: Princeton UP, 1971.

Shelley, P. B. *Shelley's Poetry and Prose.* Ed. Donald H. Reiman and Sharon B. Powers. New York: Norton, 1977.

Thorslev, Peter L., Jr. "Wordsworth's *Borderers* and the Romantic Villain-Hero." *Studies in Romanticism* 5 (1966): 84–103.

Woodman, Ross G. "Shaman, Poet, and Failed Initiate: Reflections on Romanticism and Jungian Psychology." *Studies in Romanticism* 19 (1980): 51–82.

Wordsworth, William. *The Poetical Works of William Wordsworth.* Ed. Ernest De Selincourt and Helen Darbishire. 2nd ed. 5 vols. Oxford: Clarendon, 1952–59.

———. *The Poetical Works of Wordsworth.* Ed. Thomas Hutchinson. 1904. Rev. Ernest De Selincourt. London: Oxford UP, 1936.

———. *The Prelude 1799, 1805, 1850.* Ed. Jonathan Wordsworth, M. H. Abrams, and Stephen Gill. New York: Norton, 1979.

Wordsworth, William, and Dorothy Wordsworth. *The Early Letters of William and Dorothy Wordsworth, 1787–1805.* Ed. Ernest De Selincourt. Oxford: Clarendon, 1935.

MITZI MYERS

Romancing the Moral Tale

Maria Edgeworth and the Problematics

of Pedagogy

I do not know whether many people realize how much more than is
ever written there really is in a story. . . . Between the lines of every
story there is another story, and that is one that is never heard and
can only be guessed at by the people who are good at guessing.

Frances Hodgson Burnett[1]

Autobiography is not so much a mode of literature as literature is a
mode of autobiography.

James Olney[2]

Miss Edgeworth—she's *very* clever, and best in the little touches
too. I'm sure, in that children's story—(he meant "Simple Susan")
—where the little girl parts with her lamb, and the little boy brings
it back to her again, there's nothing for it but just to put down the
book, and cry.

Sir Walter Scott[3]

hildren's literature from the more distant past poses unusual
problems of critical access. Too often, it is treated as an unproblematic "mirror" of social reality, or it is dismissed as lacking literary interest because it is "didactic." Especially is this true of that
genre literary historians label the "Moral Tale." Whether a category so
broad that it spans at least a half-century's output and confounds verse
with prose, factual dialogue with fictional narrative, empiricist science

96

with Evangelical religion, and hack with genius really forms a helpful classification is not a question that arises. Commentators evidently recognize it when they see it, and with downright hostility or urbane critical amusement, they sidestep it as quickly as possible. From the Romantics right down through such recent literary surveys as Humphrey Carpenter's and Geoffrey Summerfield's, hasty analysis climaxes in premature evaluation.[4]

It would be easy to amass a roll call of patronizing dismissals, but let the magisterial F. J. Harvey Darton represent the most generous attitude. Darton concedes more space to the form and more merit to its practitioners than do most historians of juvenilia, though his initial definition of "children's books" as "printed works produced ostensibly to give children spontaneous pleasure" and his chronicle of "the history of fairy-tales and nursery rhymes, in their progress towards becoming the true natural staple of the juvenile library" (1, 84) show clearly where his heart lies. On the one hand, the moral tale is a hardy perennial: "it is not dead now," he writes in 1932; "It probably never will be dead in English until the United States cease altogether to speak that tongue." On the other, it is the product of a particular class and culture, yet somehow bracketed off from the stirring events of its Georgian genesis: "one thinks of the middle-class parlours with little girls falling asleep under a rational discourse by papa. The Moral Tale was the chronicle of solid quiet England, in staid homes remote from personal emotions or unstable ideals. Nor had it any contact with events that were shaking the nations, nor with the wonder and visions of beauty that were at that very time stirring in English poetry. The Georgian child knew nothing of such things. Even the fairies were in hiding" (210, 197). Thin, pat, preachy, epitomizing closure and one-dimensionality, the moral tale here typically comes off as the stepsister foil to the fairy tale's Cinderella powers, its open-endedness and susceptibility to multivalent imaginative appropriations. Moral tales, it would seem, are easily caught and caged; fairy tales aren't.

Darton's amused—and confused—depiction is all the more arresting since it comes from a historian whose perspective on English children's books is presumably indicated by the subtitle *Five Centuries of Social Life* and who describes his study as "a minor chapter in the history of English social life" (vii). Despite his undeniable merits and wide-ranging knowledge, Darton's Whiggish historical model of progress from quotidian instruction toward the escapist delight of fairy tale and fantasy obscures his ability to read Georgian moral tales from within their own discourse, code, cultural system, or ideology, whatever name we choose to give their distinctive signifying practices. Supposedly descriptive, the critical paradigm inherited from the Romantics by Darton and his successors in children's literary history is in actuality prescriptive and ahistorical. It sets up a binary hierarchy of fairy tale versus moral tale that not only hampers research into a germinal period of children's literature but also forestalls informed discussion of broader issues, such as the relation of instruction to delight or of gender to genre or of adult writer to child audience (including the author's own inner child self).

Evading Darton's post-Romantic bias by more self-consciously contextualizing moral tales would require research into all those elements assembled in his stereotypical portrayal and then some, such as authorial subjectivity and class relations.[5] Here I want only to check the fit between that stereotype and one story, Maria Edgeworth's "Simple Susan." Exploring ways that this fiction eludes the binary opposition of moral tale and fairy tale (and the broader cultural contraries which this opposition implies), I am especially concerned to demonstrate how the woman writer's appropriation of children's literature opens up important issues for a feminist theory of reading. Edgeworth's subtle rewriting and personalizing of moral tale conventions illuminates themes central to Georgian female life and to contemporary feminist critique as well: the relation between nurturance and autonomy, connectedness and individuation, child and parent, dependence and dominance, feeling and reason, and, finally, between experience and the discursive practices that configure or constitute it.

Much as Edgeworth herself demonstrates that the values centered around "simplicity" are the story's locus of power and that her simple heroine is no simpleton, I want to argue that "Simple Susan" is anything but a one-dimensional work. Often considered the best of Edgeworth's moral tales for children, it is richly revelatory both for its personal subtext and its interplay of the generic and the generic, strands woven together in the story's idealizing figuration of maternal values textualized in pastoral space. Dry "Utilitarian" though she is often labeled, Edgeworth overwrites the conventions of the rational moral tale with another story, a pastoral romance of child empowerment perennially popular with girl readers and deeply satisfying to the author herself.[6] Edgeworth as writer-daughter, I will show, fantasizes a family romance in which she remothers herself by rescuing her parents, in effect giving birth to the familial status and the ideal self she desires, while creating a textual *locus amoenus* that embodies maternal values and thus remothers her child readers as well.[7] Without breaking the moral tale's generic contract, Edgeworth represents herself as woman and re-presents growing up gendered in Georgian culture.

It is curious that Darton's little scene should star a boring papa in the role of rational pedagogue, for the Georgian period initiated the great age of the mother-teacher and of educational forms that discursively function as mothering presence for the child reader.[8] Edgeworth and her sister writers appropriated for children's literature what still remains perhaps its core genre, the less stylized, more realistic pastoral—or more properly, georgic, for it treats of endeavor rather than love—that emerged in poetry, painting, and fiction in the latter half of the eighteenth century, the kind of semi-realistic, semi-Arcadian idyll now typically associated with William Wordsworth's name. Since such domesticated pastoral forms were early claimed by Hannah More as peculiarly the province of woman and of maternal values, it says much about the canonical status of writing for children and writing by women that Wordsworth's female predecessors in thematizing the commonalities of daily and rural life should be dismissed by modern literary historians as a "monstrous regiment" of women, purveyors of a genre that is "very limp—handfuls of little stories about ordinary children discovering the nature of the world around them by careful observation and reflection. There was no vital spark" (Muir 82; Carpenter 2).[9] But if, on the one hand, female stories of everyday school and family life like Edgeworth's "Simple Susan" eventuated in the more polished psychological realism of nineteenth-century novels for the nursery (such as Harriet Martineau's *The Crofton Boys*, 1841), they also demonstrate complex textual affinities with fairy tale, fantasy, and romance.[10] Anticipating generic blends like Frances Hodgson Burnett's *The Secret Garden* (1911), for example, Edgeworth's "Simple Susan" situates realistically depicted children within a landscape invested with mythic resonance and moral magic.[11] Such stories may lack outright fairy godmothers, but they endow their heroines with nurturing powers and inscribe maternal ideology in the very form of their feminized pastorals.[12]

Though Darton's rational father is thus off the mark in one way, he is nevertheless very much apropos in another, for patrilineal preoccupations dominate Edgeworth criticism. Whether Richard Lovell's influence was for worse (as most critics have lamented) or for better (as some nineteenth-century readers and Marilyn Butler, Maria's authoritative biographer, have argued), his impact on his daughter and her writing and Maria's positioning as daddy's girl occupy center stage. What little serious discussion of the daughter's writing for children does exist typically devotes more space to the parent than to the author herself or considers the two a unit, with Maria an amanuensis wielding her father's pen or a puppet ventriloquizing his ideas.[13] And just as parent and child appear homogeneous, so the rationalistic forewords framing most of Maria's tales are read as seamlessly continuous with the stories that follow.[14] The preface to the *Parent's Assistant* (1796), for example, reads like a set piece for critics with romantic proclivities to quote and deplore—and they do. (Sometimes one wonders if dismissive critics have read farther than the preface.) It assures parents that "care has been taken to avoid inflaming the imagination, or exciting a restless spirit of adventure, by exhibiting false views of life, and creating hopes, which in the ordinary course of things, cannot be realized," and it rightly observes that no one has proved that all children prefer fairy stories to "imitation of real life." "But supposing that they do prefer such tales, is this a reason why they should be indulged in reading them?" it continues. "It may be said that a little experience in life, would soon convince them, that fairies, giants, and enchanters, are not to be met with in the world. But why should the mind be filled with fantastic visions, instead of useful knowledge? . . . Why should we vitiate their taste, and spoil their appetite, by suffering them to feed upon sweetmeats?" (*Works* 10: viii). Exemplifying the outmoded historicism that still addresses earlier juvenile literature, both tale and teller are reduced to unproblematic illustrations or reflections of something extrinsic. Ergo, the educationally progressive preface must dictate the story; the daughter's fiction must simply parrot her educator father.[15]

Such simplistic equations leave no gap for the woman writer to tell her own story, which turns out to be a complex negotiation of the paternal *and* maternal narratives and languages made available to her by her culture, a dual self-inscription. Edgeworth's official public persona (much to her and her family's lifelong amusement) was that of the bluestocking educator, cool mistress of the culture's master discourse; no woman of the period could write more rationally and commonsensically than Edgeworth when she chose—and she sometimes converted scrawled notes from her father into the considered prefaces that bear his initials. Edgeworthian forewords are written in the language of the culture's parent—Reason, the father's tongue, and they are addressed to a parental audience. Frequently that audience is envisioned as maternal, for example in the "Address to Mothers" that Maria wrote to preface the *Continuation of Early Lessons* (1814), and the heartening message is that mother-educators possess every rational capability and are the vanguard of progressive instruction. But if Maria Edgeworth demonstrates both personally and theoretically how women can appropriate reason to speak with discursive and parental authority, she writes her juvenile stories from another position as well, the child's place.[16] She overlays their rational morality and cause-effect plots with an alternative discourse that privileges affiliation over achievement, human interrelatedness over scientific reason: a "different voice" of need, nurture, and even "nonsense" (a favorite term of Maria's for the playful and the nonrational), a language culturally ascribed to women and to children.[17] She liked to think of herself as her father's representative, but her stories also represent herself. They are the site of maternal longing and magical thinking as much as reason and "useful knowledge," of feelings as well as the "facts" that the preface lauds. Pragmatic and domesticated, Edgeworthian "fantastic visions" nevertheless narrativize female fantasy (*Works* 10: vi, viii).

At the manifest level, the Edgeworthian moral tale seems a fiction of common sense (and has often been called such), thoroughly rational and realistic, demonstrating through both its explicitly endorsed values and its narrative strategies bourgeois empiricist convictions of everyday experience as the source of knowledge. The linear plot appropriate to such a world view enacts the protagonist's learning process or failure to learn; the pedagogical process itself generates the rational plot, which links causes and consequences and displays the uses of foresight and analytical assessment. Characters learn virtues like industry and honesty, and character development typically takes place through contrast, the lazy boy throwing into high relief the industrious hero. With their domestic realism, an empirically produced insistence on the worth of everyday little things, and their domestic heroism, the conferring of dignity on the small acts of courage available to children, Edgeworth's stories can be read as a feminization of patterns of thought and modes of relating oneself to the world that Western culture has traditionally ascribed to men. Maria Edgeworth's appropriation of paternal narrative structures and language has, as I have argued elsewhere, much to offer girl readers.[18] But such an account neglects the affective dimension of the fictional world that she creates in response to the family world that had created her.

Far from being a monovocal genre isolated from real issues and real children, as Darton's summation suggests, the moral tale offers Maria Edgeworth a location and a locution for addressing precisely those "personal emotions" and "unstable ideals" from which Darton would divorce the genre. For Maria herself as well as for the child characters in her stories and the real child readers (originally her many young sisters and brothers) for whom the fictions were composed, the moral tale offers a literary space in which narrative events function as nurturing environment. First, I will sketch the complex family situation which generated both the writing of the stories and their most resonant themes and characterizations. The quest for, or maintenance of, a safe home place and the satisfying empowerment of juveniles who transcend the binaries of adult and child, agency and communion, logic and love, which are central to the achievement of "Simple Susan" and other stories in the *Parent's Assistant*, dominate Maria Edgeworth's life script as well as her textual inscriptions. For her as for the child hero of "Forgive and Forget," the moral tale's literary space becomes "a little garden of my own," within which an authorial psychic narrative is embedded (*Works* 10:323).[19] (Since Edgeworth's passion for gardening colors many letters and provides the name for her autobiographical child character Rosamond, of "Purple Jar" fame, it's not surprising that her pastoral tale functions as a metaphoric "room of one's own.") Second, I will explore how "Simple Susan" as story and Susan as child-woman complement, contest, and ultimately decenter the rational educational discourse epitomized in the preface to the *Parent's Assistant*. Maria Edgeworth's public allegiance to the reason that linguistically and literally parents her stories is delicately disrupted and transformed by the gendered subjectivity inscribed in the tales. Rescuing the genre from Dartonian charges, such a dual contextualization demonstrates the rich imaginative and cultural uses of the "rational" tale for the woman writer in Georgian England.

How Maria came to writing and what her writing meant in her life are central to understanding her themes and by extension those of other female authors of the period.[20] Her early childhood was unhappy. Her mother, the least loved of Richard Lovell's four wives, died when she was five, and within a month Maria had a beautiful and brilliant step-mother. Honora Sneyd, the prototype of the rational maternal educator in the "Purple Jar" and other Rosamond stories, was the initiator of the scientific child observation and the realistic story method that ground the Edgeworth educational enterprise, though her husband usually receives the credit. Her stepdaughter respected her, feared her, tried to please her, and must have deeply envied her central place in Richard Lovell's mind and heart. The second Mrs. Edgeworth died when Maria was twelve, and at school—she had been sent away at seven—the girl received a remarkable letter, written by her father at Honora's deathbed. Brokenhearted, oddly brusque, the father both urges his eldest daughter to forgive her stepmother for being perhaps too meticulously rational and to emulate Honora's extraordinary virtues; most important to the love-starved child, the letter avows her father's interest in her and her improvement. After a couple of unsettled years in England following the father's third marriage, the family moved to Ireland, and Maria had her first real home. She also had more of her father's undivided attention than she would ever have again, as he completed her schooling, setting her to translating educational works and to writing stories of her own. His third wife was unlike Honora, and Maria took her stepmother's place as Richard Lovell's intellectual companion.

After Maria's own education had concluded, she strategically revived the ambitious project begun in Honora's day; it became a vocation for her, and it provided a way to maintain what she liked to call a partnership with her father. Indeed, all her life she used her writing for children and adults alike as counters for winning family attention and affection. Everyone was involved in reading and editing her work. Stories were written as gifts and surprises for family members, especially her father. Honora had left a manuscript notebook and a small volume privately printed in 1780; in 1796, the first version of the *Parent's Assistant* was published, publicly reinstating the family educational plan to produce stories, lessons, and a manual for parents which would not be completed until 1825, years after Richard Lovell's death. In 1798, Richard Lovell married, for the fourth and last time, a bright, talented woman a year younger than Maria. Initially very upset at the prospect of a formidable rival, Maria, courted by both lovers, grew to cherish this "mother" and lived affectionately with her till her own death in 1849. The first child of this marriage, Frances Maria, born in 1799, conjoined her mother's and her sister's names and became Maria's deeply beloved surrogate daughter.

Ironically, young Fanny would win her father's commendation as "prudence itself," while the official family reading of Maria's character always remained that captured in the imaginative, imprudent Rosamond, thoughtless and talkative, who never looks before she leaps (Butler and Butler 209–10). Though Edgeworth gently mocks the imperfect little girl, so vividly real and eager for love, she relished imaging herself as Rosamond into her old age, and she used the child's part and her role as children's author to help satisfy her "inordinate desire to be beloved." This relational capacity, this need to receive and bestow love, was, her father pronounced, her greatest failing (quoted in Butler 477).[21] But as Maria's stories demonstrate to those who see past the preface, and as her letters still more openly proclaim, she herself highly values eagerness of feeling. More than the prudence and rational foresight Rosamond forever struggles—and never quite manages—to master, Maria's most resonant stories valorize the affiliative— spontaneous sympathy, empathetic interdependence with others.

Its autobiographical genesis during the late nineties and the rich symbolic systems within which its heroine is articulated and objectified render "Simple Susan" an authorial self-representation related to, yet very different from the series of tales about the giddy child Rosamond and her rational, Honora-like mother.[22] Maria's own craving for love, often attributed to faulty fictional characters like Rosamond, also generates and grounds the story of Susan, the almost perfect daughter, almost magically beloved, who transcends the binaries of child and adult, dependence and dominance, as she emulates her mother, saves her father, and is crowned heroine by her entire community. Not included in the first or second editions of the *Parent's Assistant*, "Simple Susan" was added along with several more tales to the revised and enlarged third edition of 1800.[23] Imaginatively transforming the anxieties of Maria Edgeworth's family life, the story of Susan, the ideal child, was a gift to the father by a daughter fearing disempowerment and displacement. The story woos the father, becoming part of the real life triangular courtship in which Maria played uneasy third, courted by both her father and younger stepmother-to-be. Susan, the story child, is a fictional daughter presented for paternal approval by her surrogate mother Maria, just as was the real-life Fanny, who, fittingly, grew up to be as highly valued by the father as Susan herself—three daughters, two of whom are simultaneously mother-figures as well.[24] With its symbiotic fusions of daughter-mother and child-adult, its ascription of paternal potency to maternal feeling, the story's emotional subtext thus fantasizes the family romance, at the same time that it enriches the moral tale's lesson of virtue rewarded.[25]

"Simple Susan" can't be understood as a story celebrating the triumph of empiricist reason or of Richard Lovell Edgeworth, Enlightenment theorist. Nor does it support clichés about the didactic father's suppressing the artistic daughter. The story works not through intellectual persuasiveness or informational content but through affective power. It thus problematizes pedagogy as it romances the moral tale. Marrying paternal and maternal narrative strategies even as it explores competing value systems, the fiction demonstrates how the moral tale at its best engages emotions and issues as supplely as any fantasy form. It shows too how the new Georgian literature for children could at once criticize old story traditions and exploit their folk motifs. In what still offers a useful entry into the world of Edgeworth's juvenile tales, Anne Thackeray Ritchie long ago noted how Maria's stories elude the dichotomy of "fantastic visions" and "useful knowledge" set up in the preface to the *Parent's Assistant*.[26] Rather, the stories' child power and moral magic effect a rapprochement between rational tale and fairy tale, a literary space where dream reward and active endeavor come together: "They open like fairy tales, recounting in simple diction the histories of widows living in flowery cottages, with assiduous devoted little sons, who work in the garden and earn money to make up the rent. There are also village children busily employed, and good little orphans whose parents generally die in the opening pages. Fairies were not much in Miss Edgeworth's line, but philanthropic manufacturers, liberal noblemen, and benevolent ladies in travelling carriages, do as well and appear in the nick of time to distribute rewards or to point a moral" (Ritchie, ix). What she fails to note, however, and what is most interesting is that these commonsensical fairy godparents exist at the periphery of Edgeworth's pastoral world; they do not typically generate action, but simply validate what's already been achieved by the child hero or heroine.[27]

The real fairy godmother is the author herself, whose daughter-heroine gratifyingly rescripts the plots of real life in a symbolic drama as wish-fulfilling as any fantasy. At once child and mother to her parents in the story, Susan performs similar roles for her creator, empowering her as child, authorizing her as teacher. Recent analysts of traditional romance and fairy tale such as Anne Wilson and Derek Brewer argue that their logic is not that of quotidian rationality, but of sub-

jective dream, a spontaneous emotional reaction that transforms the
world as protagonist, reader, and author wish, thus transforming the
imaginers as well. Enacting psychological conflicts and problems, such
fictions metaphorically offer solutions, not as rules of conduct but as
imaginative projections of emotions, dilemmas, and maturational patterns. Such psychic narrativizing is not limited to fantasy, as Brewer's
discussion of the slippages between fairy tale and realistic novel in so
rational a writer as Jane Austen indicates. Indeed, Barbara Hardy suggests, making up stories about ourselves is so primary a mental act
as to call into question "our commonly posited antagonism between
dream and realistic vision" (13).[28] And between moral tale and fairy
tale, I would add: for Edgeworth's ostensibly mimetic moralism is not a
transparent representation of external reality, but a controlling, ordering, and manipulating of experience that, like the "fantastic visions"
it repudiates, makes "possible the full enactment of the protagonist's
wishes." Via misfortunes, quests, tests, contests with villains, and help
from donor figures, Edgeworth's heroine struggles toward her final triumph, and here too, as in folk story, the "acclaim of the world" also
seems to signify "the fact that the hero now sees himself as he wishes
to see himself" (Wilson, *Traditional Romance* 58).

Edgeworth's "fairies, giants, and enchanters" are as thoroughly
rationalized as her pastoral setting is localized. Yet because masculinist
and maternal narratives of experience are so deeply embedded in our
culture, the modes of relating to the world that her personages embody
and the spatial ordering of her value systems are as meaningful as more
magical stories and as psychically relevant to other readers as to the
author herself. Edgeworth structures her plot and theme around evocative traditional customs and folk ceremonies.[29] Naturalistically depicted
in loving detail, May Day queens and processions, sacrificial lambs, and
customary land usages come to emblematize two contrasting modes of
relating to the world, two systems of values, two languages, litigious
Lawyer Case pitted against the heroine. Susan's story is about mothering, daughtering, and varieties of fathering both wise and villainous.
It is about love and logic, dominance and dependence, separation and
connection, bounded places and open spaces. A girl at the threshold
age of twelve, Susan is part child, part adult, exemplifying the best of
both worlds. She is a mediatory figure who reconciles contradictions in
herself and tests the values of others, and she is appropriately environed
in a pastoral space that objectifies the relational matrix of personal de-

velopment.[30] Susan's miniature garden world is an idyllic landscape of the mind—for both author and characters, it epitomizes what Gaston Bachelard calls "felicitous space" (xxxi).[31] It is child space, maternal space, family space.

In this fresh and fragrant mental garden, Edgeworth as author situates a heroine who is much more than a remarkably likable model for young readers to emulate. Susan is also more directly the heroine as the author's daughter, a remothered ideal self, a perfectly responsive daughter, ingenuous and hopeful, who is also a perfectly responsive mother, ingenious and dependable. An emblem of empowered daughterhood and maternal values, Susan almost magically succeeds at every endeavor. Though she undergoes trial after trial and must make a series of ritual sacrifices, eventually everything she touches turns almost literally to gold. Virtually everyone in her little community loves her wholly—"we can do nothing without *you*, dear Susan," they exclaim—and several become moral-tale counterparts of the conventional fairy-tale helper figures, one after another singing her praises to the fairy godparents in gentry guise who validate her active virtues. Her mother's health and her father's freedom both depend upon her love and her resourcefulness in surmounting the obstacles continually renewed by ogre-like Lawyer Case and his ill-educated children, who stand for the separatist, legalistic, entrepreneurial values threatening Susan and the whole village community. Simon Pugh's semiotic reading of eighteenth-century gardens and the ideology of enclosure illuminates the village's struggle to maintain its communal values against the Cases' usurpation: the children's "customary place of meeting is at a hawthorn, which stands in a little green nook, open on one side to a shady lane, and separated on the other side by a . . . hedge from the garden of an attorney," who wishes to appropriate and enclose it for his sole use (*Works* 10: 13, 9). Edgeworth would not need to belabor the point for her Georgian audience; the spatial symbolism set up in this opening paragraph is at once realistically allusive and timelessly evocative.

The very embodiment of maternal altruism, Susan figuratively and literally nurtures and nourishes not only her younger brothers, her ailing mother, and her impotent, though brave father, but the entire little community, from the toddling Mary, whom she mothers and to whom she confides her special knowledge of cowslips and violets, to the resident gentry, the symbolically named Somers family.[32] For Susan's story is a May pastoral, beginning with the traditional May Day ceremonies still enacted in her "retired hamlet on the borders of Wales, between Oswestry and Shrewsbury" and concluding with plans for a communal celebration on the twenty-fifth of May, Susan's birthday, when "all the lads and lasses of the village shall have a dance" in her honor (9, 58). Indeed, the whole unusually long story (it amounts to a novelette) honors Susan, who moves through its pages haloed by a language of renewal, recreation, and collaborative, reciprocal love. As Scott's admiring comment indicates, Susan Price has a little lamb. (The gift of her mother, it is named Daisy though it is male.)[33] She also has a pet guinea hen, tends chickens and bees, and generously shared her childhood basin of bread and milk with a friendly pig, only observing mildly when he usurped too large a share, "Take a *poon*, pig." Imagery marrying nature and nurture thus surrounds the heroine, whose favorite place for sewing—appropriately nest-like—is her "little honey-suckle arbour" (*Works* 10: 25, 10). When her sickly mother is no longer able to function, Susan bakes bread and sells it, and we remember, as she assumes other maternal roles, that "lady," the honorific for woman, originally meant "loaf kneader, loaf giver." She makes broth and tea to feed her mother, seasoning the latter with rosemary, the herb of remembrance. Susan is associated with eggs, mead, honey, and flowers as well; her very name means "lily" (curiously anticipating "Lilias," the mother's name in Burnett's commingling of garden place and preservative love). Although the plot line concerns saving the father who has been drawn for the militia—and the story exclaims, "Happy the father who has such a daughter as Susan!"—Susan is above all affiliated with the mother and with those activities and empathetic values conventionally defined as maternal.

One beautifully realized scene illustrates especially well Susan's symbiotic continuity with her mother and the contours of maternal altruism.[34] Watching over her mother's sickbed, Susan muses, "How can I be grateful enough to such a mother as this? . . . She taught me to knit, she taught me every thing that I know . . . and best of all, she taught me to love her, to wish to be like her." Just then her village friends come caroling in the May, with pipe, tabor, and flowers, but Susan declines her crown: "my mother is ill, I can't leave her, you know," and she takes up her mother's unfinished knitting, going on with the row in the middle of which her mother's hand had stopped. Since the stitchery itself literalizes interdependence, woman's "embeddedness in lives of relationship" and her homely skills of familial and communal nurture, Susan's small act deftly affirms both maternal values and the daughter's growing maturity (*Works* 10: 12, 17–18; Gilligan 171).

Yet the story is not at all sentimental, nor does it portray women as ineffectual angels in the house. Susan feels deeply, but she also reasons well, acts prudently, bubbles over with ideas for earning money to procure a substitute for her father, and displays enviable self-command when she must seemingly sacrifice her guinea hen, new dress, and beloved lamb. Much as Edgeworth's ethic uniting rational restraint *and* expressive feeling informs the scene of Susan's parting with her lamb to the butcher (with its poignant line, "It will not bleat to-morrow!"), so Susan's success unites the efforts of self *and* others (*Works* 10: 39). As if to underline the value of both self-reliance and interdependent love, the final sum is half earned by Susan's work and half given by the friends who value her. Susan's "simplicity"—her spontaneity, directness, generous feeling, and sensible activity—is clothed in imagery of nature and connection; from lambs to knitting, it is all of a piece. Susan herself centers a web of communal feeling that unites the villagers, and the values she embodies are enacted even more explicitly in spatial terms. Susan stands for one way of relating to objects and others in the world, a language of love and collaborative activity.

Lawyer Case, his brutal son, and his selfish daughter Barbara represent an alternative discourse, as they spitefully pursue the virtuous Prices throughout the story. Fairy-tale ogres and wicked stepsisters brought up to date, they repeatedly exemplify legalistic, competitive, separatist, acquisitive modes of behavior culturally ascribed to masculine endeavor and personality structure. The persecution of the Prices begins when Farmer Price refuses to back Case's desire to engross the "little green nook" sacred to the village children's May Day ceremonies and pastoral play. Barbara seizes as her prisoner Susan's guinea hen, which has wandered into the Cases' enclosed yard; her father finds out a flaw in Price's lease and lays claim to his farm as well; Susan's lamb is prey for Case to serve up to the gentry in hopes of becoming the agent of the Somers family. In contrast to the story's several caring father figures, Case epitomizes androcentric "agentic" values at their worst, and the story repeatedly draws attention to its organizing structure as a conflict between the lawyer and Susan and what each emblematizes. When Susan's recapitulation of her mother's virtues saves her father, preserves the children's nook, and indeed turns the whole village into one big garden and family, the narrator sums up slyly, "You see, at last, attorney Case, with all his cunning, has not proved a match for 'Simple Susan'" (*Works* 10: 60). Case and what he stands for are ritually expelled from the village family as the story concludes; he goes abroad to prey upon a wider world.

Like *The Secret Garden*, then, with which it has so much in common—from its emblematic tame lambs and May Day processions to its thematic preoccupation with georgic work and moral magic—"Simple Susan" has as its ideological and spatial genesis a place sacred to children, a nook which the story endues with maternal nurturing powers that expand it to embrace a community, yet which also remains situated within a larger patriarchal world. In both stories, the values associated with childish simplicity, mothering, and communal endeavor contest and transform alternative value systems, yet do not ultimately displace patriarchal social codes. Exploring the forms of empowerment available to children and to women, both fictions traffic in fairy-tale helper figures and espouse moral conversion effected from within, a magic that derives not from unearned external intervention, but from self-help and human caring. Each realistically rewrites the Cinderella plot at the heart of most stories for the young. And however fresh the green pastoral haze that renders these affiliated tales so delightful, their female authors are as socially pragmatic as they are psychically revisionary. Although the big house epitomizing male tenure of land and law remains solidly in place at each tale's conclusion, those who inhabit the house have been taught and transformed by alternative values embodied in the young and the motherly. Both stories realize fantasies of female nurturance, for the author herself as well as her characters.[35]

Each can also be read as a parable of female authorship and self-inscription. If Edgeworth herself needs familial love too much, the author's sanctioned linguistic creativity generates a heroine who transforms fault to transcendent merit. Women's educational function authorizes access to rational discourse; it also offers a way of making public a private language of desire and discontent. Instructive tales like "Simple Susan" aid the woman writer in negotiating the empowering and silencing fictions of man and woman presented to her by her culture. If neither Susan nor Edgeworth can voice her needs or represent herself directly, the educational author can situate her heroine within an admiring fictive world and create the blind Welsh harper, the story's final donor-helper figure, who sings for all the world to hear his ballad of "Susan's Lamentation for her Lamb," thus securing the last bit of money Susan needs to save her parents. (Not surprisingly, Llewellyn turns out to be even more of a folk-tale figure than first appears, since he travels in rags as a test and isn't as poor as he looks.) Camouflaged behind her educational rationale, the female sage supplies the chorus of village characters who celebrate Susan's active virtues and generous love, thus giving speech to both Susan and to the authorial child within. "Simple Susan," then, is a nurturing fantasy masquerading as rational moral tale, a story whose affinities are with a tradition of feminine storytelling rather than masculine rational endeavor. What the story valorizes is not scientific objectivity, but gendered subjectivity, empowerment through affiliation within the domestic frame of reference that mattered most to Maria, who once thus described to Scott "the old end of the fairy tale: 'And so they lived very happily all the rest of their days'—home must have been always omitted at the end of this sentence; but it could have been nowhere else" (*Private Letter-Books* 266–67). Edgeworth liked to tell inquirers that she personally had "no story to tell," but her moral tales are simultaneously cover-up and revelation (Edgeworth family, *Memoir* 3: 259). The factual footnotes in "Simple Susan" refer to the doings of real-life Irish girls; the spirit of the story is Maria's own.[36]

The critical discourse of children's literature these days (like most critical discourse) is a site of struggle, though here much effort goes toward *constructing* a canon rather than deconstructing one. In creating a "great tradition," we must forbear a Leavisian privileging of one strand at the expense of all others and a post-Romantic valorizing of the child as imagination incarnate.[37] Remembering that both "child" and "children's literature" are shifting cultural constructs, we will be freed to look within the dull "plain wrap" that currently envelops historical genres like the moral tale and to release their plurality of meanings. Romancing the moral tale, then, means attending to culturally specific forms and functions—the shapes that the generic, the genderic, and the generational take in particular cases. It means being attentive to nuance and to context and reading this literature as seriously as we do its more overtly magical counterparts. It means rethinking the easy dichotomies that structure so much children's literary criticism and respecting the authors of the past and the psychic uses of their "moral" fictions for them and for their readers. It means remembering the testimony of those past readers, like the little girl who suddenly accosted

Maria Edgeworth at a crowded London party, "looked at her hard, and said, 'I like simple Susan best,' and rushed away overwhelmed at her own audacity" (Thackeray 127)–or like the adult reader Scott, who somehow managed to be at once a student and admirer of Edgeworth's and a partisan of Edgar Taylor's *German Popular Stories*.[38]

Scott paid Edgeworth's realistic Irish scenes tribute for inspiring his Scottish novels, and if he preferred "our old wild fictions" to shallow "histories of Tommy Goodchild" "crowned with temporal success," he also appreciated Edgeworth's "great genius" in "the more modern path." "I think the story of Simple Susan in particular quite inimitable," he notes, and he humorously describes the tiny author herself as "quite the fairy of our Nursery-tale the Whippity Stourie . . . a sprite who came flying in through the window to work all sort of marvels. I will never believe but what she has a wand in her pocket and pulls it out to conjure a little before she begins to write" (*Letters* 7: 312; 8: 56).[39] Scott knew that the fairies weren't really "in hiding" in Georgian England, if readers can only recognize them. Perhaps we would do better to emulate his liberal literary tastes than his reactionary romantic politics.

NOTES

I am grateful to the National Endowment for the Humanities for the fellowship during which I completed much of the research for this essay.

1. Quoted from v of Burnett's original preface for *The Little Princess*, which is appropriately titled "The Whole of the Story."
2. Olney's proposal for his 1981 NEH seminar on "Autobiography and the Humanities" is quoted in Sidonie Smith 3.
3. Scott's observation to Mrs. John Davy, Dec. 1831, is quoted from her family journal in John Gibson Lockhart's life, 10: 144.
4. Sylvia W. Patterson's title, "Eighteenth-Century Children's Literature in England: A Mirror of Its Culture," epitomizes attitudes to representation and referentiality now being interrogated.
5. The same kind of historicized scrutiny that moral tales solicit also needs to be applied to the conventional pieties of fairy tale supporters. Alan Richardson's "Wordsworth, Fairy Tales, and the Politics of Children's Reading" in this volume is a useful start in the right direction. Despite their seemingly disparate designs on the child, the period's romantics, realists, and religionists come together in using the child and its literature to encode their own needs and fantasies. I am grateful to Alan Richardson for allowing me to read his essay in manuscript.

6. Even so astute a critic as Brian Alderson, who speaks appreciatively of Edgeworth's merits, brands her on the strength of the preface to *Parent's Assistant*.

7. Contemporary feminist declarations of the mother's centrality in women's writing range from the psychologically based work of Americans like Nancy Chodorow and Carol Gilligan to the more linguistically focused French feminist theory of Hélène Cixous, Luce Irigaray, and Julia Kristeva, whose maternal metaphorizing has recently been critiqued by Domna Stanton. Judith Kegan Gardiner argues that in some modern women's adult novels, the heroine is "her author's daughter"; I would extend her insight to embrace the whole of a story for juveniles as a narrative space encoding a wish for remothering.

8. Pastoral is one such form; another is the mother-child dialogue particularly favored by women writers who wished to inform juvenile readers about the natural world. For further discussion, see Ruth Bloch; Jane Rendall, "The Case for 'Maternal Education'" 109–25; Myers, "Impeccable Governesses"; Marion Amies; and Ann B. Shteir.

9. More comments on pastoral forms and "the characteristics of female genius" in *Essays on Various Subjects, Principally Designed for Young Ladies* (1777). Since "their simplicity is their perfection," such genres are particularly suited to women, who play no part in the public world and are not classically trained for more difficult literary kinds. She prophesies women's appropriation of domestic fiction, arguing for their "peculiar talent" in writing "the *vraisemblance* to real life," which especially "consists in the art of interesting the tender feelings by a pathetic representation of . . . minute, endearing, domestic circumstances," instructing indirectly through events themselves (7–8, 11–12). She had already produced a female pastoral which encodes mother-daughter relationships in its literary shape: *The Search After Happiness: A Pastoral Drama for Young Ladies* (1773), in which daughters find the happiness they seek in pastoral retreat with an all-wise mother figure.

10. Much of the Georgian period's adult realist fiction also draws on fairy tale motifs. See, for example, Derek Brewer's analysis of the "fantasies of the family drama" embedded in Jane Austen's novels (149). Since Austen publicly acknowledged her debts to Edgeworth, it is tempting to connect the pastoral enclosure in her juvenilia *Catharine or the Bower* with Edgeworth's garden hideaways like that of Simple Susan.

11. So little is the female tradition in children's literature recognized that Valerie Sanders has recently claimed Martineau's tale as an "important break in children's literature, since most of her recent predecessors, Maria Edgeworth . . . for instance, had supplied their child-heroes with the guidance of an often priggish and solemn parent" (90). In fact, the heroes and heroines of the *Parent's Assistant* are remarkably self-reliant

and independent as well as psychologically realistic; indeed, several are orphans who must make their own way entirely. Nor does Sanders note the key role that the mother of Hugh (the child hero) and the values of home play in Martineau's school story (90). Julia Briggs's similarly teleological reading of the female tradition makes E. Nesbit pivotal.

12. The literature on pastoral is very large and increasing daily. Helpful re-thinkings of pastoral forms are especially abundant in the Renaissance and Romantic periods, critics as distant chronologically as Louis Adrian Montrose and Stuart Curran arguing that pastoral forms are functional, performing real cultural work, rather than being nostalgic, escapist forms cordoned from life, as Laurence Lerner, Renato Poggioli, and Kathryn Hume have implied. Reproblematizing pastoral goes back to William Empson, though as Paul Alpers notes, his observations are slippery. The double voicing or doubled vision of pastoral to which Empson called attention in his germinal work—the mediation of class and age differences, the putting of the complex into the simple—has proved useful to many critics of children's literature, as in the dissertation of Phyllis Bixler Koppes, who finds the pastoral tradition constitutive of many juvenile classics. However, despite Koppes's interest in Burnett, she, like most readers of pastoral, there gave greatest attention to the genre's male progenitors, Rousseau and Wordsworth. Similarly, Peter V. Marinelli's chapter on the pastoral of childhood considers only male variants, and anthologies of pastoral (Frank Kermode, John Barrell and John Bull) typically define the genre solely in terms of male verse and drama for adults. Andrew V. Ettin typically states, "Pastoral society is predominantly male" (146), while Ann Messenger analyzes pastoral poetry as a "trap" for the woman writing to adults. Little theoretical consideration of female juvenile pastoral exists outside Elizabeth Francis's brief review essay and suggestive observations in more specialized essays like U. C. Knoepflmacher's study of E. Nesbit and Lissa Paul's suggestions about feminist approaches. Demystifications of Romantic associations of the male child with natural settings, like Marlon B. Ross's and Alan Richardson's in *Romanticism and Feminism* and Susan M. Levin's work on Dorothy Wordsworth, and provocative analyses of women and nature, like Sherry B. Ortner's much debated essay and Carol Fabricant's study of the eighteenth-century garden as the repository of female mysteries, clear the way for consideration of Georgian women's contribution to pastoral. The generic categories of "idyllic realism" and "narrative of community" recently suggested by Shelagh Hunter, P. D. Edwards, and Sandra A. Zagarell for some adult nineteenth-century writing might also be usefully applied to juvenile fiction. For realistic shifts in Georgian pastoral art, see John Barrell.

13. Both educational historians like Marjory Lang and feminist literary historians like Sandra M. Gilbert and Susan Gubar advance such notions. The latter critics read Edgeworth as a self-deprecator downgrading "her own 'feminine' fiction in terms of her father's commitment to pedagogically sound moral instruction," "a creature of her father's imagination" constrained to ventriloquize patriarchal Enlightenment theories (146, 148). As Toril Moi objects to their general account of how patriarchal ideology affects the woman writer, "feminists must be able to account for the paradoxically productive aspects of [the] patriarchal ideology" they would elude (Moi 64; see 57–69). As a matter of fact, Honora Sneyd Edgeworth, Richard Lovell's second wife, pioneered the family principle "that the art of education should be considered as an experimental science" and that practice rather than theory should ground educational philosophy, as the Edgeworths' handbook for parents explains (*Practical Education* 2: 734). Marjory Lang has useful things to say about Edgeworth's stories as socializing narratives that reveal a period's educational ideals, but for her Maria Edgeworth is a group voice and her stories are useful for the cultural information we can extrapolate from them. The most notable thing about her literary treatment of the tales is that there isn't any. The same must be said of Mary V. Jackson's overview of the period, where Edgeworth's story rates a one-paragraph plot summary, replete with trivial errors indicating hasty reading (163–64).

14. Some prefaces bearing Richard Lovell's initials were written by Maria from his notes; some prefaces for her adult fiction he clearly wrote himself. It is indicative of Maria's growth in personal and creative self-assurance that the prefaces she wrote in maturity after her father's death are playful, covertly autobiographical, and remarkably attentive to the child's point of view. See, for example, the dialogue between two children that introduces *Little Plays for Children* (1827).

15. Some critics grow troubled when Edgeworthian educational theory fails to account fully for Edgeworthian imaginative practice, since the former is taken to generate the latter (e.g., Harden 39–40). Others take the opposite tack that the stories somehow succeed despite the dead weight of educational ideas (e.g., Thwaite 74; Darton 140, 142). For an excellent example of how post-Romantic definitions of children's literature warp critical judgment, see Marilyn Gaull. Because eighteenth-century thought on juvenile literature "specifically excluded what we normally consider to be the very essence of children's literature: fairy tales, adventures, romances, tales of magic, and nursery rhymes," Edgeworth's "concern with the commonplace, with the authentic voice, with the terrestial life" can only be strengths in her adult fiction; they necessarily "limited her juvenile writing" (50, 57). The numerous factual errors and false

inferences Gaull packs into her brief overview testify to Romanticists' lack of interest.

16. One nineteenth-century biographer records Edgeworth's being asked "how she came to understand children as she did, what charm she used to win them. 'I don't know . . . I lie down and let them crawl over me'" (Thackeray 127). Between 1764 and 1812, Richard Lovell Edgeworth fathered twenty-two children by his four wives, so Maria, born in 1768, had ever fresh sources for reexperiencing childhood at first hand.

17. Though they do not sufficiently consider the interplay of gender and language or historical specificities, Nancy Chodorow's and Carol Gilligan's works have become standard starting places for considering women as relationally defined beings, and the growing body of feminist revisions of psychoanalytical and moral theory informs my approach to women's moral tales. Representative analyses of culturally produced "male" rationality include the studies of Evelyn Fox Keller, Genevieve Lloyd, and Sara Ruddick.

18. See my "'A Taste for Truth and Realities'" and "Socializing Rosamond."

19. Indeed, it can be argued that attitudes toward home, the "good place" however envisioned, are the core of children's literature. See Clausen, Waddey, and Frey and Griffith (227–32) for suggestive generalizations. Women writers, however, seem specially drawn toward domestic and garden enclosures, microcosms which function for them, in Gaston Bachelard's phrase, as "dominated worlds," allowing them "to be world conscious at slight risk" (161). Peculiarly the locus of "longing," as Susan Stewart suggests, miniatures also model the way the world works. The binaries "agentic" and "communal" (terms which I take from Nancy Chodorow's application of David Bakan's philosophical categories to culturally masculine and feminine ways of being in the world) themselves reflect the way spatial imagining encodes values: "agency manifests itself in the formation of separations; communion in the lack of separations. . . . Agency manifests itself in the urge to master; communion in noncontractual cooperation," embeddedness and relational sharing rather than domination and demarcation of space ("Family Structure and Feminine Personality" 55–57). The conflict between Susan and Lawyer Case is enacted in precisely these terms. Judith Fryer traces women writers' spatialization of values into the twentieth century. For Edgeworth's gardening passion, see Christina Colvin and Charles Nelson.

20. Charles Lamb's example suggests that male authors might also be illuminated by such an approach. For an application to Mary Wollstonecraft, see my "Pedagogy as Self-Expression." For fuller discussion of the links between Edgeworth's early life and her writing for children, see my "The Dilemmas of Gender" and Butler's biography.

21. Virtually the same phrases—"this inordinate desire to be loved, this impatience of not being loved"—reprove the heroine in *Helen* (1834; 1: 67).

22. Rosamond stories appeared in several collections from 1796–1821. Most are collected together in the 1825 *Works* (11: 146–392).

23. Like "Simple Susan," some other tales also notably empower children searching for home, safety, and love; maternal fusion and fairy-tale motifs shape the narrative strategies of "The Orphans" and "The Basket-Woman," for example. The expanded 1800 edition of the *Parent's Assistant* (6 vols.) has been reprinted by Garland in two volumes. Whereas Edgeworth's 1796 arrangement reflected a class division in its two volumes, the 1800 version throws interesting light on gendered virtues as well. "Simple Susan," for instance, is paired in volume 2 with a Rosamond tale, "The Birth-Day Present." Both are stories about the female child's need for love and both value generous feeling, but the bracketing calls still more attention to Susan's heroism. Rosamond must learn a lesson; Susan teaches even adults. In the 1825 *Works*, the stories have been rearranged to give "Simple Susan" the pride of first place. Fantasies of children who rescue parents and restore families also appear in stories for adults; Maria's anxiety over the possible disruption of the connection to her family engendered by her only proposal in 1802 surfaces in *Madame de Fleury* (1809) and *Emilie de Coulanges* (1812) in the two sets of *Tales of Fashionable Life*, both written long before publication. Elise Boulding offers a modern clinical perspective on such nurture of adults by children.

24. Those who read Maria as daddy's passive victim should recall Jane Gallop's insight that the daughter's seduction entails the father's seduction as well. Maria's maternal investment in Fanny is powerfully revealed in an 1826 letter recounting how the newborn was symbolically delivered from the biological mother into the sister-mother's hands, so that Maria could present the child to her father as the daughter of all three (MacDonald 98; see also 179–81). In a letter composed around 1798–1800, Richard Lovell testifies to the perfect daughterhood achieved by heroine, fiction, and author, "I have been reading *Simple Susan* this half hour and am really charmed with it—the perfect elegant simplicity & accuracy of description, the discrimination of character & the pathos which are to be met with in every page—will if it becomes known *at present* give it the preference of every story of the sort that has yet been written in any language" (quoted in Butler 160). Maria replied, "Thank you, my dear father and most kind partner, for your partiality for 'Simple Susan'" (Edgeworth family, *Memoir* 1: 102). The story was finished shortly after the marriage in 1798; the baby's 1799 birth slightly preceded the story's 1800 publication. In the manuscript draft of the tale in the

family papers at the Bodleian (MS Eng misc e1462), the Susan character and the work as a whole are called Marianne, a variant on Maria's and her birth mother's name which is also used for the heroine of "The Cherry Orchard," another story about community and being loved dating from this period.

25. Philippa Pearce, contemporary writer of juvenile fiction, wisely notes that "in children's books we should be prepared to find the fantasies as well as the realities of the author's childhood. Even what seems fairly realistic may have been heightened and distorted for a private purpose" (76). More theoretically, Dominick LaCapra observes that an author's written texts and "lived" text interact in ways far more subtle than cause-effect sequence, questioning as well as supplementing one another (60–61). Recent revisionist studies of autobiography that I have found helpful include work by Linda Anderson and Sidonie Smith and anthologies edited by Shari Benstock, James Olney, Domna Stanton, and Bella Brodzki and Celeste Schenck.

26. Although her father occasionally disparaged Edgeworth's work, Anne relished her as a child and continued to do so as an adult. Ritchie became a writer for children herself, as well as a critic. Her several prefaces to Edgeworth's fiction all remain worth reading.

27. Lee Edwards notes that female "fantasies of resolution" often seek to unite love and work as the paradigmatic marriage plot does not. But because feminist analysis has seldom noticed children's tales, much less engaged them within their historical environment, the way that stories like Edgeworth's reconcile active work and emotional reward is missed or misread. Writing in 1978 when feminist analysis stereotypically read mothering as repressive, Lynne Agress briefly dismisses the work of Edgeworth and her sister writers as passive and sexist: "females were too shallow even to be portrayed as criminals." Her own bias similarly leads her to assert without evidence that *The Parent's Assistant* refers to mothers, since the real parent must be the father; in actuality, the title was bestowed by the publisher, has no such reference, and was much disliked by the author (95, 91).

28. "Like most works of fiction," Hardy continues, "personal history is made up of fantasy and realism," the polarity between the two being "another instance of convenient fiction" (14). "*Everything's* a story. You are a story—I am a story," Burnett's *Little Princess* similarly suggests (123). Asking *Who Am I This Time?* Jay Martin's recent overview argues, is basic in studying our transactions with fiction.

29. Comparison with historical accounts like those of Bob Bushaway, Lillian Eichler, Christina Hole, William Hone, and William Walsh demonstrates Edgeworth's accuracy and alertness to suggestive nuance.

30. It's worth recalling that twelve was a traumatic age for Maria, who was facing adolescence and her father's third marriage. Years later she thanked her aunt, a surrogate mother figure, for being "constantly partially kind to me from the time I was a child with inflamed eyes and swelled features for whom nobody else cared" (*Letters from England* 15). She was afflicted with a serious eye problem about the time of the remarriage, perhaps in response. An unloved Cinderella who felt within herself unrecognized powers, Maria "seemed to have spent her childhood looking for friends," and she dedicated much of her mature emotional and creative energies to keeping them (Butler 75).

31. Bachelard's description of his philosophical investigations of "topophilia" or "eulogized space" aptly captures the informing motif of Edgeworth's narrative: "to determine the human value of the sorts of space that may be grasped, that may be defended against adverse forces, the space we love" (xxxi).

32. Like one of the fictional boys, one of the younger brothers whom Maria helped educate was named William.

33. We need not resort to heavy-handed psychoanalytic readings to find this feminized lamb's provenance, loss, and magical restoration charmingly suggestive when set against the Edgeworths' contemporaneous domestic reorganization. When Susan yields up her cherished pet to preserve the family, she wins every heart, gaining universal acclaim and getting the lamb back too in a triumphal procession cheered on by the whole village. Recently printed by Susan Levin (238–41) and speculatively dated 1805, Dorothy Wordsworth's "Mary Jones and her Pet-lamb" similarly uses a girl's lost lamb to explore familial fantasies. Although Dorothy could thus have seen Edgeworth's story, I am not arguing for influence, but rather for a woman's tradition of thematizing emotional conflicts and ambivalences through natural images, a tradition that has more in common with the preservative love Sara Ruddick has recently analyzed in *Maternal Thinking* than with the modes and genres we usually characterize as "Romantic." Levin's (52–58) and Meena Alexander's (69–70) thoughtful analyses of this tale might usefully be supplemented by considering women writers for children as well as male Romantic poets. *Simple Susan*, for example, is specifically alluded to or revised in many later women's works, such as Barbara Hofland's "The Village Florist" and Juliana Horatia Ewing's *Mary's Meadow*. Edgeworth was widely read right into the twentieth century, influencing Kate Greenaway, among others.

34. Nancy Chodorow argues that because boys and girls are mothered differently, crucial differences in male and female personality and orientation to external relationships develop: "From the retention of preoedipal

attachments to their mother, growing girls come to define and experience themselves as continuous with others; their experience of self contains more flexible or permeable ego boundaries. Boys come to define themselves as more separate and distinct, with a greater sense of rigid ego boundaries and differentiation. The basic feminine sense of self is connected to the world, the basic masculine sense of self is separate." Girls mature with "a basis for 'empathy' built into their primary definition of self. . . . a stronger basis for experiencing another's needs or feelings as one's own" (*Reproduction* 169, 167).

35. See Phyllis Bixler's "Gardens, Houses, and Nurturant Power in *The Secret Garden*" in this volume; I regret that my essay was composed without its assistance.

36. Bertha Coolidge Slade notes that Susan is indebted to the sister of Peggy Langan, granddaughter of the model for Thady in *Castle Rackrent* (18).

37. In identifying the ways empiricism slides into idealism in the classic realist novels for adults enshrined by F. R. Leavis's work, Catherine Belsey's essay also illuminates the overlap of fairy tale and moral tale conventions in the Georgian fictions that parented realist novels for the nursery. Belsey's chapter calling for a new critical practice grounded in clarification of the contradictory discourses that texts smooth over is also useful (*Critical Practice* 125–46). Though she does not sufficiently consider post-Wordsworthian changes in concepts of the child and its literature, Felicity A. Hughes usefully suggests how realist fiction came to be considered adult fare, while fantasy was assigned to children; since her essay appeared in 1978, a remarkable valorization of that assignment has been taking place.

38. Childhood memories of "Simple Susan" abound in nineteenth-century records; like Anne Thackeray, Emily Lawless records a charming story. A party of young people on a train with two elderly ladies recount the delight the story had given them, how they had illustrated it and other tales and daringly forwarded their signed drawings to the famous author herself, who was of course overhearing it all and, "like an answer out of a fairy tale," much pleased to tell them " 'What must she have thought of such children?' " and how she had treasured their work (199).

39. Scott's acknowledgment of his indebtedness in the last chapter of *Waverly* (1814)—repeated in the 1829 general preface to his novels—initiated an enthusiastic friendship, correspondence, and visits (see 493, 523 of edition cited). In his edition of the letters, H. J. C. Grierson notes that Scott's children were brought up on the moral poetry of Ann and Jane Taylor, along with Edgeworth and their father's lore (7: 310n). In contrast to Peter and Iona Opie, whose epigraphs from Scott and others prefacing their fairy tale collection float free of context (11–12), Grierson does

fuller justice to the complexity of Scott's literary response. The Whippity Stourie was not only small like Edgeworth, but also noted for her pranks and her association with children; for an interesting example, see Katharine Briggs (430–31).

WORKS CITED

Agress, Lynne. *The Feminine Irony: Women on Women in Early-Nineteenth-Century English Literature.* Cranbury, NJ: Associated UP, 1978.

Alderson, Brian. "Literary Criticism and Children's Books; or, 'Could Be Worse.'" *Responses to Children's Literature: Proceedings of the Fourth Symposium of the International Research Society for Children's Literature.* New York: Saur, 1980. 59–75.

Alexander, Meena. *Women in Romanticism: Mary Wollstonecraft, Dorothy Wordsworth, and Mary Shelley.* Women Writers Series. Savage, MD: Barnes and Noble, 1989.

Alpers, Paul. "Empson on Pastoral." *New Literary History* 10.1 (Autumn 1978): 101–23.

———. "What Is Pastoral?" *Critical Inquiry* 8.3 (Spring 1982): 437–60.

Amies, Marion. "Amusing and Instructive Conversations: The Literary Genre and Its Relevance to Home Education." *History of Education* 14.2 (1985): 87–99.

Anderson, Linda. "At the Threshold of the Self: Women and Autobiography." *Women's Writing: A Challenge to Theory.* Ed. Moira Monteith. Sussex: Harvester; New York: St. Martin's, 1986. 54–71.

Bachelard, Gaston. *The Poetics of Space.* 1958. Trans. Maria Jolas. Boston: Beacon, 1969.

Barrell, John. *The Dark Side of the Landscape: The Rural Poor in English Painting, 1730–1840.* Cambridge: Cambridge UP, 1980.

Barrell, John, and John Bull, eds. *The Penguin Book of English Pastoral Verse.* 1974. Harmondsworth: Penguin, 1982.

Belsey, Catherine. *Critical Practice.* London: Methuen, 1980.

———. "Re-reading the Great Tradition." *Re-Reading English.* Ed. Peter Widdowson. London: Methuen, 1982. 121–35.

Benstock, Shari, ed. *The Private Self: Theory and Practice of Women's Autobiographical Writings.* Chapel Hill: U of North Carolina P, 1988.

Bixler, Phyllis. "Idealization of the Child and Childhood in Frances Hodgson Burnett's *Little Lord Fauntleroy* and Mark Twain's *Tom Sawyer.*" *Research about Nineteenth-Century Children and Books: Portrait Studies.* Ed. Selma K. Richardson. Urbana-Champaign: U of Illinois Graduate School of Library Science, 1980. 85–96.

Bloch, Ruth. "American Feminine Ideals in Transition: The Rise of the Moral Mother." *Feminist Studies* 4.2 (June 1978): 101–26.

Boulding, Elise. "The Nurture of Adults by Children in Family Settings." *Research in the Interweave of Social Roles: Women and Men* 1 (1980): 167–89.

Brewer, Derek. *Symbolic Stories: Traditional Narratives of the Family Drama in English Literature.* Cambridge: Brewer; Totowa, NJ: Rowman and Littlefield, 1980.

Briggs, Julia. "Women Writers and Writing for Children: From Sarah Fielding to E. Nesbit." In *Children and Their Books: A Celebration of the Work of Iona and Peter Opie.* Ed. Gillian Avery and Julia Briggs. Oxford: Clarendon, 1989. 221–50.

Briggs, Katharine. *An Encyclopedia of Fairies, Hobgoblins, Brownies, Bogies, and Other Supernatural Creatures.* New York: Pantheon, 1976.

Brodzki, Bella, and Celeste Schenck, eds. *Life/Lines: Theorizing Women's Autobiography.* Ithaca: Cornell UP, 1988.

Burnett, Frances Hodgson. *A Little Princess: Being the Whole Story of Sara Crewe Now Told for the First Time.* New York: Scribner's, 1905.

———. *The Secret Garden.* 1911. New York: Dell Yearling, 1982.

Bushaway, Bob. *By Rite: Custom, Ceremony, and Community in England, 1700–1800.* London: Junction, 1982.

Butler, Harriet Jessie, and Harold Edgeworth Butler, eds. *The Black Book of Edgeworthstown and Other Edgeworth Memories, 1585–1817.* London: Faber, 1927.

Butler, Marilyn. *Maria Edgeworth: A Literary Biography.* Oxford: Clarendon, 1972.

Carpenter, Humphrey. *Secret Gardens: A Study of the Golden Age of Children's Literature.* Boston: Houghton, 1985.

Chodorow, Nancy. "Family Structure and Feminine Personality." *Woman, Culture, and Society.* Ed. Michelle Zimbalist Rosaldo and Louise Lamphere. Stanford: Stanford UP, 1974. 43–66.

———. *The Reproduction of Mothering: Psychoanalysis and the Sociology of Gender.* Berkeley: U of California P, 1978.

Clausen, Christopher. "Home and Away in Children's Fiction." *Children's Literature* 10 (1982): 141–52.

Colvin, Christina, and Charles Nelson. " 'Building Castles of Flowers': Maria Edgeworth as Gardener." *Garden History* 16.1 (1988): 58–70.

Curran, Stuart. "The Pastoral." *Form and British Romanticism.* New York: Oxford UP, 1986. 85–127.

Darton, F. J. Harvey. *Children's Books in England: Five Centuries of Social Life.* 1932. 3rd ed. Rev. Brian Alderson. Cambridge: Cambridge UP, 1982.

[Edgeworth family.] *A Memoir of Maria Edgeworth, with a Selection from Her Letters by the Late Mrs. Edgeworth.* Ed. by her children. 3 vols. London: Privately printed Joseph Masters and Son, 1867.

Edgeworth, Maria, and Richard Lovell Edgeworth. *Practical Education.* 2 vols. London: Johnson, 1798.

[Edgeworth, Maria.] "The Cherry Orchard." *Early Lessons.* 10 parts. London: Johnson, 1801. 10: 53–109.

———. *Continuation of Early Lessons.* 2 vols. London: Johnson, 1814.

———. *Helen: A Tale.* 3 vols. London: Bentley, 1834.

———. *Letters from England, 1813–1844.* Ed. Christina Colvin. Oxford: Clarendon, 1971.

———. *Little Plays for Children.* Vol. 7 of *The Parent's Assistant.* London: Hunter and Baldwin, Cradock, and Joy, 1827.

———. *Tales of Fashionable Life.* 3 vols. London: Johnson, 1809.

———. *Tales of Fashionable Life.* 3 vols. London: Johnson, 1812.

———. *The Parent's Assistant.* 1800. 3rd ed. 6 vols., in 2. Classics of Children's Literature, 1621–1932. New York: Garland, 1976.

———. *Works of Maria Edgeworth.* 13 vols. Boston: Parker, 1825.

Edwards, Lee. "Love and Work: Fantasies of Resolution." *Frontiers: A Journal of Women Studies* 2.3 (Fall 1977): 31–38.

Edwards, P. D. *Idyllic Realism from Mary Russell Mitford to Hardy.* New York: St. Martin's, 1988.

Eichler, Lillian. *The Customs of Mankind, with Notes on Modern Etiquette and the Newest Trend in Entertainment.* Garden City: Doubleday, 1924.

Empson, William. *Some Versions of Pastoral.* Norfolk, CT: New Directions, 1950.

Ettin, Andrew V. *Literature and the Pastoral.* New Haven: Yale UP, 1984.

Ewing, Juliana Horatia. *Mary's Meadow and Letters from A Little Garden.* London: Society for Promoting Christian Knowledge, [1886]. *Mary's Meadow* was originally published in *Aunt Judy's Magazine* from November 1883 to March 1884.

Fabricant, Carol. "Binding and Dressing Nature's Loose Tresses: The Ideology of Augustan Landscape Design." *Studies in Eighteenth-Century Culture.* Vol. 8. Ed. Roseann Runte. Madison: U of Wisconsin P, 1979. 109–35.

Francis, Elizabeth. "Feminist Versions of Pastoral." *Children's Literature Association Quarterly* 7.4 (Winter 1982): 7–9ff.

Frey, Charles, and John Griffith. *The Literary Heritage of Childhood: An Appraisal of Children's Classics in the Western Tradition.* Westport, CT: Greenwood, 1987.

Fryer, Judith. *Felicitous Space: The Imaginative Structures of Edith Wharton and Willa Cather.* Chapel Hill: U of North Carolina P, 1986.

Gallop, Jane. *The Daughter's Seduction: Feminism and Psychoanalysis.* Ithaca: Cornell UP, 1982.

Gardiner, Judith Kegan. "The Heroine as Her Author's Daughter." *Feminist Criticism: Essays on Theory, Poetry, and Prose.* Ed. Cheryl L. Brown and Karen Olson. Metuchen, NJ: Scarecrow, 1978. 244–53.

———. "On Female Identity and Writing by Women." *Writing and Sexual Difference.* Ed. Elizabeth Abel. Chicago: U of Chicago P, 1982. 177–92.

Gaull, Marilyn. *English Romanticism: The Human Context.* New York: Norton, 1988.

Gilbert, Sandra M., and Susan Gubar. *The Madwoman in the Attic: The Woman Writer and the Nineteenth-Century Literary Imagination.* New Haven: Yale UP, 1979.

Gilligan, Carol. *In a Different Voice: Psychological Theory and Women's Development.* Cambridge: Harvard UP, 1982.

Harden, Elizabeth. *Maria Edgeworth.* Boston: Twayne, 1984.

Hardy, Barbara. "Towards a Poetics of Fiction: An Approach through Narrative." *The Cool Web: The Pattern of Children's Reading.* Ed. Margaret Meek, Aidan Warlow, and Griselda Barton. London: Bodley Head, 1977. 12–23.

Hofland, Mrs. [Barbara]. "The Village Florist." *Farewell Tales.* London: Newman, 1840. 87–107.

Hole, Christina. *British Folk Customs.* London: Hutchinson, 1976.

———. *English Custom and Usage.* 2nd ed. rev. London: Batsford, 1944.

———. *English Traditional Customs.* London: Batsford, 1975.

Hone, William. *The Every-Day Book and Table Book; or, Everlasting Calendar of Popular Amusements, Sports, Pastimes, Ceremonies, Manners, Customs, and Events.* 3 vols. London: Tegg, 1835.

Hughes, Felicity A. "Children's Literature: Theory and Practice." *ELH* 45.3 (Fall 1978): 542–61.

Hume, Kathryn. *Fantasy and Mimesis: Responses to Reality in Western Literature.* New York: Methuen, 1984.

Hunter, Shelagh. *Victorian Idyllic Fiction: Pastoral Strategies.* London: Macmillan, 1984.

Jackson, Mary V. *Engines of Instruction, Mischief, and Magic: Children's Literature in England from Its Beginnings to 1839.* Lincoln: U of Nebraska P, 1989.

Keller, Evelyn Fox. *Reflections on Gender and Science.* New Haven: Yale UP, 1985.

Kermode, Frank. *English Pastoral Poetry from the Beginnings to Marvell.* London: Harrap, 1952.

Knoepflmacher, U. C. "Of Babylands and Babylons: E. Nesbit and the Reclamation of the Fairy Tale." *Tulsa Studies in Women's Literature* 6.2 (Fall 1987): 299–325.

Koppes, Phyllis Bixler. "The Child in Pastoral Myth: A Study in Rousseau and Wordsworth, Children's Literature and Literary Fantasy." Diss. U of Kansas, 1977.

LaCapra, Dominick. "Rethinking Intellectual History and Reading Texts." *Modern European Intellectual History: Reappraisals and New Perspectives.* Ed. Dominick LaCapra and Steven L. Kaplan. Ithaca: Cornell UP, 1982. 47–85.

Lang, Marjory. "Maria Edgeworth's *The Parent's Assistant* (1796): A Document of Social Education." *History of Education* 7.1 (1978): 21–33.

Lawless, Emily. *Maria Edgeworth.* English Men of Letters Series. London: Macmillan, 1904.

Lerner, Laurence. *The Uses of Nostalgia: Studies in Pastoral Poetry.* New York: Schocken, 1972.

Levin, Susan M. *Dorothy Wordsworth and Romanticism.* Douglass Series on Women's Lives and the Meaning of Gender. New Brunswick: Rutgers, 1987.

Lloyd, Genevieve. *The Man of Reason: "Male" and "Female" in Western Philosophy.* Minneapolis: U of Minnesota P, 1984.

Lockhart, J. G. *Memoirs of the Life of Sir Walter Scott.* 10 vols. Edinburgh: Robert Cadell; London: Houlston and Stoneman, 1848.

MacDonald, Edgar E., ed. *The Education of the Heart: The Correspondence of Rachel Mordecai Lazarus and Maria Edgeworth.* Chapel Hill: U of North Carolina P, 1977.

Marinelli, Peter V. *Pastoral.* The Critical Idiom. London: Methuen, 1971.

Martin, Jay. *Who Am I This Time? Uncovering the Fictive Personality.* New York: Norton, 1988.

Martineau, Harriet. *The Crofton Boys: A Tale.* London: Charles Knight, 1841.

Messenger, Ann. "Women Poets and the Pastoral Trap: The Case of Mary Whateley." *Eighteenth-Century Women and the Arts.* Ed. Frederick M. Keener and Susan E. Lorsch. Contributions in Women's Studies, no. 98. New York: Greenwood, 1988. 93–105.

Moi, Toril. *Sexual/Textual Politics: Feminist Literary Theory.* London: Methuen, 1985.

Montrose, Louis Adrian. "Of Gentlemen and Shepherds: The Politics of Elizabethan Pastoral Form." *ELH* 50.3 (Fall 1983): 515–60.

More, Hannah. *Essays on Various Subjects, Principally Designed for Young Ladies.* London: J. Wilkie and T. Cadell, 1777.

———. *The Search After Happiness: A Pastoral Drama for Young Ladies.* 1773. *The Works of Hannah More.* 2 vols. New York: Harper, 1854. 1: 110–19.

Muir, Percy. *English Children's Books, 1600 to 1900.* New York: Praeger, 1954.

Myers, Mitzi. "The Dilemmas of Gender as Double-Voiced Narrative; or, Maria Edgeworth Mothers the *Bildungsroman.*" *The Idea of the Novel in the Eighteenth Century.* Ed. Robert W. Uphaus. East Lansing: Colleagues, 1988. 67–96.

———. "Impeccable Governesses, Rational Dames, and Moral Mothers: Mary Wollstonecraft and the Female Tradition in Georgian Children's Literature." *Children's Literature* 14 (1986): 31–59.

———. "Pedagogy as Self-Expression in Mary Wollstonecraft: Exorcising the Past, Finding a Voice." *The Private Self: Theory and Practice of Women's Autobiographical Writings.* Ed. Shari Benstock. Chapel Hill: U of North Carolina P, 1988. 192–210.

———. "Socializing Rosamond: Educational Ideology and Fictional Form." *Children's Literature Association Quarterly* 14.2 (Summer 1989): 52–58.

———. " 'A Taste for Truth and Realities': Early Advice to Mothers on Books for Girls." *Children's Literature Association Quarterly* 12.3 (Fall 1987): 118–24.

Olney, James, ed. *Autobiography: Essays Theoretical and Critical.* Princeton: Princeton UP, 1980.

Opie, Peter, and Iona Opie. *The Classic Fairy Tales.* 1974. New York: Oxford UP, 1980.

Ortner, Sherry B. "Is Female to Male as Nature Is to Culture?" *Women, Culture, and Society.* Ed. Michelle Zimbalist Rosaldo and Louise Lamphere. Stanford: Stanford UP, 1974. 67–87.

Patterson, Sylvia W. "Eighteenth-Century Children's Literature in England: A Mirror of Its Culture." *Journal of Popular Culture* 13.1 (Summer 1979): 38–43.

Paul, Lissa. "Enigma Variations: What Feminist Theory Knows About Children's Literature." *Signal* 54 (Sept. 1987): 186–202.

Pearce, Philippa. "The Writer's View of Childhood." *Horn Book* 38.1 (Feb. 1962): 74–78.

Poggioli, Renato. *The Oaten Flute: Essays on Pastoral Poetry and the Pastoral Ideal.* Cambridge: Harvard UP, 1975.

Pugh, Simon. *Garden-Nature-Language.* Manchester: Manchester UP; New York: St. Martin's, 1988.

Rendall, Jane. *The Origins of Modern Feminism: Women in Britain, France, and the United States, 1780–1860.* Themes in Comparative History. London: Macmillan, 1985.

Richardson, Alan. "Romanticism and the Colonization of the Feminine." *Romanticism and Feminism.* Ed. Anne K. Mellor. Bloomington: Indiana UP, 1988. 13–25.

Ritchie, Anne Thackeray. Introduction. *The Parent's Assistant; or, Stories for Children.* By Maria Edgeworth. London: Macmillan, 1897. vii–xiii.

Ross, Marlon B. "Troping Masculine Power in the Crisis of Poetic Identity." *Romanticism and Feminism.* Ed. Anne K. Mellor. Bloomington: Indiana UP, 1988. 26–51.

Ruddick, Sara. *Maternal Thinking: Toward A Politics of Peace.* Boston: Beacon, 1989.

——. "Remarks on the Sexual Politics of Reason." *Women and Moral Theory.* Ed. Eva Feder Kittay and Diana T. Meyers. Totowa, NJ: Rowman and Littlefield, 1987. 237–60.

Sanders, Valerie. *Reason Over Passion: Harriet Martineau and the Victorian Novel.* Sussex: Harvester; New York: St. Martin's, 1986.

Scott, Sir Walter. *The Letters of Sir Walter Scott, 1821–1823.* Ed. H. J. C. Grierson. Vols. 7 and 8. London: Constable, 1934, 1935.

——. *The Private Letter-Books of Sir Walter Scott.* Ed. Wilfred Partington. New York: Stokes, 1930.

——. *Waverley.* 1814. Ed. Andrew Hook. Harmondsworth: Penguin, 1972.

Shteir, Ann B. "Botany in the Breakfast-Room: Women and Early Nineteenth-Century British Plant Study." *Uneasy Careers and Intimate Lives: Women in Science, 1789–1979.* Ed. Pnina G. Abir-Am and Dorinda Outram. The Douglass Series on Women's Lives and the Meaning of Gender. New Brunswick: Rutgers UP, 1987. 31–43.

——. "Linnaeus's Daughters: Women and British Botany." *Women and the Structure of Society: Selected Research from the Fifth Berkshire Conference on the History of Women.* Ed. Barbara J. Harris and JoAnn K. McNamara. Durham: Duke UP, 1984. 67–73.

Slade, Bertha Coolidge. *Maria Edgeworth, 1767–1849: A Bibliographical Tribute.* London: Constable, 1937. The birthdate has since been corrected to 1768.

Smith, Sidonie. *A Poetics of Women's Autobiography: Marginality and the Fictions of Self-Representation.* Bloomington: Indiana UP, 1987.

Stanton, Domna C. "Difference on Trial: A Critique of the Maternal Metaphor in Cixous, Irigaray, and Kristeva." *The Poetics of Gender.* Ed. Nancy K. Miller. New York: Columbia UP, 1986. 157–82.

Stanton, Domna C., and Jeanine Parisier Plottel, eds. *The Female Autograph.* New York: New York Literary Forum, 1984.

Stewart, Susan. *On Longing: Narratives of the Miniature, the Gigantic, the Souvenir, the Collection.* Baltimore: Johns Hopkins UP, 1984.

Summerfield, Geoffrey. *Fantasy and Reason: Children's Literature in the Eighteenth Century.* Athens: U of Georgia P, 1985.

Thackeray, Miss [Anne Isabella]. (Mrs. Richmond Ritchie). *A Book of Sybils:*

Mrs. Barbauld, Miss Edgeworth, Mrs. Opie, Miss Austen. London: Smith, Elder, 1883.

Thwaite, Mary F. *From Primer to Pleasure in Reading: An Introduction to the History of Children's Books in England from the Invention of Printing to 1914 with an Outline of Some Developments in Other Countries.* 1963. Rev. ed. Boston: Horn Book, 1972.

Waddey, Lucy. "Home in Children's Fiction: Three Patterns." *Children's Literature Association Quarterly* 8.1 (Spring 1983): 13–15.

Walsh, William S. *Curiosities of Popular Customs and of Rites, Ceremonies, Observances, and Miscellaneous Antiquities.* 1897. Philadelphia: Lippincott, 1925.

Wilson, Anne. *Magical Thought in Creative Writing: The Distinctive Roles of Fantasy and Imagination in Fiction.* South Woodchester: Thimble, 1983.

——. *Traditional Romance and Tale: How Stories Mean.* Ipswich: Brewer; Totowa, NJ: Rowman and Littlefield, 1976.

Zagarell, Sandra A. "Narrative of Community: The Identification of a Genre." *Signs: Journal of Women in Culture and Society* 13.3 (Spring 1988): 498–527.

PATRICIA DEMERS

Mrs. Sherwood and Hesba Stretton

The Letter and the Spirit of Evangelical

Writing of and for Children

The beginning of true religion, my dear, is to know we are sinners.
M. M. Sherwood, *The History of the Fairchild Family*, 31

Sin, like righteousness, is a spiritual force.
Hesba Stretton, "Only a Dog," *The Christmas Child
and Other Stories*, 72

lthough the "Big Six" (Blake, Wordsworth, Coleridge, Byron, Shelley, Keats) are now having to share the field with sisters, wives and lovers, they have yet to make room for Mary Martha Butt Sherwood (1775–1851) and Sarah Smith, or "Hesba Stretton" (1832–1911). Once lionized and now forgotten, these two of the Religious Tract Society's best-selling authors deserve consideration, especially in today's revisionist atmosphere. Margaret Nancy Cutt has labelled Mrs. Sherwood as "at heart a Romantic" and Hesba Stretton as writing from a "natural romanticism" (*Mrs. Sherwood* 37, 134). Yet the understanding of Romanticism that emerges from their allegories, tracts, family stories, and melodramas reflects not only on their vastly different temperaments and experiences but on the increasingly individualistic perception of Romanticism which flourished in Evangelical circles.

Doreen Rosman has already dismantled some of the stereotypical assumptions of Evangelicalism's denigrators and popularizers alike. Far from being joyless, grim, Bible-quoting isolationists, Evangelicals were anxious, affectionate parents who, although they encouraged religious precocity and rigor, usually reigned in homes where an "underlying happiness" (115) was the norm. Furthermore, though critical of the "insatiable thirst for fiction" (191), Evangelicals regarded literature "as an adjunct of civilization, whose advance was thoroughly congruent with the concerns of religion" (194). Mining the work of Sherwood and Stretton for the type of the Evangelical matriarch—ferocious, intransigent, and coldly didactic—is a form of what Nancy Miller would call underreading: retaining the archetype and dismembering the subject. In reclaiming Sherwood and Stretton as Romantic Evangelicals this essay will strive for the goals of overreading, "of reading for the signature, . . . put(ting) one's finger . . . on the place of production that marks the spinner's attachment to her web" (Miller 288).

The first problem to be addressed is, clearly, the ways in which these women can be considered part of the expanding corpus of Romantic works, for they appear to fall through the cracks of both traditional and theoretical conceptions of Romanticism. Their writing contains little of what Harold Bloom would call the egotistical sublime of William Wordsworth with its "defiant humanism" saluting the possibility of an "earthly paradise" (Bloom 126), and none of the "gnostic rapture" of William Blake (Wellek 129). They do not dabble in "the revolutionary liberalism preached by Godwin" nor in "the exclusive idealism of Shelley" (Huxley 64). Moreover, their imprints make it clear that these women are engaged not in "spilt religion" (Hulme 118), T. E. Hulme's blunt appraisal of Romanticism, but in serving their dogma straight and undiluted. Neither are they striving "to naturalize the supernatural and to humanize the divine" with the resolve "to give up [some] of the dogmatic understructure of Christianity," which "display of integrity" M. H. Abrams defines as "the Romantic enterprise" (68); rather than giving up any part of the Christian understructure they reinforce it with single-minded determination. Although more readily located within the heterodox theories challenging the canon, the works of Sherwood and Stretton, in which nature or circumambient conditions are often repressive, do not entirely reflect contemporary theorizing about the "politics of gender" implied in the "masculinist metaphors of power" in Romantic "self-questing and visionary conquest" (Ross 49). In contrast to Anne Mellor's claim about the assumption "deeply imbedded" in early nineteenth-century writing, which she labels "a concept of the self as a power that gains control over and gives significance to nature, a nature troped in their writings as female" (8), Sherwood, in particular, is concerned less about controlling or conquering nature and more about transcending or allegorizing it as a testing ground and model for heaven. As well, both Sherwood and Stretton, so determinedly self-possessed, would disappoint theoretical arguments about gender as a means of depriving women of authority and speech. Monique Wittig's insistence on gender as an "ontological joke" or a "conceptual maneuver" (67) to the contrary, there is nothing crablike or apologetic about the actions and words of Sherwood in appointing herself to organize catechetical schools in India, or of Stretton in working alongside Dr. Barnardo and Angela Burdett Coutts, publicly canvassing for a London branch of the Society for the Prevention of Cruelty to Children and recording accurately the conditions of slum living.

In what special sense, then, are these Evangelical women also Romantics? Though their settings range from exotic Calcutta bazaars to the industrial tenements of London, both see their protagonists' zealous religion as shaped by the realistic and often crushing demands of their locale. The natural scene is in many ways their primary subject, a stimulus for spiritual lessons. For the Romantic Evangelicals Christian hope and fortitude, as opposed to any stylized lassitude or despondency, remain uppermost. Their seeing into the life of things is, without contradiction or irony, simultaneously domestic and eschatological. Their characters' zeal in finding and defining an earthly home prompts their almost automatic longing for a heavenly home. Theirs is a consciously double vision, glimpsing the eternal in the natural, the sublime in the quotidien. This doubleness, which pervades their work, underlines the essential connection with and difference from their Romantic contemporaries. Unlike Wordsworth's climactic and transfigurative moment in the Simplon Pass or Percy Shelley's contemplation of Mont Blanc, the whole Evangelical narrative originates in and is suffused with the certainty of an otherworldly immanence. Through their particular fusions of character and setting they re-interpret Samuel Taylor Coleridge's wish for his infant son, in "Frost at Midnight"; though the shapes are not always "lovely" nor the sounds "intelligible," Sherwood and Stretton both discern in the natural scene "that eternal language, which thy God / Utters, who from eternity doth teach / Himself in all, and all things in Himself" (lines 59–62, in *Poems* 242). The rephrasing of this Coleridgean wish in more overtly moralistic terms lies at the heart of the Evangelical enterprise for children.

Sherwood and Stretton write about grace, temptation, sin, forgiveness, death, heaven, and hell. These subjects constitute their "world of the deep interior," which is anything but "morally ambivalent" (Frye, "Drunken Boat" 19). Objects of nature, whether real or imagined, are for these Evangelicals akin to what they were for Coleridge: "a symbolical language for something within . . . that already and forever exists" (Frye, "Drunken Boat" 11). However, if there is such a thing as an Evangelical equivalent for the Romantic metaphor of the correspondent breeze, which Abrams has traced to illustrate the interchange between outer motions and interior powers, then it would have to be the transcendent heavenly vision. Such a vision does not lead to what G. Wilson Knight has described as a "living paradise" (82). Emphasis is on the yearning and the potential. It is an aptitude or a gift of the pure in heart, a harmony between interior and exterior, which Coleridge termed "this strong music in the soul" ("Dejection: An Ode" 60, in *Poems* 365). Such a heaven-envisioning power, though closely related to the Romantic temperament, also exemplifies to a certain extent Alice Jardine's interpretation of the text that must always be read "*both*" ways: "transparently and opaquely," what it signifies being "always both possible and impossible" (114–115). Of course Sherwood and Stretton would insist on the real possibility of heaven, for, however thorny, imprisoning, or squalid the way, their conviction of the rightness of the straight, narrow but ultimately salvific path remains unshaken.

Groans and eschatological longings are prominent in the stories of both Sherwood and Stretton. Mrs. Sherwood concentrates on cherubic orphans whose goodness and unquestioned rewards definitely overshadow any suffering they may endure. These children usually effect long-lasting changes in adults too. On her deathbed the destitute servant Susan Gray, whose maidenly reserve has been maligned by local gossips, convinces a clergyman to tell her true story. The proselytizing Anglo-Indian Little Henry catechizes his Hindu bearer and, in the last stages of his fatal illness, even converts his worldly adoptive mother to the habit of daily Bible reading. Sherwood favors uncomplaining valetudinarians in her children. The piety of the Huguenot schoolgirl, Aimée, in *The Flowers of the Forest* (1830), is so mesmerizing that she steadies the curé's resolve to leave the Church of Rome; as a way of counseling readers "that adversity is the shining time of the Christian," Sherwood lets the first-person narrator of *Ermina* (1831) outline the differences between her vanity and the absolute sobriety of her sickly friend Anna (169). Even in the disguise of an Elizabethan romance, in

The Mirror of Maidens (1851), Sherwood essentially tells of the schooling of a haughty spirit, with Mildred Howard contrite at last, thanks to the example of the selfless Katharine Arden.

The children in Hesba Stretton's stories suffer from more than sickness, dislocation, and gossip: existence itself is a struggle for these waifs and city arabs. In *Pilgrim Street* (1867) Tom Haslam, with a father who is an idle ticket-of-leave man, endures his shabby life in the hope of helping his younger brother to an education. *Little Meg's Children* (1868) has a heroine who pawns her clothes to feed her younger siblings. *Alone in London* (1869) is the story of Tony, who sleeps in a box and spends his days sweeping passageways and running errands to help support Old Oliver and the man's granddaughter. Although the heroine of *Jessica's First Prayer* (1867) is neglected, abused, and abandoned by her drunken mother, the child sits in rapt attendance at chapel. Far from being pristine exemplars or mouthpieces for an eschatological reward, Stretton's children individualize and concretize any visionary capacity by being actively involved in transforming their world.

Just as Mrs. Sherwood and Hesba Stretton present characters enduring different hardships to reach differently understood states of peace, their concepts of sin are also contrasted. In the epigraph from Sherwood, Mrs. Fairchild is lecturing her children, Lucy, Emily, and Henry, on one of her own childhood failings and using the incident as a platform to catechize. Both parents evidently favor this method. One of the most unforgettable and talked-about episodes of *The Fairchild Family* is the father's reaction to the children's quarrelling. His grisly lesson involves taking the youngsters to see the rotting corpse of a fratricide hanging on a gibbet to impress them with the fact that "our hearts by nature, my dear children, are full of hatred" (59). Despite all the middle-class parental tenderness, concern, and watchfulness, and the absolute goodness of some child characters, Sherwood's uniformly stern tales are all rooted in this acknowledgment of an innate sinfulness. The epigraph from Stretton is part of the narrator's admonitions in the middle of a poignant story of a young bride's jealousy of a dog, which happened to be the pet of her husband's first and much-mourned wife. Although "Only a Dog" moves briskly, Stretton never sacrifices psychological complexity for narrative momentum; instead, through telling objects and events, she shows how the Vicar's veneration of his first wife, his "poor little girl," and his bereavement are reflected in his almost fraternal bond with Jock, and how Nelly's unadmitted jealousy of the dead becomes more and more prominent as

Jock is removed further and further from the center of the home. Less histrionically than Sherwood, Stretton acknowledges the subtleness of sin and its prominence and indomitability in human affairs.

Religion as a necessary, moral code of ethics is a guiding force in their fiction. And yet, although each writes about issues of the day— with Sherwood concentrating on Bible training, parental duties, and the temptations of barracks life and Stretton addressing the problems of industrial life and undernourished, illiterate children—neither promotes an established denomination as offering the needed solutions. Religion concerns the generous, beneficent heart; it is based on an absolute trust in biblical promises, especially the Beatitudes, rather than on church membership and attendance. Mrs. Sherwood's religion has been variously labelled as Calvinist, Methodist, and Millenarian; in fact, one of her students describes Sherwood at last as "a universal heretic" (Royde Smith 187). Stretton was at best a disillusioned Evangelical; intensely critical of preachers, she usually left the service before the sermon and made exceptions for very few speakers, George MacDonald being one.

Alike though their responses to institutional religion may be, their writing is marked with such contrasting attitudes toward the experiences of life, and especially of womanhood, that it would be unwise to stress a sisterly connection. Too many paradoxes keep them apart. Sherwood, the mother of a large family of natural and adopted children, accompanied her husband to four different Bengal posts. As a result of her fame and productivity as a writer (over four hundred titles have been assigned to her), she became the main support of the family. Yet the mothers in her fiction are, if not neglectful, often such earnest moralizers that there is little hint of approachability. India inspired no travelogues or poetry but remained, despite all the accurate topography and Hindu vocabulary, the home of a culture of disease, profligacy, and disorder, which Sherwood's anglophilic judgments censured at every turn. Her voluminous writing, carefully channelled to the Religious Tract Society or Evangelical publishers, reveals almost nothing of the private life of this prim matriarch. Stretton, by contrast, never married and seems to have been in agreement with one of her spinster-characters' assessments of marriage as a "misfortune" (*Christmas Child* 11). Acute, impatient and tart, she was nevertheless a fond aunt and a shrewd businesswoman; her writing about destitute children netted her fame and considerable wealth. Yet her scenes of family life—even if they do not feature parents, who are often absent, negligent, or dead— are warm, and the sentiments describing the usually experimental or adoptive family unit are ardent and enthusiastic. Stretton shows a real and compassionate understanding of emotional dilemmas, like the instant education of a teenaged prostitute, the heartsickness of a daughter who marries without her father's consent, and the emptiness of the life of an upright but parsimonious bachelor. Her insights are just as keen, in stories intended for adults, when she confronts the problems of the attractive heiress or the doctor in love with the wife of a patient.

By comparing the accomplishments of Sherwood and Stretton in specific genres, I plan to illustrate some of the differences between these two best-selling authors that biography only hints at. In their work and in the clearly distinguished transcendent visions of each, we gain some understanding both of the flexibility of the Romantic ethos and of the changing nature of Evangelicalism throughout the nineteenth century.

As the more linear and thesis-bound storyteller, Sherwood wrote three allegories: *The Indian Pilgrim* (1818), *The Infant's Progress, from the Valley of Destruction to Everlasting Glory* (1821), and *The Latter Days* (1833). The earlier two, both Bunyanesque redactions begun in India, are overtly, gruesomely catechetical. The first, adapted to "the Oriental taste," was designed to instruct the Hindu. Accordingly its main character Goonah Purist, "or the Slave of Sin," seeks salvation from Hindu, Mohammedan, and finally Christian guides. The first Christian Goonah Purist meets is a Catholic priest who proves to be a notably poor catechist, withholding "the Bible from . . . the common people" and "suffering it only to be in the hands of the priests" (46); Romanists are stock figures of abuse throughout Sherwood's writing. When Goonah Purist encounters a Bible-carrying *"feringhee,"* which Sherwood's glossary defines as "a Frank or European," his spiritual fortunes start to improve. In contrast to the nondescript terrain of *The Infant's Progress* Sherwood successfully presents the journey of Goonah Purist to the City of Mount Zion in a realistically detailed India. Passing through the City of Vanity, for instance, the pilgrim is jostled in a crowded bazaar.

> The streets themselves were filled with traffickers, each with his basket of wares—Mussulmauns, with their great mustachios, and

> turbans, and muslin garments, some on foot, some on horseback, and some in *palanquins;* Bramhuns, with bare heads and sanctified aspects—*fakeers*, bedaubed with mud and mire, their matted locks spreading over their bare backs—women, with painted eyelids, bracelets, ear-rings, and nose jewels, mincing as they walked, their *bangles* tinkling on their ancles, affectedly drawing their veils over their faces which never knew shame—bulls, consecrated to the idols of the city, with burnished horns, and crowned with garlands of white jessamine. (137–38)

Even Sherwood's unconcealed disapproval of Oriental women does not warp this scene of meticulously recorded street life. Yet topographic realism is strictly subservient to Sherwood's catechetical purposes.

Though "composed in the East-Indies" in 1814, *The Infant's Progress* reveals no influence of the Indian locale, for the topography is deliberately abstract and non-picturesque. It opens in a village called Family Love after a white-robed visitor has convinced a particular husband and wife to flee for their lives, having assured them that their son, Humble Mind, and daughters, Playful and Peace, will be looked after. The neighbours, however, are openly skeptical: "What is this *Conviction-of-Sin*, which is come unto the child? What sin can this little boy have been guilty of? But that same Evangelist, who turned the heads of his father and mother, is, it seems, frequently meddling with him; so that, unless we can hit upon some method of diverting his thoughts from the communications of that enthusiast, the boy will never be good for anything as long as he lives" (13). This is the secular view that provides the recurring but inept counterpoint to Evangelist's main theme, a denigrating judgment on Mr. Worldly-Prudence, Filthy Curiosity, and their ilk. Thinking "themselves wiser than their Maker, . . . they take the sling and the stone from the hand of the youthful pilgrim, and put on him the armour of Saul; they rob him of his Bible, and fill his mouth with the words of man's wisdom" (23). In addition to upholding the Bible as the natural weapon against all personifications of worldliness, Sherwood's allegory is suffused with scriptural texts; through paraphrase, allusion, and—most often—direct quotations, the Authorized Version supplies the unabashed clichés of every conversation. The malicious sprite of the piece, Inbred-Sin, is, in his own words, "not what you think: I am your friend, your brother, nay, I am your very self" (33). A bully and a coward, he can be reduced to skulking and even forced to disappear when characters like Evangelist, the

Old Interpreter, Law, Orthodox, and Discipline enter the scene. Under the tutelage of the shepherd Sincerity the children concentrate on the Scriptures, with the younger ones memorizing "certain portions" and the eldest reading passages "in the original language" (52). The girls are six and eight years old; their brother is ten, yet the narrator "strictly require(s) of them all to take up their cross; to crucify the flesh with its affections and lusts" (47). The only hint of frivolity or recalcitrance comes from Playful, who is properly sobered by the pious death of her younger sister. Though addressing herself to children, Sherwood makes few concessions to simplify or soften her message. At Peace's funeral Mr. Orthodox lectures her tearful siblings, without the slightest trace of facetiousness, on the complex notion of the communion of saints: "Now this mystical union . . . is neither a fancied nor a figurative thing, but a sacred reality. When you were joined to Christ, my children, sin lost its absolute power over you: the Holy Spirit at that time entered your hearts, and you became temples of the living God" (173). Sherwood's overriding purposiveness quite naturally insists on the reality of the mystical.

Children are expected to assent to, if not understand, difficult concepts in her allegories, but at times the protracted tedium of these works exhausts even the willing reader's patience. In *The Latter Days* she embarks on a gloomy apocalyptic commentary through the first-person relation of Nicodemus; encrusted with biblical texts as footnotes and including "much awful instruction" (273), his unsectioned, unrelieved account tells of his new employment in the service of an unseen master called the Lord King of Kings, and of his encounter with this Master's Intendant, Mr. Fitz-Adam; His mismanaging housekeeper, Madame le Monde; and His one-time scribe, greedy Father Peter. Fuelled with her unconcealed biases, *The Latter Days* is more taxing than any of Sherwood's redactions of John Bunyan.

Stretton's understanding of allegory itself is vastly different. Less indebted to literary models and less concerned with abstruse concepts, she deals feelingly and effectively with an issue of her time, the horrid destruction of war. As she explains in the Preface to *Max Kromer: A Story of the Siege of Strasbourg* (1871), the tale was prompted by her firsthand experiences while returning from Switzerland at the time of the siege and seeing "how children were involved in the keen suffering of the war" (5). Stretton makes her setting and characters, both realistically and figuratively described, the vehicles of her theme that Christ "was being crucified afresh in Strasbourg" (129). The adolescent boy-narrator who, with his sister, is sent from London to live with their paternal grandmother, while their explorer-father is busy in Africa, arrives in the old walled city shortly before the German siege. The contrast between the beautiful descriptions of Strasbourg and its surrounding countryside at the outset and the war-torn remnants—"the graves, . . . and the ruined houses, and the households, almost like those of Egypt" (139)—frames Max's account. In the face of military might the Cathedral, significantly, becomes the symbol of an unconquerable spirit as well as a haven for the homeless and wounded; Max underscores the connections between church and home by commenting that his grandmother, "though a Protestant, loved the cathedral as dearly as her own home" and by relating how "streams of people were pouring out of their homes to seek refuge in the churches" (71). The domestication of this welcoming religious haven is quite distinct from Sherwood's allegories, in which homes are consciously abandoned and the journey is all.

The siege has devastating effects on all the lodgers of Madame Kromer's house. Two of them, Sergeant Klein and Louise, are killed, and the narrator-observer reverses his early pronouncement, "War brings glory" (19), when he feels "the dull, dead misery of . . . disappointment" (129) and "an agony of grief and terror such as [he] had never felt before" (134). The model Max draws on to hint at the indescribable bombardment is Zephaniah: "That day is a day of wrath, a day of clouds and thick darkness, a day of the trumpet and alarm against the fenced cities, and against the high towers" (77, cf. Zephaniah 1: 15–16). His exegetical comments reinforce the particularity of Stretton's anti-war allegory:

> But in those times there were no cannon, no batteries, or shells, to add to the horrors of the battle. If the old prophet could only come back again, and if the words had been put into his lips, he might have so told it, that people hearing of it, who had never seen the horrors or felt the terrors, would have vowed, with a solemn vow, that there should be no war like that again in a Christian country. (77)

While Sherwood abstracts in her allegories, making characters and setting further her catechesis, Stretton, in the few of her stories that might qualify as allegorical, always personalizes, letting fully rounded and usually fallible characters and their awareness of their environment be the means of conveying the related or contrapuntal meaning.

A similar divide between character-mouthpieces in educational situations in Sherwood's family stories separates them from the more insightful and varied characterizations and heart-wrenching struggles of Stretton's street arabs and waifs. *The Fairchild Family* is a typical Sherwood offering: carefully arranged vignettes, each teaching a distinct lesson and concluding with a prayer and hymn. Stern disciplinarians, the Fairchilds lecture to their relatively tame children against greed, envy, quarrelling, and disobedience; yet they are not such paragons that they are averse to using themselves as lessons by negative example. At one point Mrs. Fairchild admits to her daughter, who has been envying her sister's playthings, "My heart . . . is no better than yours," and relates her adult fears to the child's pettiness: "There was a time that I was very envious. When I was first married, I had no children for seven or eight years. I wished very much to have a baby, as you wished just now for Emily's doll; and whenever I saw a woman with a pretty baby in her arms, I was ready to cry for vexation" (49–50). There is an essential purposiveness about the settings, too. The attic room is a place to confine Henry when he has pilfered an apple; the grove is a location for Sabbath hymns; the overgrown Blackwood is the eerie spot where the fratricide is on display. In her family stories Sherwood's romanticism concerns the level gaze of parental discipline and its duties, not of transforming, but of molding the young to the correct state of listening to the Lord as a disciple (from *discipulus:* he who attends) should.

Sherwood was also partial to making children themselves the leaders, model recipients of the kingdom (Mark 10: 15). *The History of Little Henry and His Bearer* (1814), a tract set in India, is the story of an orphan's conversion to Christianity and of the effects of his piety and early death on the adults who care for him. Eight-year-old Henry catechizes Boosy, his bearer, directs the man's conversion (with its consequent loss of caste), and, even on his deathbed, effects a change of heart in his worldly adoptive mother, "who became a more serious character, and daily read Little Henry's Bible" (59). A complementary tract, *The History of Little Lucy and Her Dhaye* (1823), highlights the importance of the Bible, too, since the child's turning from Sinbad stories to sacred texts signals not only her own change but the beginning of her Indian nurse's conversion as well. Sherwood's children are often little saints. The piety of the English boarder in *The Flowers of the Forest* sets her apart from the other girls; the Christian education of the boy-narrator in *The Babes in the Wood of the New World* (1830) instigates the peaceful conclusion; and the impeccable virtue of Henry

Milner is amply demonstrated in his four-volume *History* (1822–37). The reverence with which the narrator recalls his upbringing, in one of Sherwood's Houlston Tracts, *The Happy Family* (1838), accounts for his fond, almost over-fond and unreal, adulation when he speaks of the Sabbath walks and his father's reading of Bunyan that is still so vividly memorable that he is "often filled with a longing desire to be absent from the body and present with Him at whose right hand are joys evermore" (14). Sherwood's families and their intensely catechetical milieux are not so much human-centered as they are heaven-directed.

In Stretton's family stories children suffer more acutely, and the very earnestness of their struggle for physical existence usually corresponds to a growing, experiential understanding of the spiritual life. Scavenging for food and shelter leads Stretton's waifs to a knowledge of grace and heaven. The places of her stories, rather than being the mere backdrops or platforms from which Christian principles are propounded, are actually the testing ground where they are shaped and learned. Readers must first feel the desolation and joylessness of Jessica's "home" before they can appreciate the surprise and mystery that this "little heathen" (*Jessica's First Prayer* 35) experiences in an Evangelical chapel. Stretton takes pains to convey the dehumanizing, animalistic nature of Jessica's existence as reflected in her dwelling:

> It was a single room, which had once been a hayloft over the stable of an old inn, now in use for two or three donkeys, the property of costermongers dwelling in the court about it. The mode of entrance was by a wooden ladder, whose rungs were crazy and broken, and which led up through a trap-door in the floor of the loft. The interior of the home was as desolate and comfortless as that of the stable below, with only a litter of straw for the bedding, and a few bricks and boards for the furniture. Everything that could be pawned had disappeared long ago, and Jessica's mother often lamented that she could not thus dispose of her child. (28)

Although Stretton makes no bones about the pharisaism of the verger and many members of the congregation, she is also explicit about the awesome haven the church affords her "drudge and errand-girl" as early as Jessica's first visit; Stretton's description of this moment is based on contrast, between what the child has known and what she has just discovered: "Thinking sadly of the light, and warmth, and music that were within the closed doors, she stepped out into the cold and darkness of the streets, and loitered homewards with a heavy heart"

(38). Just as she makes compelling links between character and place, Stretton also uses climatic conditions to communicate changes in mood and fortune, a linkage most noticeable in *Alone in London.* Tony is the unreclaimed, unchurched innocent whose slow movement toward incorporation in a family, along with a knowledge of Christ, begins with a self-styled baptism: in his own words, "washed myself early in the morning, afore the bobbies were much about, . . . in the fountains at Charing Cross" (32). But Tony's way is hard, and abrupt changes in the weather usually warn of impending misfortune. His purchase of ill-fitting, mismatched boots (which will cause his accident and broken leg) is transacted in a dingy market, while "it was cold, and a bitter, keen east wind was searching every corner of London streets" (82). When Dolly, Old Oliver's granddaughter and the child whom Tony has come to love as a sister, starts to decline, Stretton prepares the readers for Dolly's fatal sickness by describing the weather:

> But when the summer was ended, and after the damp warm fogs of November were over, and a keen, black frost set in sharply before Christmas—a frost which had none of the beauty of white rime and clear blue skies, but which hung over the city like a pall, and penetrated to every fireside with an icy breath; when only the strong and the healthy, who were well clothed and well fed, could meet it bravely, while the delicate, and sickly, and poverty-stricken, shrank before it, and were chilled through and through, then Dolly drooped and failed altogether. (108–9)

Of course not all of the poor are benevolent, nor are all families secure. Stretton designs *Pilgrim Street* as a study in contrasts—between families, fathers, and brothers. Tom discovers the Bible through the warm hospitality of the Pendleburys. His own father, the ex-convict, presents such a contrast to Nat Pendlebury and to the Heavenly Father whom Tom is coming to know that the boy is continually remarking on the difference:

> "Father" had two sounds for Tom, one so full of gracious comfort, and of peace passing all understanding, that an hour ago he could not refrain from whispering it to himself over and over again. But the other sound was one of shame, and misery, and dread, and his lips trembled when he had to utter it aloud. Only an hour since his heart had seemed full of music and singing, as he looked up to the narrow strip of sky lying above the streets, and said, 'Father!' But now the

word that had been like a tone out of an angel's song had become a hateful and jarring sound. (119–20)

Tom cannot persuade the sneering Haslam who taunts his son, berating his new-found religion: "A fine father! . . . and thou'rt a nice one, to call God father! Does he know thou'rt ragged and clemmed? Why, I serve the devil, and he's a better master" (134). So unnatural and perverse is Haslam that he sets out to ruin his younger, more impressionable son as a kind of sadistic vengeance. His attempted arson at the mill precipitates the catastrophe and brings about the final, fatal confrontation between Tom and his father. In recounting the boy's heroic effort to rescue Haslam, Stretton emphasizes the differences between two types of vision. While the trapped arsonist, "his eyes glaring with terror," stands "fascinated and paralyzed, . . . too bewildered to see that he could himself reach the ladder by which his son was ascending," Tom climbs the ladder alone, "his upturned face shining in the lurid light with a strange smile upon it" (180–81). The fact that Tom had forced his way onto the ladder with the proclamation, "He is my father, I tell thee, . . . and he doesn't love God!" intensifies the contrast between the light-hating madman and the illumined child. The active, engaged social conscience of Stretton's characters, proven and illustrated by the very trials of their existence, is neatly summarized by the old doctor, who serves as a peace-maker in her short story "The Worth of a Baby": "Christianity means being like Christ, each one of us in our station" (*Christmas Child* 147).

If the Romanticism of Sherwood's and Stretton's allegories consists of the various ways they meshed and juxtaposed literal and symbolic terrains and characters, and of their family stories in their different methods for making domestic incidents and literary settings the occasion for either parental instruction or the exercise of a social conscience, then their melodramas, in their displays of intense emotion, are clearly the most Romantic examples of their work, and the ones which best illustrate the distinct predilections of these Evangelicals. The examples I have chosen to discuss, Sherwood's *The History of Susan Gray* (1802) and Stretton's *Little Meg's Children* (1868), are both books that established and secured their authors' reputations; Sherwood's was published before her departure for India, and in advance of the publication of her book Stretton was enough of a best-seller in Paternoster Row that she was able to bargain for an unprecedented high rate of payment with bonuses as part of her agreement with the Tract Society.

As early as *Susan Gray*, a blending of caution and pathos, Sherwood's narrative already discloses the tension, which seems to me characteristic of all her writing, between telling a tale well for its own sake and tailoring it to a doctrinal formula, between a Romantic expressiveness that runs the risk of enthusiasm and abundance and a matronly discipline exercising ultimate control. Sherwood's saga of an orphaned servant-girl, related on her deathbed to a clergyman who becomes her biographer, is intended to affirm the doctrine of the wages of sin; Sherwood herself often intrudes as a censorious, proscriptive voice: "And I pray you, my good girls, do not deceive yourselves, nor suppose, because you see many bad women around you, that God will spare them for their numbers. . . . All bad people will have their portion in the lake which burns with brimstone and fire" (22). Biblical warnings clearly lessen the attraction of the narrator's chattiness. When she is apprenticed to a notorious gossip, Susan finds Mrs. Bennett's "light discourse . . . so unpleasant," and goes to such lengths to point out this distaste, that a reader might be forgiven for agreeing with Mrs. Bennett's assessment of the precisian: "You have lived with the old folks till you are got so starched and precise, that you are quite tiresome" (53). Sherwood's version of a purified Pamela resists the advances of a philandering soldier; though trembling with emotion at the man's declaration of love and promise of marriage, the nineteen-year-old saint insists on confessing her weakness to the ministering clergyman: " 'Oh! most honoured Sir,' said Susan Gray, 'what will you think of me when I tell you that I did not try to get away from the Captain, but that I listened to him for a long while?' " (145). Painfully self-conscious, Susan is much more at ease when, hovering above the re-cast event, she can hit her homiletic stride as the tried but good woman. Although a potential tug-of-war between honor and passion is inherent in Susan's tale, Sherwood prefers to concentrate on the cardboard moral exemplum: "Remember Susan Gray, and let her example be ever in your mind; and let it not be your wish to be rich and great, to seek for distinction and pleasure in this world, but to do your duty in that humble state in which God has placed you" (191–92).

Stretton narrates *Little Meg's Children*, yet she allows her ten-year-old heroine ample scope for instructing her younger brother and for dealing with the denizens of Angel Court, the dismal yard in East London where the child nurses her dying mother and tries to hold the family together during their sailor-father's absence. Old beyond her years, Meg wears the "anxious air of a woman upon her face, with deep

lines wrinkling about her forehead, and puckering about her keen eyes"
(11). Stretton makes this precocious, stunted child of poverty a credible
ingenuous character, and the griminess of her surroundings immediate
and palpable. Her treatment of "Angel Court" is actually based on observation of an East London alley called "Cherubim Court." In "Three
Hours with the Boys' Beadle" (collected with Stretton's *Log Book* in the
Shrewsbury Library), Stretton remarks on the irony of the designation:

> a strange name truly . . . there was a flagged pavement, thick with
> old mud which the rain had not altogether washed off, and with the
> dust and soot of a dry day, and about it were crawling half-naked
> children of all ages and sizes covered with grime and dirt; while
> their drunken mothers lolled in the door-ways, or upon the window
> sills, gossiping and quarrelling with one another. (126)

A practical meliorist, Meg is not obsessed with notions of depravity or
sinfulness; she silences her brother's reference to their father's wicked-
ness "when he's drunk," deliberately throwing "a cloak over her father's
faults" (25). But her trust in providence and ignorance of sex make her
a genuine innocent. When the teenaged prostitute Kitty, whom Meg
has befriended, intervenes to help her in dealing with the pawnbroker
(one of Kitty's clients), Stretton allows the vulnerable and the knowing
to complement one another in this exchange:

> "Meg," she said, "you let me do that sort o' work for you always.
> They'll cheat you ever so; but I wouldn't, not to save my life, if you'll
> only trust me. You ask me another time. Is that the way God takes
> care of you?" "He does take care of me," answered Meg, with a
> smile; "or may be you wouldn't have come into the shop just now,
> and I should have got only tenpence. I suppose that's taking care of
> me, isn't it?" "I don't know," said Kitty. "Only let me do that for you
> when you want it done again." (78)

Meg's hope is as mysterious for Kitty as is Kitty's acumen for the
ten-year-old. Without sermonizing or resorting to metaphors, Stretton
makes the girls' candid exchanges intuitive and affecting, reverber-
ating with innuendo. Her subtlety is actually more literal than Sherwood's figurative warnings and adjurations about docility.

The melodramas which enunciate most plainly the differences between these Romantic Evangelicals are their works intended for adults,
and so a brief final contrast will not be irrelevant. Sherwood's *Monk of
Cimiès* (1834) and *The History of John Marten* (1844) appeared toward

the end of her career, while Stretton's *Doctor's Dilemma* (1872) was one of her early novels. Sherwood did not mellow with age; her anti-Catholicism is close to rabid in these narratives. Stretton's complex examination of the plight of a young wife, running away from a loveless marriage, never resorts to caricature or stereotype; although she carefully details the legal rights of a wife, Stretton also leaves considerable room for compassion, emotional confusion, and benevolence.

One of the most exaggerated examples of Sherwood's animus toward the Church of Rome is *The Monk of Cimiès*, Edmund Etherington's first-person account of his temporary abandonment of the Church of England and lurid lapse into Catholicism. He refuses to call his story a novel, insisting it is "a serious and solemn history" (124). In fact, this Gothic horror, ostensibly concerned with what constitutes the Church, is full of Capuchin and Jesuit casuistry, travestied confessions, and pragmatic ordinations, as proof of Etherington's claim that "the truth about religious houses would blister paper" (202). "Popery" is the hideous taint, figured in such metaphors as "a rusty tube" (61), "a mighty piece of mummery" (292) and "a horrible vision" (335). The erstwhile monk, moreover, has managed to use the confessional to plan murder and satisfy his lust, and has felt no compunction in calling his religious brothers "poor, frightened fools" (245). Sherwood's ludicrous concoction, riddled with errors and inconsistencies, can only have been lapped up, I assume, by like-minded extremists. The sequel to *Henry Milner*, *The History of John Marten* combines an episodic formula with anti-Catholic bigotry. Through recounting the hero's successive curacies Sherwood attempts to pull together the unresolved plot of the mammoth earlier work and, when Marten travels to Venice, introduces some surprising revelations about an English heir who "had been brought up under the gloomy and rigid domain of the priests" (429). Disclosures about Signior Giovanni, or Lord James, as he is finally addressed, become more and more dramatic, reaching their histrionic climax when Giovanni's aristocratic mother appears—like a ghost, from behind "folding doors"—"in the complete costume . . . of a Carmelite nun" (460) and renounces her son as a loathsome heretic because he is returning to the Church of England. Such an anathematizing scene cries out for horror-movie treatment.

Although it has what moviemakers would call real box-office potential, *The Doctor's Dilemma* seems only to have been discovered by George Bernard Shaw, who borrowed the title. Stretton's novel is a combination of detective mystery and protracted affair, using the alternate narration of the young wife Olivia and the young doctor Martin Dobrée, and flitting from scenes in London and the Channel Islands to France. Stretton's characters have a nobility that transcends mere letter-of-the-law observances. At one point Olivia finds refuge in a small French village, where the curé does not throw up any barriers between Protestant and Catholic, but instead welcomes Olivia and the child with whom she fled a dangerous teaching post "as if they were good Catholics" (198). Though this sense of sacrifice may make her a curiosity to some, Olivia later puts her own life at risk in agreeing to nurse her dying, fever-racked husband (the very man who has tormented and hounded her throughout), in her own words, "as I should have nursed him if he had always been tender and true to me" (215). What is most remarkable in this lengthy tale is Stretton's ability to keep the reader concentrated on the immediate event or catastrophe, like the heroine herself daring "not (to) glance beyond the passing hour, . . . not (to) conjecture what the end would be" (218).

Female characters are no less powerful or more fallible than males in the works of Sherwood and Stretton, and with sympathetic understanding, both view the child as an empowering individual. Distinctions between their Romantic Evangelicalism ultimately rest on the differences of temperament and time, differences which recent criticism on the mode of female discourse illuminates. Sherwood prescribes and sermonizes, looking back to a period of normative, inculcated values. In examining the works of Georgian women writers for children as "not just an outlet available to their sex, but a genuine vocation," Mitzi Myers identifies "in their self-conscious didacticism a resilient and purposeful maternal discourse, a female mode of cultural reform directed toward improvement of both self and community" (33, 55). Sherwood's Christian fervour heightens the purposefulness and accounts for most of the built-in social criticism of her writing. Stretton is no less purposive or critical, but the vagaries of the heart and the demands of an immediate and literal reality are the controlling features of her fiction. In attempting to mediate between American and French feminisms, Margaret Homans describes masculine language as conventionally representational, symbolic, and androcentric, while feminine language is, in large measure, literal, non-symbolic, and rhythmic; although her study of nineteenth-century women's writing goes as far as to suggest the ambivalence of these authors "about the desirability of the female discourse they tentatively explore" (21), and although Sherwood and Stretton are not discussed at all, her book does provide yet another way, in addition to the letter-spirit dichotomy, of distinguishing between these two Romantic Evangelicals. Sherwood favors a highly representational and figurative kind of acculturation in the name of catechesis, while Stretton personalizes, concretizes, and lavishly dramatizes the moral choices that for her constitute engaged Christianity.

WORKS CITED

Abrams, M. H. "The Correspondent Breeze: A Romantic Metaphor." *English Romantic Poets: Modern Essays in Criticism.* Ed. M. H. Abrams. New York: Oxford UP, 1960. 37–54.

———. *Natural Supernaturalism: Tradition and Revolution in Romantic Literature.* New York: Norton, 1971.

Bloom, Harold. *The Visionary Company; A Reading of English Romantic Poetry.* Rev. and enl. edition. Ithaca: Cornell UP, 1971.

Coleridge, Samuel Taylor. *The Complete Poetical Works of Samuel Taylor Coleridge.* Ed. Ernest Hartley Coleridge. 2 vols. Oxford: Clarendon, 1912.

Cutt, Margaret Nancy. *Ministering Children: A Study of Nineteenth-Century Evangelical Writing for Children.* Wormley: Five Owls, 1979.

———. *Mrs. Sherwood and Her Books for Children.* London: Oxford UP, 1974.

Frye, Northrop. "The Drunken Boat: The Revolutionary Element in Romanticism." Frye, *Romanticism Reconsidered* 1–25.

———, ed. *Romanticism Reconsidered.* New York: Columbia UP, 1963.

Homans, Margaret. *Bearing the Word: Language and Female Experience in Nineteenth-Century Women's Writing.* Chicago: U of Chicago P, 1986.

Hulme, T. E. "Romanticism and Classicism." *Speculations.* Ed. Herbert Read. London: Routledge and Kegan Paul, 1936. 113–40.

Huxley, Aldous. "The Cold-Blooded Romantics." *Vanity Fair* 29 (1928): 64, 104.

Jardine, Alice. "Opaque Texts and Transparent Contexts: The Political Difference of Julia Kristeva." Miller, *Poetics* 96–116.

Knight, G. Wilson. *The Starlit Dome: Studies in the Poetry of Vision.* Oxford: Clarendon, 1941.

Mellor, Anne K. "On Romanticism and Feminism." Mellor, *Romanticism* 3–9.

———, ed. *Romanticism and Feminism.* Bloomington: Indiana UP, 1988.

Miller, Nancy K. "Arachnologies: The Woman, the Text, and the Critic." Miller, *Poetics* 270–95.

———, ed. *The Poetics of Gender.* New York: Columbia UP, 1986.

Myers, Mitzi. "Impeccable Governesses, Rational Dames, and Moral Mothers: Mary Wollstonecraft and the Female Tradition in Georgian Children's Books." *Children's Literature* 14 (1986): 31–59.

Rosman, Doreen. *Evangelicals and Culture.* London: Croom Helm, 1984.

Ross, Marlon B. "Romantic Quest and Conquest: Troping Masculine Power in the Crisis of Poetic Identity." Mellor, *Romanticism* 26–51.

Royde Smith, Nancy. *The State of Mind of Mrs. Sherwood.* London: Macmillan, 1946.

Sherwood, Mrs. *Ermina.* London: Houlston and Son, 1831.

——— . *The Flowers of the Forest.* 1830. 3rd ed. London: Religious Tract Society, 1834.

——— . *The Happy Family.* London: Houlston and Son, 1838.

——— . *The History of the Fairchild Family; or, The Child's Manual; being a collection of stories calculated to show the importance and effects of a religious education.* 3 vols. London: Hatchard and Son, 1847–48.

——— . *The History of Henry Milner, a Little Boy, Who was Not Brought Up According to the Fashions of this World.* 4 vols. 1822–37. 3 vols. London: Hatchard and Son, 1831–44.

——— . *The History of John Marten.* London: Hatchard and Son, 1844.

——— . *The History of Little Henry and His Bearer.* 1814. 25th ed. Wellington: Houlston, 1829.

——— . *The History of Little Lucy and Her Dhaye.* Wellington: Houlston, 1823.

——— . *The History of Susan Gray, As Related by a Clergyman.* Bath: Hazard, 1802.

——— . *The Indian Pilgrim; or, The Progress of the Pilgrim Nazareenee (Formerly called Goonah Purist or the Slave of Sin,) From the city of the Wrath of God to the City of Mount Zion.* 1818. Wellington: Houlston, 1825.

——— . *The Infant's Progress, from the Valley of Destruction to Everlasting Glory.* 1821. 4th ed. Wellington: Houlston, 1825.

——— . *The Latter Days.* London: Seeley and Burnside, 1833.

——— . *The Mirror of Maidens in the Days of Queen Bess.* London: Hatchard, 1851.

——— . *The Monk of Cimiès.* 1834. Manchester: Johnson, 1847.

——— . *The Recaptured Negro and the Babes in the Wood of the New World.* London: Houlston and Wright, 1860.

Stretton, Hesba. *Alone in London.* 1869. London: Religious Tract Society, 1880.

——— . *The Christmas Child and Other Stories.* London: Religious Tract Society, 1888.

——— . *The Doctor's Dilemma.* New York: Appleton, 1872.

——— . *Jessica's First Prayer.* London: Religious Tract Society, 1867.

————. *Little Meg's Children.* 1868. London: Religious Tract Society, 1875.

————. *Max Kromer: A Story of the Siege of Strasbourg.* London: Religious Tract Society, 1871.

————. *Pilgrim Street: A Story of Manchester Life.* 1867. London: Religious Tract Society, 1870.

————. "Three Hours with the Boys' Beadle." [1883?]. Local Studies Library, Shrewsbury.

Wellek, Rene. "Romanticism Re-examined." Frye, *Romanticism Reconsidered* 107–34.

Wittig, Monique. "The Mark of Gender." Miller, *Poetics* 63–73.

Childhood and Growth

George MacDonald and

William Wordsworth

*I*n his recent biography of George MacDonald, William Raeper notes that the "romantic pattern for a work of art remained MacDonald's own" (109). MacDonald is indeed a belated Romantic. His images, themes, and language derive from his great Romantic precursors, and his imagination is a product of their theories and practices. He sides with the Romantic preference for imagination over mechanical reasoning, and follows Romantic thought by conceiving of imagination as "that faculty in man which is likest to the prime operation of the power of God" (*Dish of Orts* 2). Imagination perceives truth; it is not a diverting faculty or a means of creating private dreams. For this reason its creations are instructive. The poet remains a responsible human spokesman, and his art is a moral art. MacDonald offers little that is new in the movement of ideas; he re-Christianizes Romanticism. Scholars have traced the influence of German Romanticism on MacDonald's writing, but aside from Stephen Prickett, who discusses MacDonald in the context of Victorian Romanticism's debt to Samuel Taylor Coleridge and William Wordsworth, and M. Jadwiga Swiatecka, who shows how MacDonald's idea of the symbol derives from Coleridge, no one has studied MacDonald's close relationship to his English Romantic forebears. In this essay, I discuss MacDonald's interpretation of Wordsworth and show how Wordsworth informs Mac-Donald's children's fiction. Since MacDonald's Wordsworth is what we might call a distinctly Blakean Wordsworth, I shall also draw on MacDonald's interest in William Blake.

In his essay on Wordsworth, MacDonald sees him as a Christian pantheist who "saw God present everywhere; not always immediately in his own form, it is true; but whether he looked upon the awful mountain peak, sky-encompassed with loveliness, or upon the face of a little child, which is as it were eyes in the face of nature—in all things he felt the solemn presence of the Divine Spirit" (*Dish of Orts* 247). His emphasis is on Wordsworth's relation to nature: "Nature laid upon the storehouse of his mind and heart her most beautiful and grand forms, whence they might be brought, afterwards, to be put to the highest human service" (249). To Wordsworth, nature was "a power of good, a world of teaching, a strength of life" (250). MacDonald also saw in Wordsworth a connection between nature and childhood. This connection is most evident in what MacDonald calls "that grandest ode that has ever been written": Wordsworth's "Ode: Intimations of Immortality from Recollections of Early Childhood" (256). Like Wordsworth, MacDonald was fostered alike by beauty and by fear. Both writers lost their mothers when they were eight years old, and this loss left them seeking nurture and comfort in nature.

In MacDonald's novel *The Seaboard Parish* (1868), a conversation between the narrator, Mr. Walton, and the doctor, Turner, furnishes evidence that Wordsworth's ode inspired MacDonald's use of the child as an image in his own work. As the two men stand on the open moor, the fresh breeze reminds them of their past. The breeze itself is Wordsworthian. It is a therapeutic wind "that calls up a kind of will in the nerves to meet it," a sort of correspondent breeze (311). There is in a strong wind, as Wordsworth says, "some working of the spirit" (*Prelude* [1850], 12.331). Walton recalls a beautiful summer day in his childhood when the complement of nature and the pearl buttons he wore opened his young mind "to the enjoyment of the eternal paradise around me" (312). Turner replies that maturing has brought a more complete understanding of "what Wordsworth says about childhood" (312). He continues by voicing the Romantic faith in the imaginative and intuitive qualities of childhood. It is, he says, "a mercy that we were not born grown men, with what we consider our wits about us. They are blinding things those wits we gather. I fancy that the single thread by which God sometimes keeps hold of a man is such an impression of his childhood as that of which you have been speaking" (312). Walton remarks on "thoughtless youth's . . . unconscious intercourse with beauty," and the surrounding heaven of infancy: the child's world is "so at variance with sin" (312). "A sense of purity" is all about the child, but as yet he neither feels nor thinks of such things. Only later, when "he is conscious of so much that is evil and so much that is unsatisfied in him," does the mature man long "after the high clear air of moral well-being" (313).

Here MacDonald departs from Wordsworth, for whom Nature's power is ultimately in its evocation of childhood, or, more precisely, in its power to raise remembrances of childhood in the poet's mind:

> O joy! that in our embers
> Is something that doth live,
> That nature yet remembers
> What was so fugitive!
> ("Immortality" ode 133–36, in *Poetical Works* 461)

For the mature man can no longer feel the "aching joys" and "dizzy rapture" of youth ("Tintern Abbey" 84–85, qtd. in *Dish of Orts* 249), nor can he sense "Delight and liberty" or glory and freshness since these are, even in the "Immortality" ode, "of a dream" (lines 140, 5, in *Poetical Works* 461, 460). The early love of nature becomes a sympathy with the still, sad music of humanity, that "primal sympathy" that remains in the "soothing thoughts that spring / Out of human suffering" ("Immortality" ode 185–188, qtd. in *Dish of Orts* 28). But these soothing thoughts are thoughts of the past: nature is inextricably bound up with the child that Wordsworth was, the child that intimates to the grown man a time of not knowing death, a time of immortality. Childhood, then, remains just that: it is of short duration; it is a fleeting moment and nothing can bring back its hour of splendor. Matthew in "The Two April Mornings" mourns the death of his daughter, but seeing a blooming girl one morning, he does not wish that she were his (lines 43, 56, in *Poetical Works* 381).

For Wordsworth childhood is bound by time; it passes. For MacDonald, the opposite is true; childhood is a state of being which everyone must aspire to. In this he is more akin to Novalis and Blake than to Wordsworth. MacDonald's first published book is a translation of *Twelve Spiritual Songs of Novalis* (1851), and he had in his library "a facsimile of the original *Jerusalem* and an early hand-coloured reproduction of *The Marriage of Heaven and Hell*, besides *Gilchrist's Life*" (Greville MacDonald 554–55). His bookplate is an adaptation of Blake's engraving, "Death's Door," from Robert Blair's *The Grave*. "Where there are children, there is the golden age," writes Novalis in *The Disciples at Sais* (168), and following Blake, who notes that "Some

Children are Fools & so are some Old Men" (794), MacDonald confesses in a sermon preached in Brighton, in June 1857, "that there are children who are not childlike" (*Unspoken Sermons* 3). What matters is not the child herself, but the invincible "idea of childhood which moved in the heart of God when he made that child after his own image" (5). Childlike innocence is a quality inherent in everyone (like poetry); it may be latent or muted by sin and age, but it cannot be annihilated, and it partakes of God.

In "Tintern Abbey" and elsewhere, Wordsworth speaks of the passing of childhood. Memory, prompted by nature, keeps the child present in the adult's mind. Yet nostalgia is inescapable; nature recalls the past, and its power is thus evanescent. In moods of weariness and melancholy nature raises his mind with a sense sublime to an understanding of the harmony of the world, and it does this through its power of tranquil restoration that conjures up feelings and remembrances of the past. These remembrances are at the heart of Wordsworth's moral being. In the "Immortality" ode, Wordsworth depicts the change in nature herself as the man grows. She is no longer a mother, but a stepmother, and man is her "Inmate" (line 82, in *Poetical Works* 461), a word that casts shades of the prison house over nature. Nature, perhaps recalling Blake's Nurse from *Songs of Experience* or the stepmothers of folk tales, does all she can to make her foster-child forget his childish glories. But, of course, those must not be forgotten. Earlier, in "Tintern Abbey," Wordsworth concluded that even if he had not been taught to see the associations which nature impresses on man, he would have turned to his sister Dorothy, in whose voice he catches "the language of . . . [his] former heart" and "former pleasures," and to whose mind he looks to be a "mansion of all lovely forms," and whose memory will be "as a dwelling-place / For all sweet sounds and harmonies" (lines 117–18, 140–42, in *Poetical Works* 165). The power of nature, once again, rests in this power of association with the past.

For MacDonald, nature has a separate power. He is untroubled by the possibility that nature may form us, that is, that it may reduce us to mere receivers of impressions. The tension between individual imagination and the force of environment, which is evident in Wordsworth, does not appear in MacDonald's work. "There *is* a purity and state in that sky," Mr. Walton remarks in *The Seaboard Parish* (313). There is rest and peace in nature, "to rouse my dull heart to desire it and follow after it," that cannot be found in "the science the present day is going wild about" (313). Nature, MacDonald says elsewhere, is like "a beautiful old grandmother" from whom "so many of God's loveliest influences come to us" (*What's Mine's Mine* 212). This glosses MacDonald's many wise grandmother figures in his fantasies and children's stories. Still, MacDonald cautions us not to suppose that nature's power, no matter how efficacious for good, is sufficient. First, "the soul must be tuned to such things." "When we understand the word of God, then we understand the works of God," MacDonald writes in his essay on Wordsworth (256). The child's soul is so tuned. Wordsworth's famous lines from the "Immortality" ode—"But trailing clouds of glory do we come / From God who is our home" (MacDonald's transcription, *Seaboard Parish* 315)—MacDonald interprets not "that we must have had a conscious life before this life," but rather as illustrating our foundation in God: all the life in us comes from God, all the sin from ourselves. And we "cannot be the creatures of God without partaking of his nature" (315). The clouds of glory we trail are our consciences, our "admiration of what is pure and noble" (315).

In *The Hope of the Gospel* (1892), MacDonald quotes all of the fifth stanza of the "Immortality" ode with the comment:

> Whoever has thus gazed on flower or cloud; whoever can recall poorest memory of the trail of glory that hung about his childhood, must have some faint idea how his father's house and the things in it always looked, and must still look to the Lord. With him there is no fading into the light of common day. He has never lost his childhood, the very essence of childhood being nearness to the Father and the outgoing of his creative love; whence, with that insight of his eternal childhood of which the insight of the little ones here is a fainter repetition, he must see everything as the Father means it. (55–56)

To the perfectly childlike, familiarity will never breed apathy. "To cease to wonder is to fall plum-down from the childlike to the commonplace—the most undivine of all moods intellectual" (*Hope of the Gospel* 57). What MacDonald finds missing in Wordsworth's poem, he finds in Henry Vaughan's "The Retreat": "the hope of return to the bliss of childhood" (*England's Antiphon* 256). Retreat does not involve regression. MacDonald's children—the Light Princess, Photogen and Nycteris ("The Day Boy and the Night Girl"), Princess Irene, and the others—cannot remain as they are; they must carry on the feelings of childhood into the powers of adulthood. Those who will remain childish, like the fairies in "The Carasoyn," remain spoiled and silly, never growing in wisdom. Wordsworth irrevocably loses childhood, but he feels that he has "abundant recompense" in his new sober pleasure. This will not satisfy MacDonald: "We may be comforted for what we lose by what we gain; but that is not a recompense large enough to be divine: we want both" (*England's Antiphon* 256).

The paradox MacDonald detected in Wordsworth is that for Wordsworth the mind of man is greater far than this earth in which he dwells, and yet this world is all there is. Stephen Prickett notes two positions here: the " 'Naturalist' position, [which] claims to find values inherent in Nature itself"; and the transcendental position, which "purports to discover in the shifting ephemera of the natural world evidence, or symbols, of a hidden and unchanging reality of absolute forms 'behind' the mere appearances of things" (160). Prickett calls these positions the "Naturalistic" and the "Platonic," and he suggests that MacDonald was "perhaps the first Victorian critic to point out that this 'contradiction' in Wordsworth mirrored the classic Christian paradox of God as *both* immanent in Nature and transcendent over *and* beyond it" (161–62). Blake had noted this paradox earlier in the century when he observed in Wordsworth the Natural Man rising up against the Spiritual Man continually. But for MacDonald, the Spiritual Man in Wordsworth was always stronger than the Natural Man who would rise up against him: as an example of this, MacDonald quotes Wordsworth's sonnet of 1819, "Composed During a Storm," in which a person "suffering tumult in his soul" goes forth without seeking the "sure relief of prayer." The storm smites his soul, but in the midst of his dread, a blue space opens in the storm clouds, an "unlooked for . . . minister / Of providential goodness ever nigh!" (*Dish of Orts* 253; lines 1–2, 13–14, in *Poetical Works* 209). Here and throughout Wordsworth's poetry, MacDonald sees a pattern he was to utilize in his own work, a spiral pattern which moves the child from harmony to dislocation and back to harmony.

Life is a spiral. The metaphor receives concrete expression in "Cross Purposes" (1867) when Alice and Richard, on their educative journey, descend the spiral-stair inside a great tree. The spiral journey, as M. H. Abrams describes it in *Natural Supernaturalism*, "is a spiritual way through evil and suffering which is justified as a necessary means to the achievement of a greater good; and usually, although with greater or less explicitness, this process is conceived as a fall from unity into division and into conflict of contraries which in turn compel the movement back toward a higher integration" (193). Characters may return to their point of origin, but with a difference. This explains why, in MacDonald's fairy tale "The Golden Key" (1867), the principal characters, in their journey through life, discover that the oldest and wisest man of all, the old man of the fire, is a mere baby, the Christ child. Only he can instruct Tangle how to find the country from whence the shadows fall. As well, after their journeys are complete, Tangle and Mossy find themselves young and beautiful. They have learned the lesson of the beautiful yet ancient grandmother: "It is very idle to grow old" (*Complete Fairy Tales* 216). MacDonald does not long "for a restored Paradise: for even in the ordinary history of man, no man or woman that has fallen can be restored to the position formerly occupied . . . They must be restored by attaining something better than they ever possessed before" (*Dish of Orts* 234).

Childhood is separate from nature, and nature is separate from childhood. Each is autonomous. Despite this, MacDonald follows Wordsworth in endowing nature with a formative influence on the growing child. In his essay, "A Sketch of Individual Development," first published in the *British Quarterly Review* (1882) and reprinted in *A Dish of Orts*, he outlines the four births which constitute his doctrine of becoming. These four births and consequent development have their roots in Wordsworth who, like MacDonald, envisaged life as a growth from the "fair seed-time" of infancy through "unripe" years of "animal activities" to mature consciousness. From birth, MacDonald begins his essay, "each succeeding consciousness dims—often obliterates—that which went before, and with regard to our past as well as our future, imagination and faith must step into the place vacated by knowledge" (*Dish of Orts* 43). At each successive stage of growth, as Wordsworth points out in the "Immortality" ode, man "perceives [childhood glory] die away" (line 75, in *Poetical Works*, 460). For both Wordsworth and MacDonald it can only be recovered through the imagination, which, as Marilyn Gaull notes, serves "as mediator between man and nature" (304). But where Wordsworth associates imagination with memory, which overcomes periods of weariness and which is a recurring rather than continuous power, MacDonald describes it as a permanent state of communion with God: "a wise imagination . . . is the presence of the Spirit of God" (*Dish of Orts* 28). To Wordsworth, it gives glimpses of man, a "creature divine" (*Prelude* 10.424); to MacDonald, it gives glimpses of God, the Divine. Blake's comment on Wordsworth clarifies the difference: "Imagination is the Divine Vision not of the world, or of Man, nor from Man as he is a Natural Man, but only as he is a Spiritual Man" (783). As Geoffrey Hartman has eloquently shown in

Wordsworth's Poetry, 1787–1814, Wordsworth avoids apocalypse. Mac-Donald, on the other hand, heralds it; *The Princess and Curdie*, for example, ends with a battle that draws its power from MacDonald's use of the images and language of Revelation.

MacDonald speaks, as Wordsworth does in the second book of *The Prelude*, of the difficulty we have in tracing the origins of our awareness. He follows with an analysis of what he calls the child's first birth, "before the first moment of which his memory affords him testimony" (*Dish of Orts* 44). This is the completely unthinking time that Wordsworth describes where the infant babe lies cradled in his mother's arms, "love's purest earthly fount" (247), who beautifies the whole universe. In language reminiscent of this great passage, MacDonald describes the infant: "enfolded with an atmosphere of love, the sky over him is his mother's face; the earth that nourishes him is his mother's bosom" (44). She is the "source, the sustentation, the defence of his being." In this region of "unquestioned security" the child first comes to know what God is: his mother's face "is God, her bosom Nature, her arms Providence." Here is MacDonald's myth in miniature. Man, coming from God, finds himself in the arms of a providential nature; if he realizes this and submits to it he need only look up to see the face of God. Nature for both Wordsworth and MacDonald was a surrogate mother, a conscience-figure: "In childhood," MacDonald writes of Wordsworth, "even his conscience was partly developed through the influences of nature upon him" (247).

This first birth is a time of irresponsibility; the child is one with his surroundings. But he is still a seed, or, in MacDonald's more ambiguous and less felicitous phrase, a "visible germ" (45). He "floats" towards the second birth, the time when he learns "that the world is around and not within him." The first birth is physical; the second is the gaining of self-consciousness, and it corresponds to that time in Wordsworth when nature becomes an object prized for her own sake—that is, when the child perceives an external world. The emphasis in MacDonald, however, is not on nature, but on the self. His analysis of the child's growth is more meticulous than Wordsworth's, for whom nature is the constant focal point. MacDonald grants nature a large share in the child's development, but it is only, he realizes, incidental. This is why he so often places his young children—Gibbie (*Sir Gibbie* 1879), Diamond (*At the Back of the North Wind* 1871), Mattie Kitley (*Guild Court* 1868)—in the city, only to move them to the country after the development of their ideal personalities. The child now becomes aware of his own desires, his own likes and dislikes, and through these, MacDonald claims, he begins to recognize "the existence and force of Being other and higher than his own" which is manifest as "*Will*" and is "in opposition to his desires" (*Dish of Orts* 46). This gives rise to the strife which initiates the necessary growth; as Blake wrote in *The Marriage of Heaven and Hell*, "Without Contraries is no progression" (*Complete Writings* 149). And out of this conflict results "the third birth of the human being."

This third birth is the consciousness on the part of the child of the resisting will of the mother, and with it that other crucial element which ranges itself with the mother—"we call it *Conscience*." MacDonald refers to the conscience as "her," suggesting the succession of grandmother figures in his fantasies and children's stories. Experiencing the resisting will of the mother and conscience, the child learns obedience to something beyond himself, something greater than himself. At this very moment the heaven of childhood recedes and yet comes closer: "It is farther, yet closer—immeasurably closer" (47). Growth is a spiral movement away from childhood, yet ever moving back to the essential purity of childhood. The possibility held out here is never felt in Wordsworth's poetry. Wordsworth sees the raptures of youth "for ever flown" and is almost touched to tears at the realization that books read in his youth are now "Dead in my eyes, dead as a theatre / Fresh emptied of spectators" (*Prelude* 5.546–52). The third stage in the development of MacDonald's child is decisive; the child becomes "conscious of himself as capable of action—of doing or of not doing." Action is necessary for growth, and true action is always good; evil is the frustration of action. Those who perform faithfully what has been given them to do succeed.

Not until after this third birth does the individual enter the larger world of man and nature. Now the most important birth of all "*may* begin to take place": that is "the birth in him of the Will—the real Will." This is to say, the child is oriented to God: "When the man, listening to his conscience, wills and does the right, irrespective of inclination as of consequence, then is the man free, the universe opens before him" (48). The truly free man is he who fully serves God; to serve another is to degenerate into a tyranny of the self or a tyranny of a neighbor, both of which destroy individuality. This fourth birth "with most . . . takes years not a few to complete." Its accomplishment requires active determination, not passivity, and it is the dynamics of this birth which constitute the mythical quests of MacDonald's fiction.

The fourth birth is most often preceded by a fall into moral and spiritual night, in which the young person wanders lost, alone, perplexed and despairing. MacDonald elsewhere affirms that this is the archetypal Christian tragedy, which

> corresponds more or less to the grand drama of the Bible; wherein the first act opens with a brilliant sunset vision of Paradise, in which childish sense and need are served with all the profusion of the indulgent nurse. But the glory fades off into grey and black, and night settles down upon the heart which, rightly uncontent with the childish, seeks knowledge and manhood as a thing denied by the Maker, and yet to be gained by the creature; so sets forth alone to climb the heavens, and instead of climbing, falls into the abyss. Then follows the long dismal night of helpless despair; till at length a deeper stratum of the soul is heaved to the surface. ("Broken Swords" 214)

This is the basic pattern of nearly all of MacDonald's novels and fantasies. It is also paradigmatic of much Romantic narrative, the circuitous yet progressive self-education and self-discovery. Wordsworth's *Prelude* is one of these crisis-autobiographies, and MacDonald clearly read it as such. He describes Wordsworth after his experience of the French Revolution: "Dejected even to hopelessness for a time, he believed in nothing" (*England's Antiphon* 304). Later "the power of God came upon Wordsworth," or, as MacDonald puts it in the novel *What's Mine's Mine* (1886), "it was Wordsworth's bitter disappointment at the out-come of the French Revolution . . . that opened the door to him" (217). On his second visit to France, Wordsworth saw the failure of the revolution, and the experience shattered his mental equilibrium; his sleep was filled with "ghastly visions . . . of despair / And tyranny, and implements of death" (*Prelude* 10.402–3). Turning to abstract science in vain, Wordsworth entered the dismal night "in heart and mind benighted." But the poem had not begun in utter loss of hope, nor would it end so. Through communion with nature, with Dorothy, and with Coleridge, Wordsworth finds an enriched awareness and the poem ends where it began, only with a surer sense of direction and mission.

MacDonald describes a similar process in the "Sketch of Individual Development." The youth, all youth, is restless for movement and knowledge. He is constantly questioning, and consequently the "world begins to come alive around him" (*Dish of Orts* 49). Nature awakens the youth's mind to beauty; it arouses his imagination. In Wordsworthian language, MacDonald depicts the youth as he lies on a sunny river bank gazing "into the blue heaven till his soul seems to float abroad and mingle with the infinite made visible, with the boundless condensed into colour and shape." Nature arouses great emotions, but the youth is dissatisfied; he wants a "deeper waking" and "greater beauty." Nature itself is not sufficient; there must be something more, "an unknown ideal of Nature," and more important, a human ideal. Like Wordsworth, who felt the brotherhood of man through nature, MacDonald's imagined youth now fancies himself a liberator, a "champion of the weak" and "friend to the great" (50).

At college, the youth confronts, as had Wordsworth at Cambridge, the spectre of science, which binds his feelings "even as in a chain" (*Prelude* 3.169). Once the visible universe "with microscopic view / Was scanned" (*Prelude* 12.91–92), it was rendered dull and inanimate. The fear arises that nature is truly cold and indifferent and that we receive but what we give. Wordsworth finds his way out of dejection in the face of the old leech gatherer, the natural man ("Resolution and Independence," *Poetical Works* 155–57). MacDonald finds renewal of hope in the love of a woman. Love brings life back into the earth; the flowers appear as they did in his boyhood, only they have "a yet deeper glow, a yet fresher delight, a yet more unspeakable soul" (*Dish of Orts* 53). A feeling is here of something more precious than early childhood, a feeling which is missing in Wordsworth. Wordsworth expresses an inescapable feeling of nostalgia. For MacDonald, the love of a woman brings to man, "for his own," that infinite that Wordsworth's nature only intimates.

But the spectre of selfhood is never far away. That self, that "radiant of darkness" (54), Anodos's Shadow in *Phantastes* (1858), arrives on the scene to imprison the young man once more. After the vision, the clouds again enclose him, only to be blown away by a renewed awareness of the "changelessness amid change, the law amid seeming disorder, the unity amid units" (55). Through the scientific view of creation and evolution (MacDonald, like many of his Victorian contemporaries, interprets Darwin's theory of evolution as teleological) impelling us toward some future perfection, and the vision of "the oneness of the universe" (57), the young man's hope is kept alive. He realizes that life without God is not worth living. Everything, including science, is rooted in the unseen. Art makes visible the invisible, and he turns to poetry. He keeps perpetually before him a "live ideal" (75), a something greater than man, towards which he aspires. MacDonald could never assent to Wordsworth's exclamation: "Here must thou be, O Man! / Power to thyself; no Helper hast thou here; / Here keepest thou in singleness thy state" (*Prelude* 14.209–11). Instead, the "existence of a God such as Christ, a God who is a good man infinitely, is the only ideal containing hope enough for man" (*Dish of Orts* 70). And having brought the individual to the end of his development, MacDonald presents him as longing for "the godlike way of being" (68), and places him within reach of "the divine nature, of the divine joy" (69). Obedience to the will of God keeps the man childlike; belief in Christ renders life holy, harmonious and poetic. This is the result of the fourth birth.

Wordsworth fears loss of childhood, a decaying of the power to discern beauty:

> I see by glimpses now; when age comes on,
> May scarcely see at all; and I would give,
> While yet we may, as far as words can give,
> Substance and life to what I feel, enshrining,
> Such is my hope, the spirit of the Past
> For future restoration.
>
> (*Prelude* 12.281–86)

Poetry here is a means of claiming past experiences from the passage of time, enshrining those "spots of time" which are continually found in Wordsworth's childhood and youth. But MacDonald carries his childhood feelings into manhood, and poetry for him is an aid "along the path to truth" (*Sir Gibbie* 149). In Wordsworth's "Peele Castle" and the "Ninth Evening Voluntary" the sunset is "past; the visionary splendour fades; / And night approaches with her shades" (see *England's Antiphon* 305–7). It is significant that MacDonald omits these final two lines in his transcription of the poem in his essay on Wordsworth in *A Dish of Orts* (255). For MacDonald, the vision did not pass.

In the "Sketch," MacDonald sees the individual's spiritual conflict in terms of a clash between science and poetry. He also dramatizes this conflict in his novels and romances. In *There and Back* (1891), Richard Lestrange has a happy childhood, but as he grows older he regards the world as an "aggregate of laws and results, the great dissecting-room of creation, the happy-hunting ground of the goddess who calls herself Science" (146). He falls into despair. But sorrow and love revive his spirits and lead him to God. At the end of the book, he does not believe in "separation any more than in death" (384). Paul Faber, the eponymous hero of another novel, "cared for nothing but science" (105). Eventually despair catches up with him, but again suffering is purgation. At the end, a "deeper, loftier, lovelier morning was dawning in Faber's world" (512). Both Anodos in *Phantastes* and Vane in *Lilith* (1895) have scientific minds, both fall into despair, and both come home uplifted by suffering and love. Curdie in *The Princess and Curdie* (1883) believes as he grows older "less and less in the things he had never seen" (180) until he too spirals upward to recovery. In *The Light Princess* (1863), MacDonald satirizes the scientific mind in the two "very wise Chinese philosophers," Hum-Drum and Kopy-Keck. The witch, Makemnoit, also represents intellect, whereas the Prince who saves the Light Princess thinks intuitively and poetically. The Princess herself must suffer grief and despair before the deeper stratum of her soul heaves itself into being.

This spiritual conflict between science and poetry is accompanied by a corresponding psychological conflict, that between libidinal and other aims. The fall into desire is as inevitable as the fall into self consciousness. Once the self perceives nature as "other," that other becomes desirable; the self seeks to exert its influence and the result is a struggle for power. The boy in Wordsworth's "Nutting" thoughtlessly yet brutally defiles the trees in his effort to gather his spoils, to enjoy self-gratification. A similar depiction of the fall into desire appears in Blake's *The Mental Traveller*. MacDonald's Light Princess is equally as thoughtless in her desire to enjoy the delights of swimming with the Prince or in swimming alone when the Prince is needed to plug the hole in the lake's bottom. Curdie, in *The Princess and Curdie*, thoughtlessly yet brutally kills a pigeon, and feels a sudden consciousness of separation as if the whole world were going to cast him out. He must learn, as all of MacDonald's characters must, that the "child is not meant to die, but to be forever fresh-born" (180). Essential childhood is fatherhood. Child Curdie sets things right in the King's house; child Diamond, in *At the Back of the North Wind*, does his father's work driving the cab and providing for his family; and young Colin, in "The Carasoyn," proves to be father to the man when he learns how to cope with the fairy fleet, something which serves him well when, as an adult, he once again must use his wits and his faith to outmaneuver the fairies.

Wordsworth's children—Edward in "Anecdote for Fathers," the little girl in "We are Seven," Johnny in "The Idiot Boy," Lucy Gray, the

Wordsworth in books 1 and 2 of *The Prelude*—are poets in their immediacy of response to nature and in their unmediated speech. They speak a pure language untainted by self-consciousness, the will to power, or the need to rationalize. Their words carry relationship and love; these children are the rock and defence for human nature. Something the same may be said for MacDonald's child characters: Irene, Curdie, and Diamond are poets who use rhyme to bring joy to darkness. Tricksey-Wee, in "The Giant's Heart," is capable of song, and so is the Prince in "The Light Princess." Often the musical and polysemous language of poetry contrasts with the hard-edged and one-dimensional language of politicians, witches, or business people. And just as often, MacDonald and Wordsworth contrast the vital and living language of an oral tradition with the fixed and bound language of print.

Wordsworth, in the well-known poems "Expostulation and Reply" and "The Tables Turned," privileges nature over the barren leaves of books, and in book 5 of *The Prelude* (71–140) he dreams of an Arab hurrying to bury two books, one a stone (*Euclid's Elements*) and the other a shell (poetry), the latter being "something of more worth" than the former (89), containing as it does "voices more than all the winds" (107). In book 2, Wordsworth points to an old inn sign on Lake Windermere's eastern shore to indicate the decline from a preliterate time to the present; rhymes over the threshold of the inn have gone, and so too has the old Lion that once adorned the inn sign, replaced by "large golden characters" (lines 149–53). The language of script is a diminishment of oral language. To make poetry work, its language must strive to return to the condition of orality, that is, to be a live thing, active and efficient. Poetic language is pleasant noise of waters, the voice of streams, the ceaseless music of the Derwent of Wordsworth's childhood.

MacDonald too speaks of poetic language as music. The music of the spinning wheel in *The Princess and Curdie* spins "songs and tales and rhymes" in Curdie's brain (186), and Diamond in *At the Back of the North Wind* conceives of poetry as music, something to dance to. The wise old owl in "Cross Purposes" cannot read the book he holds upside down, but he can sing. The ageless lady in "The Golden Key" sings songs to Tangle so wonderful that Tangle wishes they would go on forever. The language of poetry aspires to the condition of music because music communicates immediately and feelingly. This language is living the way oral language lives; voice is not disembodied but personal. The Shadows, in the story of the same name, "have no writing or printing," and "the only way they can make each other acquainted with their doings and thinkings is to meet and talk" (*Complete Fairy Tales* 102). Finally, language at its most powerful has nothing to do with words as we know them; instead it is immediate communication, communication that defeats the barriers of different languages.

In touch with this language more than anyone else is the child; many of MacDonald's child characters are poets: Tricksey-Wee and Buffy-Bob ("The Giant's Heart"), Curdie (*The Princess and the Goblin*), Diamond (*At the Back of the North Wind*), the Prince ("The Light Princess"). And all his heroes reach a state of knowing that passes understanding to become seeing. In other words, language serves only to announce vision, revelation. In "The Golden Key" Tangle learns to hear and comprehend what the birds and beasts and creeping things say "though she could not repeat a word of it" (220); she learns to understand the speaking face of nature. Curdie too, in *The Princess and Curdie*, first hears the spinning songs of the great-great-grandmother and then he sees her, that is he knows her; he is ready to experience her fire of roses as Tangle is ready to experience the Old Man of the Fire. In Wordsworth too this apocalyptic pattern of sound leading to sight recurs. The soft inland murmur of "Tintern Abbey" leads to the intensely inward vision of the Wye Valley; the sound of waters in "Resolution and Independence" is a prelude to the vision of the old leech gatherer; the hooting owls and hooting boy of "There Was a Boy" herald the visible scene's impression on his mind. This boy dies before his twelfth birthday. Perhaps, like Diamond in *At the Back of the North Wind*, he had already grown a man. For these poetic children, like the girl in "We Are Seven," or Edward in "Anecdote for Fathers," or Curdie caring for the king in *The Princess and Curdie*, or Irene who is wise beyond her years in *The Princess and the Goblin*, have something to teach the adult. They are, in their own way, prophets of nature who speak a lasting inspiration, reminding us "how the mind of man becomes / A thousand times more beautiful than the earth / On which he dwells" (*Prelude* 14.444–50; see *Dish of Orts* 263).

MacDonald's children's fantasies reflect the influence of Wordsworth in their wise children who have a bond with nature either directly or with a representative of nature in the form of a wise old woman. Although MacDonald accepts, in a way Wordsworth does not, the supernatural, his vision of nature is discernably Wordsworthian.

As inappropriate as the comparison may at first appear, Wordsworth's *Peter Bell* and MacDonald's fairy tale, "Cross Purposes," have much in common. In his letter to Robert Southey printed with *Peter Bell*, Wordsworth informs us that his poem illustrates not only that the supernatural is unnecessary to excite imaginative activity, but also that "incidents within the compass of poetic probability" are perfectly capable of calling forth Imagination (*Poetical Works* 188). On the other hand, MacDonald's story makes no claim for "poetic probability" since it has its setting firmly within fairyland, beginning in the conventional fairy-tale manner "Once upon a time" (*Complete Fairy Tales* 187).

The two works, however, outline the education in humanity, or in what MacDonald calls "essential childhood," of the main characters. Peter Bell is a ruffian, a man into whose heart "nature ne'er could find the way" (line 244, in *Poetical Works* 190). One November night he enters a "thick wood" and has an experience which changes him for the better. He comes across an apparently abandoned or lost ass, then the ass's drowned owner, and finally the dead man's son, who searches for his father. The night's events, including Peter's anger at the stubborn ass, affect his imagination in such a way that he thinks he sees and hears strange things: fairies, witches, murmurs from the earth, a ghost, and his own double. Each of these seeming supernatural visitations has a natural explanation, but Peter's mind plays him tricks; the spirits he senses are "Spirits of the Mind" (line 783, in *Poetical Works* 195). Being a "deep logician," Peter attempts to rationalize the uncanny things which appear to him, but his logic fails. His experience of death and family grief awaken his heart and mind to nature and humanity: "he sobs even like a child" (line 1119, in *Poetical Works* 198). The poem articulates what MacDonald observes in Wordsworth's poetry; man finds "a meaning in nature that he brought to it" (*Dish of Orts* 252). Peter's conscience gets the better of him, and the world that appears so threatening is, in actuality, a schoolhouse for his own betterment.

In "Cross Purposes," Alice and Richard travel to fairyland, where they learn love and interdependence. At the outset, Alice is too "silly" and Richard too "sensible," a typical separation of the sexes based on emotion and reason. Alice also holds unpleasant preconceptions about poor people, of whom Richard is one. Their trip to fairyland brings maturity and understanding. Fairyland, which to Alice is akin to reading a story-book, is MacDonald's metaphor for nature in its maternal aspect, both nurturing and disciplining. Their trials in this seemingly strange land educate the two children to know that the outward appearance of things is not necessarily trustworthy. Like Peter, Richard and Alice experience frightening spirits of the mind in the form of "lizards, and frogs, and black snakes, and all kinds of strange and ugly creatures, especially some that had neither heads, nor tails, nor legs, nor fins, nor feelers, being, in fact, only living lumps" (203). Such horrors vanish, however, when Richard controls fear and pursues his way forthrightly. Similarly, when Richard and Alice experience trial by separation, they learn that nothing can separate those who truly love except fear. Overcoming fear, the two walk away from fairyland hand in hand, a new Adam and Eve, both grown "quite man and woman in Fairyland" (208). Yet they remain children, each returning to his or her parents; maturity means leaving childish attitudes behind, but not losing the childlike spirit.

Much of this—the interest in experience as the best educator, the growth into self-consciousness, the inward journey, and imagination as a formative faculty of mind—MacDonald derives from the Romantic sensibility generally. What Wordsworth gave MacDonald was an acute appreciation of nature as imbued with a sense sublime. Primroses, snowdrops, daisies, trees, mountains, streams—all these communicate thoughts of permanence amid change. The heart attuned to nature, in both MacDonald and Wordsworth, sees into the heart of things. The heart attuned to nature is a childlike heart. MacDonald appropriates the Wordsworthian child who is an eye among the blind, who wandering in strange seas is never without an anchor. In short, MacDonald takes Wordsworth's vision of nature and the child and gives it a distinctly Christian perspective. Nature reflects God's spirit and the child must remind us of Jesus.

WORKS CITED

Abrams, M. H. *Natural Supernaturalism: Tradition and Revolution in Romantic Literature.* London: Oxford UP, 1971.

Blake, William. *Complete Writings; with Variant Readings.* Ed. Geoffrey Keynes. London: Oxford UP, 1966.

Gaull, Marilyn. *English Romanticism: The Human Context.* New York: Norton, 1988.

Hartman, Geoffrey. *Wordsworth's Poetry, 1787–1814*. New Haven: Yale
  UP, 1971.
MacDonald, George. *At the Back of the North Wind*. 1871. London: Blackie
  and Sons, n.d.
———. "The Broken Swords." *The Portent and Other Stories*. London:
  Fifield, 1924. Originally published in *The Monthly Christian Spectator*
  4 (1854): 633–40.
———. *The Complete Fairy Tales of George MacDonald*. Intro. Roger Lance-
  lyn Green. New York: Schocken, 1977.
———. *A Dish of Orts*. London: Sampson Low, Marston, 1895.
———. *England's Antiphon*. London: Macmillan, 1874.
———. *Guild Court: A London Story*. 1868. London: Sampson Low, Marston,
  Searle, and Rivington, 1881.
———. *The Hope of the Gospel*. London: Ward, Lock, Bowden, 1892.
———. *Paul Faber, Surgeon*. 1879. New York: George Routledge, n.d.
———. *Phantastes and Lilith*. Grand Rapids: Eerdmans, 1968.
———. *The Princess and the Goblin. The Princess and Curdie*. 1872, 1883. Ed.
  Roderick McGillis. Oxford: World's Classics, 1990.
———. *The Seaboard Parish*. 1868. London: Kegan Paul, Trench, Trubner,
  n.d.
———. *Sir Gibbie*. 1879. London: Dent & Sons, 1924.
———. *There and Back*. 1891. London: Kegan Paul, Trench, Trubner, 1907.
———. *Unspoken Sermons*. 1st ser. London: Alexander Strahan, 1867.
———. *What's Mine's Mine*. London: Kegan Paul and Trench, 1886.
MacDonald, Greville. *George MacDonald and His Wife*. London: Allen and
  Unwin, 1924.
Novalis. *The Disciples at Sais and Other Fragments*. London: Methuen, 1903.
Prickett, Stephen. *Victorian Fantasy*. Bloomington: Indiana UP, 1979.
Raeper, William. *George MacDonald*. Tring, Hertshire: Lion, 1987.
Swiatecka, M. Jadwiga. *The Idea of the Symbol*. Cambridge: Cambridge UP,
  1980.
Wordsworth, William. *The Poetical Works of Wordsworth*. Ed. Thomas
  Hutchinson. 1904. Rev. Ernest De Selincourt. London: Oxford UP, 1936.
———. *The Prelude: A Parallel Text*. Ed. J. C. Maxwell. Harmondsworth:
  Penguin, 1972.

JUDITH A. PLOTZ

A Victorian Comfort Book

Juliana Ewing's *The Story of a Short Life*

*C*hildhood death is a central Victorian theme. Nothing in literary history quite compares with the sudden turn between 1840 and 1910 to searching treatments of childhood death and dying both in works intended for children and those for adults. The frequent transience and brevity of children's lives was a paradox: why should such intensity of existence be so brief? "The children didn't stay; they went back again," a country woman told the Victorian diarist Francis Kilvert; it was as if "they had just come into a room and had gone out again, or had arrived from a distant journey and had started to go back immediately" (3: 242). Why should these precious lives flicker into a moment's brilliance, like that which comforted Hans Christian Andersen's Little Match Girl, only to gutter out in a wash of tears? Though the occasional Christian apologist might offer some thin rationalization, few Victorian writers found ready religious consolation. "Job!" rejoined William Canton to some pieties preferred at the loss of his daughter; "the author of Job knew more about astronomy than he knew about fatherhood" (*Invisible Playmate* 5).

The insistent attention to childhood death in late-nineteenth-century literature may seem surprising. After all, the evidence of statistics, though murky on some points,[1] clearly indicates a *falling* mortality rate for the young. Indeed the demographer P. E. H. Hair argues that since 1750 the "number of children in Britain has increased decade by decade, almost without exception" (35). By Hair's estimate, the number of children in Britain doubled between 1750 and 1850, surging from about 3,600,000 to 7,300,000, and constituting a veritable "flood of children" whose presence caused a shift in the "social mentality of the decades after 1850" (35–37). Despite differences in some details, there is a consensus among demographers that the infant mortality rate fell gradually in Britain from the mid-eighteenth century when it stood around 300–400 per 1,000 live births (McKeown and Brown 63) to 1850 when it was around 160 per 1,000 (Wrigley 166–67; Hair 39). Thus in 1750 one infant in three died, between 1850 and 1900 one in every six, and in 1950 approximately one in every thirty (Hair 40). Even though the overall mortality rates were declining, the earliest and most striking improvements were for older children. As Hair notes, the "mortality of older children fell off from . . . around 1850; that of toddlers fell off from about 1870; and that of infants from about 1900" (39). Infant mortality was not significantly reduced until after 1900; indeed, before 1900 "the figures often tended to rise rather than fall" (Wrigley 169). In a study of age-specific mortality in nineteenth-century Europe, Odin Anderson argues that before 1900 there were tremendous improvements in mortality in young adult groups "and relatively little improvement in the very young groups" (253). In partial confirmation, J. M. Winter has argued that the decline in death rates in the 1870s "can be ascribed almost entirely to improvements in the life chances of people aged 2–35" (104). Nineteenth-century improvements in nutrition and sanitation—which increased resistance and decreased exposure to infectious diseases, the major causes of childhood death—were responsible for these ameliorated "life chances" among older children. Infant diarrhea, however, remained the "scourge of infant health" until well into the second decade of the twentieth century, when greatly improved sewage systems and controls of contaminated food and milk lowered the incidence to negligible levels (Winter 109–17). Thus throughout the period 1850 to 1900, at the same time that average family size was increasing because of the improved survival of older children, high infant mortality continued to exist and to be "generally regarded as inevitable" (McKeown and Brown 48). During this period Britain became more densely populated with children than ever before in history, so parents might with reason entertain greater hopes for this hitherto unrecognized but now romantically exalted "one supreme majority" (Canton, "The Legend of Childhood," *Lost Epic* 134). But the same brutal physiological fate continued to savage infants as of old. The contrast between aspiration and fate gave rise to an extensive literature of consolation and explanation.

The late nineteenth-century emphasis on childhood death brings a new element into literature. Renaissance claims for attention to such trivial deaths had been modest or even shamefaced: " 'Tis not a life," one Beaumont and Fletcher character remarks of a dead child, " 'Tis

but a bit of childhood thrown away" (Russell 124). Most eighteenth-
and early nineteenth-century depictions of childhood death, following
James Janeway's relentlessly pedagogic *A Token for Children* (1672),
had been religiously doctrinal, easily justifying as triumphal and glori-
ous good children's extended holy dyings. Victorian treatments, however, were neither minor nor, by and large, doctrinally consolatory.

This remarkable shift in response—or, at any rate, in expression—is
rooted in Romanticism. The Romantic heritage made it impossible to
take childhood death lightly. In Wilfred Meynell's words, the Romantics virtually "discovered the child" and restored him to a place at the
center of human consciousness: "Him the Modern Poets have Set in
the Midst of us, even as he was Set in the Midst of men by the Lord"
(ii). By valorizing the child as, in Friedrich von Schiller's words, "the
lively representation to us of the ideal" (87), the Romantics freighted
the life of the individual child with new and important kinds of meaning. The child became central partly because childhood ceased to be
seen as marginal or preliminary to real life and was indeed defined
as real life in and of itself, partly because childhood was perceived as
the embodiment of nature, and partly because childhood psychological powers were increasingly seen as the foundation and model of all
substantial adult achievement.

The Romantics promoted childhood from a stage of probationary
nonage preliminary to the real business of living to a type of life
itself. Seen as more fully alive than adults, children often therefore
are addressed—and not ironically—as exemplars, preceptors, guides.
The child as teacher is everywhere in nineteenth-century literature.
William Wordsworth's "seer blest" is merely the first of many such
teachers. John Greenleaf Whittier writes: "God has his small interpreter— / The child must teach the man" (W. Meynell ii). Wilfred
Meynell's "Out of the Mouths of Babes" praises even infantine babble:

> What they say, in their nests, these dear birds,
>   Is all even:
> For their speech, be whatever their words,
>   Is of Heaven.
>
> (Canton, *Children's Sayings* 1)

Inferior, therefore, to the child, the adult "Dare not bless him!" as
Elizabeth Barrett Browning enjoins the parents of "A Child Asleep,"
but should submit to "be blessed by his peace, and go in peace" (247).

In the same vein, Elizabeth Chapman elegizes her dead nephew for his pedagogic authority:

> For me, my best instructor in the spells
> And wiles of Nature was a seven-years' boy,
> To whom, she had revealed the soul that dwells
> Beneath her careless outward robe of joy.
> She knew him true; she made him one with her,
> Her little prophet and interpreter.
>
> (sonnet 6)

Far from being innately flawed and limited as some have taught, "They erred":

> The child is, was, and still shall be
> The world's deliverer; in his heart the springs
> Of our salvation ever rise, and we
> Mount on his innocency as on wings.
>
> (Chapman, sonnet 27)

Less a departure point than a goal or center, the child is seen by Bronson Alcott, for example, as a "a Type of the Divinity. Herein is our Nature despoiled of none of its glory" (*Essays* 52). His work as a schoolmaster gave him a daily lesson in sanctity:

> Not Wordsworth's genius, Pestalozzi's love,
> The stream have sounded of pure infancy.
> Baptismal waters from the Head above
> The babes I foster daily are to me;
> I dip my pitcher in these living springs
> And draw, from depths below, sincerity.
> Unsealed, mine eyes behold all outward things
> Arranged in splendors of divinity.
> What mount of vision can with mine compare?
>
> (*Sonnets and Canzonets* no. 14)

Ralph Waldo Emerson, deferring to the insights of Alcott, the "Orphic Poet," similarly praises infancy as "the perpetual Messiah which comes into the arms of fallen men and pleads with them to return to Paradise" (54). In similar vein, Amiel apostrophizes childhood as the salvation of a fallen world:

> Blessed be Childhood which brings down something of Heaven into the midst of our rough earthliness. All the good and wholesome feeling which is intertwined with childhood and the cradle is one of the

secrets of the providential government of the world.

> Blessed be Childhood for the good it does, and for the good which it brings about carelessly and unconsciously, by simply making us love it, and letting itself be loved. What little of Paradise we still see upon earth is due to its presence among us. Without fatherhood, without motherhood, I think love itself would not be enough to prevent men from devouring each other. (30)

Rather than existing on sufferance simply as potentially valuable, the Romantic child is perceived as a figure of authority. This authority comes in part from sheer numbers. William Canton, for example, in "The Legend of Childhood," puts into the mouth of "A Philosopher" the perception:

> That ever since the articulate race began
> These babes have been the joy and plague of man!
> Unnoticed by historian or sage,
> These bright-eyed chicks have been in every age
> The one supreme majority.
>
> (*Lost Epic* 134)

The perception of this impending new force plays out into a fantasy of utopian reform in Canton's *Invisible Playmate:* "Oh man, man, what wonderful creatures these bairnies are! Did it ever occur to you that they must be the majority of the human race? The men and women combined may be about as numerous, but they must far outnumber the men or the women taken separately, and as all the women and most of the men—bad as they are—side with them, what a political power they might be, if they had their rights!" (10). Indeed, Ellen Key, Swedish educator, whose *Century of the Child* (1900) was an international best-seller at the turn of the century, similarly asserted: "When the child gets his rights, morality will be perfected" (45).

Since early life is thus precious, the truncated lives of those who have died young take on a new meaning for Romantic writers. Comfort must come not from the thought of how little is lost but rather from how completely even the youngest infant has lived. "My Baby has not lived in vain," Samuel Taylor Coleridge wrote of his son Berkeley, dead in his first year; "this life has been to him what it is to all of us, education & development!" (479) Indeed, childhood death is frequently interpreted by bereaved adults not simply as destroyer but as the preserver of the most valuable part of life which would otherwise be obliterated in normal adulthood. "Time was," Alice Meynell noted, "when childhood was but borne with, and that for sake of its mere promise of manhood. We do not now hold, perhaps, that promise so high" (28). Consequently Romantic writers suggest that the most meaningful period of a life is the earliest and that even "early deaths somehow conduce to the overall happiness of mankind," as Leigh Hunt observed in his famous essay, "Death of Little Children":

> If there were *no childhood deaths* . . . we would regard every little child as a man or woman secured, and it will easily be conceived what a world of endearing cares and hopes this security would endanger. The very idea of infancy would lose its continuity with us. Girls and boys would be future men and women, not present children. They would have attained their full growth in our imaginations, and might as well have been men and women at once. On the other hand, those who have lost an infant, are never, as it were, without an infant child. They are the only persons who, in one sense, retain it always, and they furnish their neighbours with the same idea. The other children grow up to manhood and womanhood and suffer all the changes of mortality. This one alone is rendered an immortal child. (6)

As a comforting rationalization, of course, Hunt's comments can do little to assuage a parent's grief. This praise of the dead baby evinces a profound and poignant attentiveness to the qualities of infancy, an attentiveness that keeps grief alive. But in addition his comments do suggest the possible appeal of the theme of childhood death to Romantic writers. Since the loveliness of childhood is obliterated by maturation into adulthood, the child who survives into adulthood has, in a sense, died as a child. "How the children leave us!" lamented Elizabeth Barrett Browning, "and in their places / Weary men and anxious women stand" ("And the Child Grew," *Why Weepest Thou?* 55). But if the child has died before the childlike self has been eroded by time, then he remains, in Wordsworth's formulation, "as if embalmed / By Nature—through some special privilege / Stopped at the growth he had . . . a child / And nothing more" (*Prelude* [1805] 7.400–405). Such an "embalmed" "immortal" child is privileged by death to embody perpetually those qualities only retrospectively available to survivors. Thus the child who dies remains quintessentially childlike—indeed, he is the only lasting child—and the inevitable subject of obsessive scrutiny to those who value childhood.

The increasing seriousness imputed to childhood death in the nine-teenth century grows partly from the increasing perceptions of the ordi-nary child as the living embodiment of that most powerful of Romantic abstractions, Nature. In Romantic depictions, the ordinary child is vir-tually indistinguishable from the Jungian archetype of the *puer aeter-nus*, who embodies the invincibility of the forces of nature in a self-generated atmosphere of energy (Jung 170). Schiller's great essay *Naïve and Sentimental Poetry* lays down axiomatically the connection be-tween nature and childhood: "There are moments in our lives when we dedicate a kind of love and tender respect to nature in plants, minerals, animals, and landscape, as well as to human nature in children . . . not because it gratifies our senses, nor yet . . . our understanding or taste . . . rather simply *because it is nature*" (83). To say a child is like nature is to place her within the dynamic, organic universe of Romanticism. Whether the emphasis falls on the child's natural self-completeness (what Schiller calls the "subsistence of things on their own" [84]) or on the child's power of growth, she is like nature and unlike the self-conscious adult. Wordsworth habitually asserts that "an active prin-ciple pervades the Universe" and notes "How lively this principle is in Childhood" ("Argument," *The Excursion*, book 9, *Poetical Works* 5: 286). Pervasive in nineteenth-century art and literature are depic-tions of children as manifesting this principle. They are shown as vital, whirling beings. Thus William Blake's "Nurse's Song" describes the children who "leaped & shouted & laugh'd / And all the hills ecchoed" (*Songs of Innocence* 15–16, in Blake 15). Thus Coleridge's "limber elf" in *Christabel* "Singing, dancing to itself, / A fairy thing with red round cheeks, / That always finds, and never seeks" (lines 656, 657–59, in *Coleridge* 84) shares the vitality of its original, Coleridge's own son Hartley, "a fairy elf—all life, all motion—indefatigable in joy—a spirit of Joy dancing on an Aspen Leaf. From morning to night he whirls about and about, whisks, whirls, and eddies, like a blossom in a May-breeze" (*Collected Letters* 2: 668).

Such energies link childhood in Romantic discourse to the vital powers of the universe itself. In a remarkable tour-de-force written in the manner of Thomas Carlyle's *Sartor Resartus*, William Canton gives an account of "An Unknown Child-Poem" on this theme. Allegedly written by the imaginary German poet, "Altegans," this work, "Erster Schulgang," attributes to the world's children the vivid energy, diver-sity, and dynamic potentiality of the miraculous universe of Becoming:

The poem opens with a wonderful vision of children; delightful as it is unexpected; as romantic in presentment as it is commonplace in fact. All over the world—and all under it too, when their time comes—the children are trooping to school. The great globe swings out of the dark into the sun; there is always morning somewhere; and forever in this shifting region of morning-light, the good Altegans sees the little ones afoot—shining companies and groups, couples and bright solitary figures; for they all seem to have a soft heavenly light about them! . . . The morning side of the planet is alive with them; one hears their pattering footsteps everywhere. And as the vast continents sweep "eastering out of the high shadows which reach beyond the moon" . . . and as new nations with *their* cities and villages, their fields, woods, mountains, and seashores, rise up again into the morning-side, lo! fresh troops and still fresh troops of "these small school-going people of the dawn." . . . What are weather and season to this incessant panorama of childhood? (*Invisible Playmate* 31–32)

If Canton stresses children's kinship with the dynamism of the great globe, Alice Meynell emphasis kinship with natural law and likens the just and spontaneous originality of the child to birdsong: "You cannot anticipate him. Blackbirds, overheard year by year, do not compose the same phrases; never two leit-motifs alike. Not the tone, but the tune alters. With the uncovenanted ways of a child you keep no tryst" (9). In one lovely essay, "Children in Midwinter," Meynell writes of the natural "climate" of childhood. Seeming to carry with him his own world, always a springtime world, the child usually seems out of season—glowing with a strange warmth in mid-winter and tranquil with his own coolness in summer—because he "overcomes both heat and cold by another climate, which is the climate of life" (22).

When Romantic writers elegize lost children, they do so paradoxically by stressing their prodigious vitality. Thus Mary Lamb memorializes a child in terms of her constant energy: "Thou struggler into loving arms / Young climber up of knees" ("Paternal Recollections" 398), while Mary Howitt elegizes her dead son in terms of a vitality antithetical to the very idea of death:

Beauty was on thy cheek, and thou didst seem
A privileged being, chartered from decay;
And thy free spirit, like a mountain stream
That hath no ebbs, kept on its cheerful way.
Thy laugh was like the inspiring breath of spring,

> That thrills the heart, and cannot be unfelt,
> The sun, the moon, the green leaves and the flowers,
>   And every living thing,
> Were a strong joy to thee; thy spirit dwelt
>   Gladly in life, rejoicing in its powers.
> Oh! what had death to do with one like thee . . . ?
>   ("The Child in Heaven," *"Why Weepest Thou?"* 38)

Romantic writers further tend to emphasize that childhood mental powers are normative for the adult. The child's powers of intuition, holism, play, and imagination are increasingly regarded as exemplary for the adult. Indeed, by the close of the nineteenth century, the American anthropologist Alexander Francis Chamberlain could argue that the *goal* of mankind was childhood. *The Child: A Study in the Evolution of Man* (1900) maintains that human evolution *must* and human progress *should* involve the increasing childlikeness of adults: "In a sense . . . the child is really 'father of the man' for the modern man is becoming more and more of a child, or rather, the modern child is losing less and less of childhood in the process of becoming a man" (8). As the world improves, the parent will "be like the babe [rather] than the babe like the parent. The things simply foreshadowed in the child seem to be those which will one day be the most valued possession of the race" (445). Arthur Schopenhauer was voicing a nineteenth-century platitude in observing that "Every child is to a certain extent, a genius, and every genius is, to a certain extent, a child" (Chamberlain, *Child and Childhood*, ch. 28).

The child of Romantic tradition—so fully alive, so powerful an embodiment of Nature's vitality, a prototype of the noblest human qualities—is thus too important a being to die, or, at any rate, to die unnoticed.

This exalted conception of childhood meant that the individual child's death took on new importance and demanded a worthy response. Furthermore, as Philippe Ariès has noted, the gradual leaking away of religious belief by the late nineteenth century meant "that survivors accepted the death of another person with greater difficulty than in the past" (67). The need for consolation for the loss of so precious a being as the Romantic child is responsible for a proliferation after about 1840 of a rash of "Comfort Books," works explicitly or implicitly designed to bring consolation for the loss of short-lived children. The explicit works bear such titles as *Little Angels: A Book of Comfort for Mourning Mothers;* and *Asleep in Jesus; or, Words of Consolation to Bereaved Parents;* and *Our Children's Rest; or, Comfort for Bereaved Mothers.* These are works with a clear design on their readers, usually a specifically denominational design. These readers are assumed to be either the parents or siblings of children recently dead. All these works are expressly directed to console the bereaved for their loss of a beloved child by showing them how to keep a meaningful life intact during the dying and after death. Even though these works bear ostentatiously religious titles, they offer, as do the implicit works, modes of comfort that are less doctrinally Christian than they are affective, psychological, or even magical. The implicit comfort books, among which are numbered many of the classics of Victorian adult and children's literature—works such as *The Old Curiosity Shop; At the Back of the North Wind; The Water Babies;* and the once-celebrated *Invisible Playmate*—are similarly, though more gently, tendentious.

Almost all nineteenth-century comfort books, whether explicit or implicit, make two assumptions and hold out a triple comfort. First, both explicit and implicit comfort books assume a Romantic view of childhood, a view in which childhood is at once precious, important, and exemplary. Second, the Comfort Books make plain by their elaborate schemes of rationalization or explanation that a merely religious scheme of consolation is inadequate to meet the loss of such a being.

All the comfort books I have examined are characterized by three structures of consolation, each bolstering an only partly operative religious structure.[2] First, these works create a fellowship, a community of mourners. Titles often suggest this: W. B. Clark's *Asleep in Jesus; or Words of Consolation to Bereaved Parents* (1858); the anonymous *Our Children's Rest; or, Comfort for Bereaved Mothers* (1863); *Children in Heaven; or, The Infant Dead Redeemed by the Blood of Jesus with Words of Consolation to Bereaved Parents* (1865); *"Why Weepest Thou?" A Book for Mourners* (1888); and Matthew Russell's *Little Angels: A Book of Comfort for Mourning Mothers* (1909). The texts virtually all invoke a community of shared pain and loss, and a community of joy through recollection. A common tactic of the explicit comfort books is to assemble multiple examples of suffering and response. Russell's *Little Angels,* for example, intermingles an account of his own bereavements, stretching back over forty years, with those of his parishioners and with those of historical characters. The work makes extensive citations from elegies on lost children from ancient and modern English, American, French, Latin, and Greek sources. Further, Russell cites children's epitaphs from graveyards all over Europe and relates such narratives of grief as "The Death of an Irish School-Boy" (116), "the Poor Man's Child" (4), and "The Child Who Could Never Grow Old" (140). His tactic is to document centuries of tender grief for centuries of lost children; the effect is both to authorize and dignify the grief of the mourner of the present and to enroll her in the great society of those who grieve. Such collectivism is enforced by the editorial strategy of comfort books which are organized as collections, documenting the fate of "*Our* Children" (italics mine), as J. G. titles the largest section in "*Why Weepest Thou?*" This affective language of "*our*" common experience, such as Elizabeth Barrett Browning uses in a frequently quoted poem—"How the children leave us" ("*Why Weepest Thou?*" 55)—works to bind the readers of comfort books into a common circle.

A second structure of consolation found in comfort books is that of heroic pathos. Unable to acquire heroic stature in the public world because of their youth and their frailty, dying children nevertheless become memorable figures of dignity by virtue of exercising a fortitude beyond their strength. This is the heroism in Charles Dickens's *Old Curiosity Shop* and in the tales in Frederick Faber's *Ethel's Book; or, Tales of the Angels* (1858). Dickens's little Nell, taxed beyond her strength in an exhausting trek across England, forced to play the role of parent to her feckless grandfather, resembles the dying protagonist Wilfred of Faber's story "The Weeping Angel." Initially a rosy merry child like Nell of the early chapters, Wilfred meets the Weeping Angel by moonlight. The angel weeps for man's rejection of God's glory. Wilfred joins the angel by night and pines by day, taking more and more of the sorrows upon himself. Gradually Wilfred fades into death with great tranquility and courage. "Some children belong to God and to their mothers. But some seem to belong to God only. These die soon, and they like to die. Yet they love their mothers better than other children do. Those are happy mothers who have such children. We call them God's Early Blossoms. Most mothers have one such" (Faber 138). This willing choice of death is also characteristic of heroic pathos. These child heroes, debarred from other forms of public achievement, achieve a kind of grandeur in their death. Heroic pathetic heroes are powerless figures, subject to the control of the adult world. Their weakness is innate as well as circumstantial—Nell and Wilfred are exceptionally frail, as well as dependent, children. They are exposed to unnecessary pain, pain that does not arise from the normal vicissitudes of human life but from what seems exceptional bad luck or the malignity of nature or sadistic individuals. Most important, by virtue of physical constitution, emotional sensibility, and alert intelligence, these heroes of the heroic pathetic have a special gift for suffering. They know how to make something of it. Faber is explicitly doctrinal on this point, arguing that "the souls of little children whom God makes pious very early are to God's glory what the lily bed is to your mother. When the world is very wicked, and God's glory withers and is yellow and dry, He refreshes it by the souls of little children, whom He takes to Himself" (138). For all his vulnerability and defenselessness, however, the figure of pathos is capable of a form of heroism which renders him worthy of admiration. As Schiller observed of the "naïve of temperament," the child who lives his principles regardless of limiting circumstances "puts the world to shame" and acquires a grandeur which diminishes the survivors (89, 92). By valorizing the heroic pathetic, comfort books work to emphasize the meaningfulness of the little life that is gone.

The third tactic of consolation, a somewhat uneasy one, is that of improvisational "made up" structures of explanation. Even explicitly doctrinal books such as W. B. Clark's heavily Evangelical *Asleep in Jesus* and the Presbyterian *Children in Heaven* (1866) augment the religious explanation with a raft of improvised myths. The authors of *Children in Heaven* suggest, for example, that "heaven is made up of little children" (199). This is God's express design for saving "at least half our race" and also for insuring a *cheerful* atmosphere in heaven (215). Clark supplements his stern assurances that the dead infants of saved parents will be saved with fanciful suggestions that children must die in order to be "the choristers of heaven" (34), rebuking disconsolate parents: "what if God removed thy child, to supply the room of one promoted to a higher place in the children's choir? Dost thou grudge him to God for such a purpose?" (35) Relenting, he suggests further that children in heaven will remain children until the souls of parents arrive to educate them; death in childhood will provide for interesting educational activities for both parents and children. In less explicit comfort works such as Charles Kingsley's *Water Babies* and George MacDonald's *At the Back of the North Wind*, there is an even more exuberant construction of mythic alternatives to Christian justifications for early death. Both writers reinforce a Christian vocabulary with a still deeper appeal to elemental nature: Kingsley immerses and redeems his hero in the destructive-creative element of water in a Darwinian universe of an all-generating life-force; while MacDonald transfigures and enlarges his hero by merging him with the element of air—literally in his excursions with North Wind and psychologically in his almost autistic withdrawal from the material. The proliferation of such homemade schemes of explanation as these suggests that the trauma of childhood death was increasingly hard to endure. Thus William Canton, poet and father of three dead daughters, responded to well-meant religious solace in *The Invisible Playmate:* "Dreams, dreams, and not *my* dreams—dreams that might give rest if one knew that they were only a little more than dreams" (*Invisible Playmate* 22). Far more real than any such consolation, Christian or otherwise, was the intense pain of the irrevocable loss.

With the erosion of religion, once the principal structure of consolation during the crises of human existence, it fell more and more to literature to provide a new controlling structure. In the proliferating works on childhood death written during the last decades of the nineteenth century, there is a persisting quest for an adequate consoling myth of meaning.

Among the many Victorian works treating the paradox of the life which is at once brief and full, unfulfilled yet full of value, none is more distinguished than Juliana Ewing's *The Story of a Short Life* (1885). It is a work which dignifies and sanctifies the brief life of a child by embedding that life in the human institution of the family, a family extended into history and eternity. Framed by this family, the child's short life and long dying take on a permanent value. The title of *The Story of a Short Life* (1885), also known as *Laetus Sorte Mea*,[3] makes its subject plain: the "short life" indicates a death. Because the two titles suggest both the *destined shortness* and the *happiness* of the protagonist's life ("Laetus sorte mea" means "Happy in my Lot"), it is plain that the tale is meant to be consolatory, suggesting both loss (the "lot") and a counterbalancing meaning ("laetus").

In the eleven chapters of this short novel, Ewing recounts the brief life of engaging, intelligent, spoiled Leonard, from his crippling injury at six until his death about three years later. The sole child and heir of a rich, aristocratic family, Leonard is passionate, sensitive, affectionate, and overindulged. Because his aunt has married a soldier, now commanding officer at the nearby army camp of Asholt, Leonard is permitted to visit the army camp, where he delights in his friendships with soldiers and the hope of becoming a soldier himself. This hope is smashed when Leonard is irrevocably crippled in a carriage accident.

Even as an invalid, however, he still loves the camp and hero-worships "the V.C.," a young officer whose bravery earned him the Victoria Cross. In an effort to bear his pain as heroically as soldiers bear theirs, Leonard is a characteristic exemplar of the heroic pathetic. He masters his petulant temper, compiles an anthology of the lives of heroic sufferers whom he strives to emulate (his "Book of Poor Things"), and decks himself as much as possible in soldiers' ways—their clothes, their vocabulary, their favorite hymns. Indeed, his death is a kind of soldier's death; it takes place at Asholt Camp as he listens to the nine hundred soldiers in their ugly Iron Church shout out his and their favorite hymn, the martial "The Son of God goes forth to war."

Ewing's book works to make Leonard's death bearable by making his life meaningful. That meaning comes from embedding Leonard in a series of family groups—some literally familial, some metaphorically so—in which he plays a cherished and memorable role. Because the familial institutions to which he is joined are permanent and long-enduring, he becomes the "immortal child" of a durable family community that extends from the distant past into the imaginable future.

Leonard's initial identification is with the nuclear family, his devoted parents. Leonard, used to living "at grown-up people's level" (92), is the only child of loving parents with whom he has a passionately close and rather tremulous relationship. He carries on the leading traits of both parents. "Defiantly like his father" (85), a poet, musician and aesthete, Leonard evinces the paternal sensibility, willfulness, volubility, and intelligence. Like his mother, Lady Jane, the descendent of "an ancient Scottish race, that had shed its blood like water on many a battlefield" (89), Leonard is "naturally brave" (92), has a deep respect for soldiers, and suffers from an over-scrupulous conscience. In illness, Leonard comes to resemble his parents even more, until he embodies their guiding principles. Like his mother ("Your mother's own son!" [140]), he becomes more and more morally scrupulous as he is forced to renounce the possibility of military action for the more inward, female heroism of endurance. Like his father, he channels his will to action into a preoccupation with writing (his "Book of Poor Things") and color (the choice of a properly military dressing gown). His parents' characteristics appear in Leonard's short life, but intensified, concentrated, brilliantly visible.

Leonard's identity is also linked to that of his young ancestor, the Cavalier soldier "Uncle Rupert," whose Anthony Van Dyck portrait, eyes brimming with bright tears, fascinates the child. This Rupert, who died at 17 at Naseby fighting for the king's cause, is Leonard's prototype. The child resembles his dead ancestor so much that "he might have been that other master of the same house come to life again at six years of age. . . . He was very very like Uncle Rupert" (87). Uncle Rupert is a key figure in Leonard's life. Uncle Rupert is a playmate ("Leonard did play with Uncle Rupert—the game of trying to get out of the reach of his eyes" [86]). He is a friend to whom Leonard shouts good-bye as he drives away toward his dreadful accident ("Goodbye, Uncle Rupert! . . . Uncle Rupert, I say! I am—*laetus—sorte—mea!*" [118]). He is a model of achievement ("I meant to die young, but more grown up than this, and in battle . . . I meant about Uncle Rupert's age. He died in battle" [136]). He is also a tutelary guardian who watches over Leonard both as he lives ("Uncle Rupert always looks at me" [86]) and as he dies ("He is at the end of the room there. . . . Only he is out of his frame, and—it's very odd! . . . Someone has wiped away all the tears from his eyes" [165]).[4] The association with Uncle Rupert's "brief life" (85) not only reflects glory on Leonard's "short life" but links the child to an heroic family tradition extending many centuries into the past.

Leonard also belongs to the extended family constituted by his Aunt Adelaide, her husband Colonel Jones, and their subaltern son. Leonard's snobbish and aesthetic father is initially scornful of his military poor relations, both on social and aesthetic grounds. Nephew George is assumed to be vulgar: "Is he likely to have been well brought up? However, he's 'in the Service', as they say. I wish it didn't make one think of flunkeys, what with the word service and the liveries (I mean uniforms), and the legs, and shoulders, and swagger, and ragtags, and epaulettes, and the fatiguing alertness and attentiveness of 'men in the Service'" (89). And his brother-in-law is known to be illgroomed: "the regular type. Hair cut like a pauper, or a convict . . . big, swaggering sort of fellow" (91). Yet through his aunt, uncle, and cousin, Leonard comes first to visit and then to live in the military camp he loves among the soldiers he loves. The child discovers that his "happy lot" covers both the rich grounds of the hall and the barren grounds of the camp. In the opening chapter, Leonard associates the family motto with his "Wednesday text" (96) from the Bible: "The *lot* is fallen unto me in a fair ground. Yea, I have a goodly heritage." Thus the "fair ground" (96) of Leonard's direct heritage is juxtaposed with the "acre of barren ground" (97) on which Asholt Camp is built. The "lots" of ground are geographically contiguous (as indeed the references to them are textually contiguous, on pages 96 and 97); Leonard's own heritage plainly spans both. Though Leonard's own home is vast and splendid, he prefers when possible to stay with the Barrack Master and his wife in the tiny camp "hut" (148), which resembles a child's playhouse. Leonard's extended family extends his sympathies—and eventually his father's sympathies as well—to a wider range of social and moral experience. Indeed, through the link to the Barrack Master's family, Leonard becomes a member of the still larger army family.

Leonard's identity is deepened and confirmed by his membership in the camp community. He is befriended by O'Reilly, the "owld soldier" (115) whose Irish accent and military bearing Leonard does his best to imitate: "I mean to do as like him as ever I can. I do love him so very very much" (115). He hero-worships the brave "V.C." who convinces him that all courage "counts" as military courage:

> "I thought—no matter how good I got to be—nothing could ever count up to be as brave as a real battle, leading your men on and fighting for your country, though you know you may be killed any minute. But Mother says, if I *could* try very hard . . . and keep brave in spite of feeling miserable, that then (particularly as I shan't be very long before I do die) it would be as good as if I'd lived to be as old as Uncle Rupert and fought bravely when the battle was against me, and cheered on my men, though I knew I could never come out of it alive. Do you think it *could* count up to that? *Do you?* . . . You've been in battles—do you?"
> "I do, I do."
> "You're a V.C., and you ought to know" (138).

Desperate to *count*, to be added into the great collectivity of the army's heroes, Leonard enlists his heart's energies into bravely bearing, thus becoming an honorary soldier. As Leonard learns to translate military fortitude into the practice of personal fortitude, his Colonel-Uncle makes him privy to the workings of the camp: "on special occasions, the arrangements for which were only known the night before, O'Reilly, or some other Orderly, might be seen wending his way up the Elm Avenue by breakfast time, 'with Colonel Jones's compliments, and the Orders of the Day for the young gentleman'" (146–47). Even when too ill to follow military maneuvers or watch the drills, Leonard plays the sole "soldier game" accessible to him, that of "being in hospital," with an ardent intensity of belonging that drives him to request "a blue dressing-gown of regulation colour and pattern" (148). Even The Sweep, Leonard's dog, continues his young master's adherence to the army by installing himself after the boy's death in the barrack-room: "And so, rising with gun-fire and resting with 'lights out', he lived and died a Soldier's Dog" (177). Because Leonard is "counted" as one of the military family, he is linked both to the tradition of military duty stretching back into time and also to continuing living memory: "Leonard's military friends do not forget him. They are accustomed to remember the absent" (173).

Leonard's life is further corroborated by his membership in a community of the spirit. This community of spiritual experience is a characteristically Victorian interassimilation of the aesthetic and the religious. Leonard's life is endued with spiritual resonance in three related ways: by allusive epigraphs, by his own literary composition, and by religious music. The fifteen different chapter epigraphs are drawn from sources as various as Virgil, Lady Jane Grey, John Bunyan, Jeremy Taylor, John Milton, William Shakespeare, George Eliot, and the Bible. Unusual in Ewing's work, these intertextual signals indicate the company which this short life deserves to keep—the company of Lady Jane Grey, Bunyan's Christian, and Aeneas. Another literary enterprise is the "Book of Poor Things," a beautifully lettered and illuminated collaboration by Leonard and his father which is an emblem of the boy's own life. It is a literary calendar intended to record the lives of 365 different afflicted people, one for each day of the year, who have mastered their fates. Leonard's book, like a calendar of saints, is so structured as to give to each short life in it a defined, regularly recognized annual place. Moreover, the creation of his book is a product of Leonard's aesthetic joy and evidence of his indomitable imaginative energies. Indeed, it is notable that the first entry in the book is the name of the blind organ-tuner whose happiness in his lot is also expressly aesthetic: "yes, he was always happy when meddling with a musical instrument" (144). The third community Leonard joins is that proclaimed in "The Son of God goes forth to war."[5] The community asserted in the hymn is not only religious ("Who best can drink his cup of woe, / Triumphant over pain, / Who patient bears his cross below, / He follows in his train" [167]), but, even more, musical. Ewing emphasizes the psychologically unifying power of this notably rousing hymn:

> "Tug of War Hymn" is a very good name for that hymn, because the men are so fond of it they all sing, and the ones at the bottom of the

church 'drag over' the choir and the organ. (156)

The verse the men tug with is, "A noble army, men and boys." I
think they like it because it's about the army; and so do I. (156)

The soldiers were beginning to tug. In a moment more the organ
stopped, and the V.C. found himself, with over nine hundred men
at his back, singing without accompaniment, and in unison: "A
noble army—men and boys. . . ." (168)

These descriptions suggest the soaring triumphant sense of communal
assertion to be won by singing. The formal religious consolation literally offered by the words of the hymn is reinforced by the aesthetic and
physiological consolation of the music. Moreover, the military context
in which the hymn is last sung—the nine hundred soldiers singing in
unison—anticipates the solidarity of the band to which Leonard will
belong. The literal unison in music and the literal fellowship of the
soldiers are solid precursors of the predicted community of salvation.
Leonard's life is thus amplified and ratified by its connection to the
epigraphs which link him to greatness, the calendar which fixes a recurrent communal structure of remembrance, and the music which
proclaims both the promise and the fact of unity.

Despite the shortness of his life, Leonard is successfully initiated
into a number of families extended almost to eternity: he confirms
the characteristic excellences of his parents; he triumphantly embodies
the traditions represented by his ancestral alter ego, Uncle Rupert; he
is the link that joins his parents to their military poor relations and
makes possible the extension of the family; he is a loving foster-child
of the regiment whose proclaimed ideal of fortitude he lives by; he is a
child-member of the calendar of "Poor Things" and one of the "noble
army—men and boys" whose triumph each Sunday's hymn continues
to evoke. These attachments all validate and confirm the boy's life as
notable—not only for the brief moment shared with his parents but
also as a link with the past and the future. He is bound up with the past
both of his own family and of the British army; he is equally bound
up with the future—the future of eternity as articulated in the hymn
and the future of perpetual remembrance as inscribed in the calendar. So many ways of imparting value to the short life make it *count*
as fully lived, fully honored. Fixed so permanently into so exemplary a
role, Leonard has become a Romantic "immortal child" whose death
intensifies his value.

NOTES

A portion of this essay appeared as "A Victorian Death in the Family: Juliana Ewing's *The Story of a Short Life*," in *The Child and the Family: Selected Papers from the 1988 International Conference of the Children's Literature Association*, ed. Susan R. Gannon and Ruth Anne Thompson. 1990. 40–46.

1. The "unreliability of much of the statistical evidence" (Barker 11) is a constant theme of studies of nineteenth-century demography. See, for example, Dublin, Lotka, and Spiegelman; Griffith; Hair; Krause; McKeown and Brown; Tranter; Wrigley; Wrigley and Schofield.

2. I have coined the term "Comfort Book" because of the clear intention to console embedded in the prose of all and encoded in the titles of several of the nine works I have examined. The nine are: *A Boy in the Swellings of Jordan; or, The Child in Conflict with Death* (1855); *Children in Heaven; or, The Infant Dead Redeemed by the Blood of Jesus with Words of Consolation to Bereaved Parents* (1865); *Asleep in Jesus; or, Words of Consolation to Bereaved Parents* (1856) by W. B. Clark; *Early Death: Thoughts for a Week of Mourning* (1861); *Ethel's Book; or, Tales of the Angels* (1858) by F. W. Faber; *Our Children's Rest; or, Comfort for Bereaved Mothers* (1863); *Little Angels: A Book of Comfort for Mourning Mothers* (1909) by Matthew Russell; *"Why Weepest Thou?" A Book for Mourners* (1888) by "J.G."; *Lambs Safely Folded* (1894), edited by William Wileman.

3. *The Story of a Short Life*, published as a book four days before Juliana Ewing's death in 1885, initially appeared as *Laetus Sorte Mea: The Story of a Short Life* in serial form in *Aunt Judy's Magazine* for 1882. The two versions are identical except for the addition of letter 5 on St. Martin in chapter 10 (Eden 118).

4. Leonard's words echo the concluding comfort of John Milton's "Lycidas":
> There entertain him all the Saints above,
> In solemn troops, and sweet Societies
> That sing, and singing in their glory move,
> And wipe the tears for ever from his eyes.
> (lines 178–81, in Milton 125)

The principal epigraph of *The Story of a Short Life* (84) is also drawn from "Lycidas":
> But the fair Guerdon when we hope to find,
> And think to burst out into sudden blaze,
> Comes the blind *Fury* with th'abhorrèd shears,
> And slits the thin-spun life.—"But not the praise."
> (lines 73–76, in Milton 122)

Ewing evidently sees *The Story of a Short Life* with its Miltonic echoes and

its seventeenth-century cavalier warrior as a child's version of "Lycidas."
5. For their kind assistance in locating, analyzing, and invigorating this hymn
   I wish to thank Richard Roeckelein, chairman of the Music Department
   of St. Albans School, and Robert Rutledge, my musical colleague in the
   George Washington University Department of English.

WORKS CITED

Alcott, Amos Bronson. *Essays upon Education by Amos Bronson Alcott.*
    Gainesville, Fl.: Scholars' Facsimiles and Reprints, 1960.
    ———. *Sonnets and Canzonets.* Boston: Roberts Brothers, 1882.
Amiel. "Childhood." Trans. Mrs. Humphry Ward. *In the Gardens of Child-
    hood: An Anthology in Prose and Verse for All Childlovers.* Ed. Edith Ivor-
    Parry. London: Routledge, 1913. 30.
Anderson, Odin W. "Age-Specific Mortality in Selected Western European
    Countries with Particular Emphasis on the Nineteenth Century." *Bulletin
    of the History of Medicine.* 29 (May–June 1955): 239–254.
Ariès, Philippe. *Western Attitudes towards Death from the Middle Ages to the
    Present.* Trans. Patricia Ranun. London: Marion Boyars, 1976.
Barker, Theo. Introduction. Barker and Drake 7–13.
Barker, Theo, and Michael Drake, eds. *Population and Society in Britain,
    1850–1980.* New York: New York UP, 1982.
Blake, William. *The Poetry and Prose of William Blake.* Ed. David V. Erdman.
    Commentary by Harold Bloom. 1965. Garden City: Doubleday, 1970.
A Boy in the Swellings of Jordan; or, The Child in Conflict with Death. Edin-
    burgh: Thomas Grant, 1855.
Browning, Elizabeth Barrett. *The Poetical Works of Elizabeth Barrett Brown-
    ing.* London: Smith, Elder, 1897.
Canton, William, ed. *Children's Sayings.* London: George G. Harrap, 1900.
    ———. *The Invisible Playmate, W.V. Her Book and In Memory of W.V.* Lon-
    don: Dent and Dutton, 1912.
    ———. *A Lost Epic and Other Poems.* Edinburgh: Blackwood and Sons, 1887.
Chamberlain, Alexander Francis. *The Child: A Study in the Evolution of Man.*
    London: Walter Scott, 1900.
    ———. *The Child and Childhood in Folk-Thought.* New York: Macmillan,
    1896.
Chapman, Elizabeth Rachel. *A Little Child's Wreath.* London: John Lane,
    1904.
*Children in Heaven; or, The Infant Dead Redeemed by the Blood of Jesus with
    Words of Consolation to Bereaved Parents.* Philadelphia: Presbyterian
    Board of Publication, 1865.

188 JUDITH A. PLOTZ

Clark, W. B. *Asleep in Jesus; or, Words of Consolation to Parents.* Edinburgh: Nelson and Sons, 1856.

Coleridge, Samuel Taylor. *Collected Letters of Samuel Taylor Coleridge.* Ed. Earl Leslie Griggs. 6 vols. Oxford: Clarendon, 1956–71.

——— . *Samuel Taylor Coleridge.* Ed. H. J. Jackson. The Oxford Authors. Oxford: Oxford UP, 1985.

Dublin, Louis I., Alfred Lotka, and Mortimer Spiegelman. *Length of Life: A Study of the Life Table.* Rev. ed. New York: Ronald Press, 1949.

Early Death: Thoughts for a Week of Mourning. London: Society for Promoting Christian Knowledge, 1861.

Eden, Horatia F. K. *Juliana Horatia Ewing and Her Books.* Detroit: Gale Research, 1969.

Emerson, Ralph Waldo. "Nature." *Selections from Ralph Waldo Emerson.* Ed. Stephen E. Whicher. Boston: Houghton, 1960. 21–56.

Ewing, Juliana ["Mrs. Ewing"]. *Lob Lie-By-The-Fire or The Luck of Lingborough AND The Story of a Short Life.* New York: Dent and Dutton, 1964.

Faber, Frederick William. *Ethel's Book; or, Tales of the Angels.* London: Richardson and Son, 1858.

Griffith, G. Talbot. *Population Problems of the Age of Malthus.* Cambridge: Cambridge UP, 1926.

Hair, P. E. H. "Children in Society 1850–1950." Barker and Drake 34–61.

Hunt, Leigh. "Deaths of Little Children." *Essays of Leigh Hunt.* Ed. Reginald Brimley Johnson. London: Dent, 1891. 1–7.

Jung, Carl. *The Archetypes and the Collective Unconscious.* Trans. R. F. C. Hull. Vol. 9, pt. 1. London: Routledge and Kegan Paul, 1959.

Key, Ellen. *The Century of the Child.* London: Putnam's, 1909. Trans. of *Barnets århundrade.* 1900.

Kilvert, Francis. *Kilvert's Diary: Selections from the Diary of the Rev. Francis Kilvert.* 3 vols. Ed. William Plomer. London: Jonathan Cape, 1938–1940.

Krause, J. T. "Some Neglected Factors in the English Industrial Revolution." *Population in Industrialization.* Ed. Michael Drake. London: Methuen, 1969. 103–17.

Lamb, Charles, and Mary Lamb. *Books for Children.* Vol. 3 of *The Works of Charles and Mary Lamb.* Ed. E. V. Lucas. 5 vols. 1903. New York: AMS, 1968.

McKeown, Thomas, and R. B. Brown. "Medical Evidence Related to English Population Changes in the Eighteenth Century." *Population in Industrialization,* Ed. Michael Drake. London: Methuen, 1969. 40–72.

Meynell, Alice. *The Children.* London: John Lane, 1897.

Meynell, Wilfred., ed. *The Child Set in the Midst by Modern Poets.* London: Leadenhall, 1892.

Milton, John. *Complete Poems and Major Prose.* Ed. Merritt Y. Hughes. New York: Odyssey, 1957.

Our Children's Rest; or, Comfort for Bereaved Mothers. London: James Nisbet, 1863.

Russell, Matthew. *Little Angels: A Book of Comfort for Mourning Mothers.* London: Burns and Oates, 1909.

Schiller, Friedrich von. *Naive and Sentimental Poetry and On the Sublime.* Trans. Julius Elias. New York: Frederick Ungar, 1966.

Tranter, N. L. *Population and Society, 1750–1940: Contrasts in Population Growth.* London: Longmans, 1985.

"Why Weepest Thou?" A Book for Mourners by "J.G." London: Nelson and Son, 1888.

Wileman, William, ed. *Lambs Safely Folded: Authentic Records of the Power of Divine Grace in the Hearts of Children, Early Called Home.* London: William Wileman, 1894.

Winter, J. M. "The Decline of Mortality in Britain 1870–1950." Barker and Drake 100–120.

Wordsworth, William. *The Poetical Works of William Wordsworth.* Ed. Ernest de Selincourt and Helen Darbishire. 2nd ed. 5 vols. Oxford: Clarendon, 1952–59.

———. *The Prelude: 1799, 1805, 1850.* Ed. Jonathan Wordsworth, M. H. Abrams, and Stephen Gill. New York: Norton, 1979.

Wrigley, E. A. *Population and History.* New York: McGraw Hill, 1969.

Wrigley, E. A., and R. S. Schofield. *The Population History of England, 1541–1871: A Reconstruction.* Cambridge: Harvard UP, 1981.

MICHAEL HANCHER

Alice's Audiences

The tense ambivalence that the innocent Hartley Coleridge
prompts in his melancholic father, which James McGavran
cites in his introduction above as an epitome of Romantic and Victorian constructions of childhood, finds complete expression in the various *Alice* stories, which include not only Lewis Carroll's stories about
Alice but also the stories told by himself and others about his situation as a writer for children. Carroll's narrative "Giddiness of Heart
& Brain" never overcame the "Rage & Pain" that set it going; the
bodily and psychological terrors to which Carroll subjected his long-
suffering heroine realize the "Words of Wrong and Bitterness" that as a
correspondent he casually inflicted, just joking, in letters to his "child-
friends."[1] In his relations with little girls Carroll notoriously "dall[ied]
with Wrong, that does no Harm"—or so he believed. By both demo-
nizing and trivializing such fellow adult authority-figures as the Queen
of Hearts and the White Knight, Carroll managed to exorcise their
shared "Sin / . . . sorrow & shame" and, almost incidentally, empower
the child Alice. If this "Giddiness of Heart & Brain" is a customary
defense-mechanism—"So talks, as it's most used to do"—to whom is
it talking? And how does the audience respond?

The first audience for the story of Alice's adventures is her older sister, left behind at the start of the first chapter, engrossed like an adult
in reading "a book . . . without pictures or conversations."[2] Alice left
her to chase the White Rabbit down a rabbit-hole and into a fantastic dream. But the narrator reports, near the end of the book, that on
returning from that dream Alice "told her sister, as well as she could remember them, all these strange Adventures of hers that you [meaning
the reader of *Alice's Adventures in Wonderland*] have just been reading
about" (*AW* 189; ch. 12).

Her sister responds dismissively. She "kissed her, and said, 'It *was* a curious dream, dear, certainly: but now run in to your tea; it's getting late.'" The narrator shows more appreciation; for him, as for Alice, it was a "wonderful dream." But the sister takes Alice's experience more seriously than she has let on. She stays behind, alone, "watching the setting sun, and thinking of little Alice and all her wonderful Adventures, till she too began dreaming after a fashion" (190). Her extended reverie closes the book. "First, she dreamed of little Alice herself," as Alice told her adventures. "She could hear the very tones of her voice . . . and still as she listened, or seemed to listen, the whole place around her became alive with the strange creatures of her little sister's dream."

By dreaming that Alice tells her dream again, the sister comes to have a dream that largely recapitulates Alice's own. But she only "half believe[s]" (191) this renewed dream, because she thinks she knows its immediate sources. She thinks that the phenomena that it presents are merely fantastic interpretations of ordinary sounds coming from the real world. "The rattling teacups" that she hears as she re-dreams the mad tea-party are only "tinkling sheep-bells" heard in a nearby meadow; "the Queen's shrill cries" are only "the voice of the shepherd boy." If she but opened her eyes, "the sneeze of the baby, the shriek of the Gryphon, and all the other queer noises, would change (she knew) to the confused clamour of the busy farm-yard—while the lowing of the cattle in the distance would take the place of the Mock Turtle's heavy sobs" (191–92).

Such analytic reduction of dream imagery to external sensory stimuli —in this case, intrusive sounds—was in keeping with standard nineteenth-century practice. A typical German treatise held that "every noise that is indistinctly perceived [during sleep] arouses corresponding dream-images. A peal of thunder will set us in the midst of a battle; the crowing of a cock may turn into a man's cry of terror; the creaking of a door may produce a dream of burglars."[3] Sigmund Freud thought that such accounts were not so much wrong as inadequate: they stopped short of asking why the dreamer, in responding to a given stimulus, would produce one image but not another. Instead of interpreting dreams they explained them away.[4] Alice's sister uses such analysis to explain away her own daydream, even while it is in progress. By implication she also casts doubt on its prototype, Alice's dream, dismissing it a second time. The narrator has already prepared for such a naturalistic reduction by referring the end of Alice's last adventure to an external stimulus. When the Queen for the last time orders her execution, Alice repudiates the entire court as "nothing but a pack of cards!"

> At this the whole pack rose up into the air, and came flying down upon her; she gave a little scream, half of fright and half of anger, and tried to beat them off, and found herself lying on the bank, with her head in the lap of her sister, who was gently brushing away some dead leaves that had fluttered down from the trees on to her face. (188–89)

At which point her sister wakes her up.

The sister's rationalization of Alice's dream is not satisfactory, even to herself. So she ends by perpetuating it, by imagining that "the dream of Wonderland of long-ago" might be retold by Alice, now "a grown woman," to "little children" (192), perhaps children of her own. As William Madden has remarked, "the endless retelling of Alice's dream" is, for the sister, a necessary "counterpoise" to the loss that Alice and she both suffer on awakening from dreams to the ordinary world.[5]

This conclusion to *Alice's Adventures in Wonderland* differs from the conclusion that Carroll had originally written for the manuscript version, decorated with his own illustrations, that he made as a gift for Alice Liddell.[6] In that version Alice's sister did not re-dream and criticize the illusory scenes of Alice's dream. Instead, she dreamt about the originating scene from which all these scenes derive: the now-famous boat trip up the river Isis, during which Carroll improvised stories of Alice's adventures to entertain Alice Liddell and her two sisters, Edith and Lorina (*AAuG* 89–90). That personal reminiscence was appropriate to the manuscript as a personal gift. When Carroll revised the story for publication he replaced the private reference with the paragraph already discussed. In effect he displaced one genetic account of Alice's dream (involving literary history) with another (involving causality). The causal explanation was just hinted at in the manuscript, as the cards transformed back into leaves (*AAuG* 88); in the revision the sister elaborates it. One narrative function of this change is to extend and to smooth the transition from Wonderland back to reality. The revision also gives scope to the sister's roles as reader and critic: by subjecting Alice's dream to psychological analysis she invents a leading mode of Carroll criticism.[7]

In *Through the Looking-Glass*, the second of the two *Alice* books, the primary audience is the same older sister. Though she does not dominate the close of this book as she does the first, her importance becomes obvious sooner: in the fourth chapter the narrator parenthetically remarks that "afterwards" Alice "was telling her sister the history of all this." A similar attribution appears near the end; and several other remarks allude to this narrative structure.[8] Apparently the narrator of both *Alice* books gets his information indirectly from Alice and directly from Alice's sister. He explains at one point that because Alice failed to ask Humpty Dumpty what he "paid" words with, "I can't tell *you*" (*LG* 125; ch. 6). If it weren't for that broken link, the full chain of information would have run: Humpty Dumpty to Alice, Alice to her sister, the sister to the narrator, and the narrator to "*you*." Who "*you*" are, as an audience, is a riddle worth exploring.

First, however, there are audiences within the stories to take into account, audiences much less satisfactory than Alice's sister. These audiences monitor the conversational performances with which Alice tries to establish her identity in their world; and almost always they thwart her performance. " 'Oh, there's no use in talking to him,' said Alice desperately," after a particularly frustrating effort at conversation: " 'he's perfectly idiotic!' " She says that about the Frog-Footman in *Alice's Adventures* (80, ch. 6), but the remark could apply to almost any character in either book. No one, not even the White Knight, is patient and self-effacing enough to give up the floor and hear her story out. (Her sister at least does that.) When characters *do* yield the floor for any stretch of time, instead of encouraging her to speak for herself they make her recite a prefabricated piece of discourse—a poem by Robert Southey ("You Are Old, Father William"), or Isaac Watts ("The Sluggard"). Inevitably her performance satisfies no one, not even herself. The stupid audience stultifies her.[9]

Fortunately, Lewis Carroll found quite a different audience, an ideally enabling one, in Alice Liddell and her two sisters, Edith and Lorina, for whose entertainment he "extemporised . . . many a fairy tale" on summer picnics (Carroll, "Alice on the Stage," 165). "Tell us a story," they would ask, and he would. When he stopped to "tease" them, saying "that's all till next time," they would demand more, "and he would go on." [10] After the famous boat trip, because the story had been especially good, Alice, aged ten, asked Charles Lutwidge Dodgson to write it all down for her, and he agreed.

Alice Liddell was the primary audience for this gift manuscript, but writing invites secondary readings. Displayed on the drawing-room table in Alice's home, the manuscript caught the attention of the novelist Henry Kingsley, who urged Carroll to publish it for yet other readers. Dodgson turned for advice to his friend George MacDonald, the novelist and children's writer, and MacDonald recommended some small-scale field testing: "an experiment should be made upon his young family." And so, MacDonald's son Greville recalled many years later, "my mother read the story to us. When she came to the end I, being aged six, exclaimed that there ought to be sixty thousand volumes of it" (342). According to this testimony it was an audience of children that decided on the publishing of *Alice's Adventures in Wonderland*.

The publisher became the next audience. Surely Alexander Macmillan, the head of Macmillan and Company, read some version of the story before agreeing to publish it, but there is no record of his initial response. Carroll retained editorial authority for the project, along with all the financial risk (Cohen and Gandalfo 14–15). Macmillan freely advised Carroll about details of book production; but as regards the text of *Alice's Adventures* his role in the audience seems to have been minor.

The same can't be said of John Tenniel, the artist whom Carroll hired to illustrate his story for publication (replacing the illustrations that Carroll had drawn in the gift manuscript), and whom he later persuaded to illustrate *Through the Looking-Glass*. Tenniel was a uniquely privileged reader of the *Alice* books. His illustrations, the products of his reading, control or even preempt responses that the text would otherwise prompt from its other readers.

Roman Ingarden (50–63) has drawn attention to the fact that all narrative includes "places of indeterminacy," specific spatial or temporal details about which the text is silent. Physical objects have a detailed, determinate identity, but narration can't specify all the details; it leaves that work to the audience. A hearer or reader usually fills out the sketchy narrative with imagined details drawn from experience, determining many textual indeterminacies in a process that Ingarden calls "concretization." The reader imagines the heroine to be other than bald; blonde, not brunette; not naked but clothed; dressed in a pinafore, not a business suit; impassive, not smiling. Or some other combination of features will be imagined—by a different reader, or by the same reader on a different reading. The reader will concretize a large mass of detail in the process of reading any extended text—perhaps relatively more for a text like *Alice's Adventures in Wonderland*, which contains little description.

But the reader of *Alice's Adventures* will have less work to do if she reads—as she almost certainly will—an illustrated edition; for illustrations concretize: that is, they represent acts of concretization that the illustrator has performed in reading the text; and they strongly control the reader's own work.

Carroll relies upon this function of illustration. Twice the narrator urges the reader to consult an illustration of Tenniel's to resolve an indeterminacy in the text (how the King managed to wear his royal crown over his judicial wig [*AW* 163]; what a Gryphon looks like [*AW* 138]). Even without such advice the pictures would tend to dominate the text, because the reader would normally see them before reading the words. Someone to whom the story were read aloud would have greater imaginative freedom and responsibility—unless she were shown the pictures.

Although some readers resent the power of an illustrator, preferring to visualize the story themselves,[11] children's books don't usually prompt such complaints; and few editions of the *Alice* books forego pictures. Most copies perpetuate Tenniel's reading of the two stories: unblinking, matter-of-fact, seriously amused. When Carroll chose Tenniel to illustrate the books he gave him distinctive power as a member of the audience, the first among equals. Though dozens of other illustrators have tried to usurp it, Tenniel still exercises that power.

When *Alice's Adventures* was finally published, after a famous delay caused by defects in the printing, Carroll presented a copy to Alice Liddell and many other copies to other children. For the rest of his life he continued to give copies of the *Alice* books to young girls who caught his fancy. For him they were certainly children's books. And it was as one among many "children's books" published in time for the Christmas gift season of 1865 that the English press gave the book its first praise.[12]

The book was so popular that five new editions were called for in the next three years; by 1868, twelve thousand copies were in print. A German translation appeared the year after. But hints began to appear that this was not a mere—or even a real—children's book. Reviewing the German edition, the editor of the American journal the *Nation* remarked in passing that despite its being a "book for children . . . the children care little or nothing for it, and it is to grown people that it is so charming." That remark was contradicted by a letter from a Carroll fan, an adult (a letter that apparently gratified Carroll). In the end the editor sheepishly acknowledged that "we probably generalized from too limited an experience."[13] Maybe his children didn't like the book.

But the topic would not go away; there was something unstable in the relation between this book and its audience. Another American reviewer reversed the emphasis: although (he supposed) the nonsense in the book could appeal *only* to children, Tenniel's "quaint and characteristic illustrations . . . commend themselves alike to old and young." What this reviewer found to be childish nonsense, another characterized as "grown-up humor." Shortly, in England, the *Spectator* commented that "though grown people are better able than children to enter into that wonderful production, it is by no means thrown away upon children."[14] All these prophetic misgivings about the status of *Alice's Adventures* as a children's book were expressed by 1870, within four years of the book's publication.[15]

Publication in 1872 of the sequel, *Through the Looking-Glass*, brought the same double response. The writer of the long review in the *Times* insisted, "we will not let the children monopolize" the book, adding "the only thing we fear is that they may miss the delicacy and exquisite absurdity of what they read"; he ended by strongly recommending the book to both "grown and ungrown readers . . . to all readers, be they young or old."[16]

Years later, in 1890, Carroll took up the question of audience in the preface to *The Nursery "Alice"*, a simplified version of *Alice's Adventures* that he wrote for children under five. In self-indulgently sentimental prose, he categorized the readers of the original book. (By this time more than fifty thousand copies had been sold in England alone.)

> I have reason to believe that "Alice's Adventures in Wonderland" has been read by some hundreds of English Children, aged from Five to Fifteen: also by Children, aged from Fifteen to Twenty-five: yet again by Children, aged from Twenty-five to Thirty-five: and even by Children—for there *are* such—Children in whom no waning of health and strength, no weariness of the solemn mockery, and the gaudy glitter, and the hopeless misery, of Life has availed to parch the pure fountain of joy that wells up in all child-like hearts—Children of a "certain" age, whose tale of years must be left untold, and buried in respectful silence.[17]

Here Coleridge's adult "Rage & Pain" and envy of childish joy again make an appeal for sympathy.

Whatever his original intentions, by 1890 Carroll had accepted the fact that adults enjoyed his children's books. In 1898 his first biographer noted that *Through the Looking-Glass* had recently been cited in a law case decided by the House of Lords (Collingwood 150). Since then the *Alice* books have leavened countless arguments at the bar, in the philosophy lecture-hall, and on the editorial page. Probably no other secular text is quoted so often in writing and in imagery—a fact for which Tenniel deserves some credit. Certainly no other children's book has been so thoroughly appropriated by adults.

Do children have an equal claim on these books? It is often said that they are over children's heads. Psychological subtexts aside, there are several ways that might be true.

First, the books may now be too old-fashioned. Victorian references and assumptions saturate them; they are grounded in a now-vanished experience that was common to many upper-class children a century ago. Alice's fear of being mistaken for a servant girl dates her and would alienate many children, if they understood it (*AW* 42; ch. 4). Few young children today have looked inside a Latin Grammar (*AW* 24; ch. 2). Bathing machines (*AW* 23; ch. 2) have gone the way of writing-desks (*AW* 97; ch. 7), of frumenty (*LG* 57; ch. 3) and sal-volatile (*LG* 143; ch. 7)—even shillings and pence (*AW* 168; ch. 11). Worse, the books presuppose familiarity with the nursery rhymes and didactic poems that determined much of Alice's dreaming—an ordinary Victorian child's literary knowledge, now obsolete. Bertrand Russell, who was born within a year of the publication of *Through the Looking-Glass* and was "brought up on the two books," asserted (in the course of a radio panel discussion) that such cultural obsolescence had helped to disqualify the Alice stories for children; he proposed labelling them "For Adults Only" (Porter 209, 210). Besides such contextual difficulties Russell pointed to the intellectual sophistication of the books, which he thought made them "much too difficult for children" (212). The "metaphysical points, very interesting logical points," he said, "are good for the older ponderer, but for the young only produce confusion." He concluded that *Alice* was "very useful to a philosophical lecturer who wants to liven up his stuff . . . full of philosophical jokes which are quite good for philosophical students. But I think you oughtn't to read the book before you're fifteen" (213). To which his fellow panelist, Katherine Anne Porter, replied, doubtfully, "I wonder. Probably that's true."

Teachers and children's librarians have had to deal with the problem as a practical matter. Russell's complaint that the books are too abstruse was echoed at about the same time by an annotator for the American Library Association, who found the "amusing subtlety" of the *Alice* books "more likely to appeal to adults than to most children." Nonetheless, she assigned them to the sixth grade. She included the striking comment (carried forward from an earlier edition) that Alice had "the most loyal lovers and decided haters of any juvenile heroine" (*Right Book*, 55; 3rd ed., 87). May Hill Arbuthnot, author of a standard textbook on children's literature, also acknowledges widespread hostility to the *Alice* books, which she traces to forcing children to read them at too young an age. "When college students are asked what books they remember enjoying as children there is more disagreement over *Alice* than over any other book. Some disliked it heartily or were bored by it; some say *Alice* was one of their favorite books, not as children but at the high-school age. This is perhaps where it really belongs." [18] Arbuthnot's perspective differs from Russell's, but their conclusions are roughly the same.

More recent news from the classroom suggests that the books baffle even many college students. They are too paradoxical, too open, too indeterminate, to be satisfying, especially for the "less able" (Adams 8). It is telling that at a recent MLA conference on "The Future of Doctoral Studies in English" (Wayzata, Minnesota, April 1987), three speakers independently mentioned the *Alice* books as promising additions to the doctoral curriculum. [19]

More basic than the question of appreciation is that of sheer "readability." Is the prose of the *Alice* books simply too difficult for children? Educators have developed several ways of measuring readability, usually expressed in terms of school grade level; three reputable indices are the Dale-Chall formula, the Fry readability graph, and the Flesch formula (Harrison 73–79). Applying these measures conservatively to the *Alice* books suggests that both books are appropriate to the seventh-grade level: their verbal difficulty presupposes only that the reader have reached thirteen or so. [20]

It happens that Alice Liddell was thirteen when Lewis Carroll gave her a copy of the first edition of *Alice's Adventures in Wonderland.* Of course she was already familiar with the story; when she was ten Carroll had told part of it to her and her sisters, probably in language adapted to that audience. Even in the published text the narrator is alert to the fact that not all children know the meanings of all hard words. He says that Alice was proud of knowing the word *jurors,* for "she thought, and rightly too, that very few little girls of her age knew the meaning of it at all" (*AW* 164; ch. 11). The narrator makes a small joke out of explaining the meaning of *suppressed,* because "that is rather a hard word"—especially in the context of a newspaper report of a trial (*AW* 172; ch. 11). But some hard words he takes for granted, or even puts in the mouth of his young heroine: *chrysalis* (*AW* 60; ch. 5), *contemptuously* (*AW* 61; ch. 5), *parchment* (*AW* 162; ch. 11), *indignant* (*AW* 164; ch. 11), *memorandum* (*AW* 168; ch. 11), *melancholy* (*AW* 174; ch. 11), *proboscis* (*LG* 47; ch. 3), *obstinacy* (*LG* 108; ch. 5), *attitudes* (in the sense of "postures": *LG* 140; ch. 7), *sauntered* (*LG* 150; ch. 7), *perplexity* (*LG* 198; ch. 9). Though Carroll spoke of his primary audience as ranging "from Five to Fifteen," few children in the lower half of that range would know such words.

Indeed, it is unlikely that the heroine of Carroll's *Alice* books would have readily understood such language. For the Alice *in* these books is much younger than the thirteen-year-old Alice who read the first published edition; younger, even, than the ten-year-old to whom Carroll first told the story. "I'm seven and a half exactly," Alice tells the White Queen in *Through the Looking-Glass* (99; ch. 5)—which would make her seven years old in *Alice's Adventures.* Carroll later assumed that *The Nursery "Alice"* would make an appropriate gift for well-educated children of about that age—not the more difficult *Alice's Adventures* (*Letters* 2: 991).

It is strange that when Alice Liddell was ten years old, Lewis Carroll told her a story about a version of herself at age seven: children usually like to imagine themselves as older, not younger. Admittedly there is no explicit mention of Alice's age in the first book; we know how old she is there by calculating backward from *Looking-Glass* (Carroll, *Annotated Alice,* 96, 177–78). But the photograph that Carroll attached to the end of the gift manuscript showed Alice Liddell as she had been at age seven. Carroll's partial dissociation of Alice-as-heroine from Alice-as-audience probably expresses his preference for younger children.

Though it is well known that Carroll preferred little girls to little boys, I haven't seen it remarked that the implied reader for *Alice's Adventures* is a girl like the heroine herself. After reporting that Alice "tried to curtsey as she spoke" during her early fall down the rabbit-hole, the narrator comments, "fancy *curtseying* as you're falling through the air! Do you think you could manage it?" (*AW* 5; ch. 1). That is the only passage in either book that strictly presupposes a female addressee; it might easily be overlooked or discounted, despite its placement early in the narrative. (It occurs early in the gift manuscript that Greville MacDonald liked so much [*AAuG* 4].) The question is whether, aside from such a clue, the narrative specially engages feminine interests.

The question is not a decisive one, since males too have feminine interests. Even before Alice Liddell, Lewis Carroll was the original audience for his stories; arguably he projected his own femininity upon his heroine. Male readers might participate in such projection. Or, if they read as Freudians, they might cathect Alice as the object of Oedipal desire (Schilder 291), or as the mutable embodiment of phallic fortune (Grotjahn 310–12).

The potential for female identification with Alice is more obvious. As a girl, Katherine Anne Porter was "frightened" by the stories; she found that the domestic familiarity of the setting made Alice's ordeals undeniably threatening.[21] In a more optimistic reading Nina Auerbach has commended the way that Carroll honors the "metamorphic complexity" and "latent power" of the female (168, 156).

Surveys suggest that American girls of junior-high-school and high-school age do find the *Alice* books more "interesting"—for whatever reasons—than boys do. But the same data, collected over a forty-year period, suggest that even girls find the books only weakly interesting.[22] Carroll's child-readers, from the start a population of uncertain size, have evidently waned in importance.

And yet it isn't necessary to read the *Alice* books to enjoy them. Originally Alice Liddell didn't read but heard the stories, in the first of the many formations and transformations that they would undergo. They began as oral improvisations; and though they were gradually fixed on the page and tied to visual illustrations, they retained an oral potential. (Of course audiences in general are primarily—etymologically—listeners.) Arbuthnot's further comments, based on the recollections of undergraduates, are relevant here: "Most of those who liked *Alice* as children, ten or under, had heard it read aloud by adults who enjoyed it. Those who had to read the book for themselves rarely found it funny until they were older" (292). These particular undergraduates would have been children in the 1930s, before movies and television began to control the telling of Alice's story.

Having an adult mediate the story for a child can resolve some aspects of the "readability" problem. He or she can gloss over difficult passages in advance, and can answer the child's questions as they come up. The narrator of the *Alice* books is like such an adult, often supplying helpful comments; but since he is a textual artifact he can't really be responsive. An adult reader-aloud who impersonates the narrator can adapt the story to the audience, and so recover something of the liveliness and flexibility of Carroll's first telling of the story—as Mrs. MacDonald, one of the first to read the story aloud, apparently succeeded in doing.

And yet, by a Carrollian paradox, any mediating adult who succeeds in bringing the story to life for a child must in the very process subvert the gratifying inversion of ordinary power relations that it represents. For properly, as we saw at the outset, the story belongs not to adults but to the child heroine: it is hers to tell to her older sister, who represents the world of adults. Since the story that Alice tells is not flattering to adults the sister reasonably explains it away. She also reserves the story for Alice to tell to little children later—when she has safely joined the adults. In the meantime the sister confides it to the narrator of the two *Alice* books, who, as Lewis Carroll, knows well how to exercise adult authority over his "child-friends."

Carroll is not, strictly speaking, an omniscient narrator; as we have seen, he has no idea what Humpty Dumpty "paid" words with (*LG* 125; ch. 6). But he is omnipotent. He invents and appropriates Alice's story, so that she, his heroine and his chief audience, will be wholly dependent upon him for her existence. The worst terror that Alice suffers in *Through the Looking-Glass* is the possibility (asserted as a fact by Tweedledum and Tweedledee) that she is merely a creature of the Red King's dream (*LG* 81–82; ch. 4). The question returns to her at the end, after she awakens from her own dream: "which dreamed it?" (*LG* 217, 221; ch. 12). The narrator, who has the same equivocal authority as the Red King, ends by leaving the question open, either willfully or out of ignorance. In his last sentence he passes responsibility for the question on to his audience, which he has also created: "Which do *you* think it was?" (222).

That concluding indeterminacy epitomizes the instability of both books, and the final authority of their audience. Despite having been written down, arrested, fixed in type, the *Alice* stories continue to undergo transformation, like Alice herself in her first adventures; they will not be constrained, even within the relaxed framework of reading-aloud. Carroll encouraged their proliferation of forms: he supervised the translation of *Alice's Adventures* into French, German, and Italian; he rewrote the book in language intended for the nursery; he arranged for separate publication of the preliminary version that he had inscribed as the gift manuscript for Alice Liddell. In 1886 he approved a theatrical pastiche called *Alice in Wonderland,* which melded bits from both of the *Alice* books in a way that has since become normal. There have been dozens of movies and TV productions over the years; almost all twist Carroll's two stories into one. Viewers accept this license because few people other than Carroll specialists can remember which episode belongs to which story.

The fact is that Alice's audience is very much larger than the select group—children *or* adults—who have actually read what Carroll wrote. Like Mickey Mouse, Alice lives in the popular culture; she does not need books to survive. She has escaped her narration and narrator.

Carroll made Alice a variable character when he first began to improvise her stories aloud. If the written text and Tenniel's illustrations both tended to arrest that variability by determining her history and appearance, the illustrations ironically confirmed her mutability by necessarily differing from (that is, by going beyond) what the narration specified, and by differing also from Carroll's previous illustrations.

Alice has continued to change as she has courted the audiences for plays, movies, cartoons, ballets, orchestral suites, pop songs, and T-shirts. The dreamlike, episodic structure of both books, the heavily charged psychological subtext, and the explicit privileging of pictorial illustration, have from the start led her audiences to register her story in terms of character, scene, myth, and image, rather than of plot, narrative voice, or (save for some memorable phrases) diction. Scholars may prefer the integrity of the original books,[23] but Alice's story has outgrown them. *Alice* is a happily overdetermined and polymorphous text. It thrives in an indefinite number of forms, which amalgamate differently in the experience of each viewer, hearer, and reader, old or young. The threatened disintegration of Alice's personal identity in Wonderland prefigures her actual dispersal, and renewal, among her audiences.

NOTES

A draft of this essay was read at the Carolinas Symposium on British Studies, Appalachian State University, Boone, NC, in October 1984; I want to thank Jeanie Watson for inviting it and for offering helpful comments. Linda Hancher helped me with the readability calculations. My colleagues William Madden and Gordon Hirsch have also, again, given good advice.

1. *A Selection from the Letters of Lewis Carroll to His Child-Friends* contains an often disturbing display of the rhetoric of domination and exploitation. Judging from the preface and other memoirs, the recipients found ways of denying Carroll's hostility.

2. Carroll, *Alice's Adventures in Wonderland* (hereafter cited as *AW*) 2; ch. 1.

3. P. Jessen, *Versuch einer wissenschaftlichen Begründung der Psychologie* (Berlin, 1855), 527, as quoted by Freud (57). "External sensory stimuli" is the rubric under which Freud reviews such accounts.

4. Reporting modern research, Foulkes (154–64) goes even further in belittling the importance of such stimuli.

5. Madden 372, n. 9. However, Madden generally understates the reductive strain in the sister's analysis, preferring to identify her not with the ordinary world but with the more imaginative world that Alice has revealed to her.

6. Carroll, *Alice's Adventures under Ground* (hereafter cited as *AAuG*).

7. Unfortunately this revision undermines details that survive in the essentially unrevised final paragraph. The references there to "other little children," and to Alice's making "*their* eyes bright and eager with many a strange tale," depend on previous mentions (present in the manuscript, but dropped from the revision) of "a merry party of children on board" the boat, including "another little Alice, who sat listening with bright eager eyes" (*AAuG* 89). When Carroll replaced that passage, the word "other" and the italics became pointless.

8. Carroll, *Through the Looking-Glass* (hereafter cited as *LG*) 70, ch. 4 (the passage quoted here); 17, ch. 1; 210, ch. 9 (" 'And they *did* push so!' she said afterwards, when she was telling her sister the history of the feast."); 219, ch. 12.

9. I analyze some of Alice's troubles with her interlocutors in "Pragmatics in Wonderland," and in "Humpty Dumpty and Verbal Meaning."

10. Alice Liddell Hargreaves, interview in *New York Times* April 4, 1928, as quoted by Clark (73).

11. For examples of such complaints see my *Tenniel Illustrations* 108–10; and Altick 48, 205, 357.

12. For example, the *Times* gave it a brief mention in a review that noticed seven "children's books," among other "Christmas books"; December 26, 1865: 5.

13. *Nation* 8 (April 8, 1869): 276; 8 (April 15, 1869), 295; as quoted by Matthews (85). For Carroll's response see Cohen and Gandolfo 80.

14. *Putnam's Magazine* 4 (1869): 124; *Overland Monthly* 3 (1869): 102; *Spectator* December 4, 1869: 1431; all as quoted by Matthews (86, 87, 91).

15. Cripps cites two further reviews, both English, as showing an early tendency to credit the book with a double audience (37).

   A useful collection of almost all the British reviews of *Alice's Adventures* that Carroll himself preserved (including the two cited by Cripps) has been reprinted in *Jabberwocky* 9 (1979–80). Most of them assume an audience of children for the book; but ten (out of twenty-nine) propose a double audience, one that includes adults.

   Matthews's dissertation, from which I quote review excerpts above, discusses Carroll's early reception in the United States as well as in Great Britain. The dissertations by Page, Rackin, and Rheinstein also contribute to an understanding of Alice's audience.

16. *Times*, December 25, 1871, 4; as quoted by Matthews (103–5), who in note 70 mistakenly credits the review to the *New York Times*.

17. Carroll, *Nursery Alice* [iii]. Five years earlier, in 1885, Carroll had written to a correspondent, "That children love the book is a very precious thought to me, and, next to their love, I value the sympathy of those who come with a child's heart to what I have tried to write about a child's thoughts" (Collingwood 365).

18. Arbuthnot 292; Sunderland retains this passage in the sixth edition (223). Compare Natov's opinion that "the *Alice* stories are hardly read by children anymore" and that they now speak to the identity anxieties of adolescents (48, 57).

19. Or so I remember; the published proceedings include at least one such mention (Spacks 27).

   The *Alice* books have been assimilated to the undergraduate curriculum for some twenty years (the Norton Critical Edition appeared in 1971).

20. The Fry readability graph and the Flesch formula both correlate the average length of words (in syllables) to the average length of sentences (in words). The Dale-Chall formula correlates the average length of sentences to an index of lexical unfamiliarity.

   I applied each of these measures to the same six representative passages, one hundred words long, excerpted from the *Alice* books (three passages from each). The results are as follows (figures indicate grade level):

	Wonderland	*Looking-Glass*
Dale-Chall	5.5	5.3
Fry	7.0	6.9
Flesch	7.5	7.3

Note that though the scores vary from measure to measure, the two books are very similar by any measure.

21. Bertrand Russell cheerfully responded that the story never bothered him, because "after all it was a girl who had all these troubles, and boys don't mind the troubles of girls" (Porter 209).

22. Norvell 57, 181, 318, 418. The *Alice* books typically were extracurricular reading for the students reported in this broad survey. Norvell explains how data were gathered for curricular texts (10–13), but not for extracurricular ones (14).

23. Here let me recommend the carefully produced facsimiles of the first editions of *Alice's Adventures in Wonderland* and *Through the Looking-Glass* that Macmillan published in 1984. I discuss their merits in an accompanying pamphlet, *On the Writing, Illustration, and Publication of Lewis Carroll's "Alice" Books.*

WORKS CITED

Adams, Gillian. "Student Responses to *Alice in Wonderland* and *At the Back of the North Wind.*" *Children's Literature Association Quarterly* 10 (1985): 6–9.

Altick, Richard D. *Paintings from Books: Art and Literature in Britain, 1760–1900.* Columbus: Ohio State UP, 1985.

Arbuthnot, May Hill. *Children and Books.* Chicago: Scott, 1947.

Auerbach, Nina. "Falling Alice, Fallen Women, and Victorian Dream Children." *Romantic Imprisonment: Women and Other Glorified Outcasts.* New York: Columbia UP, 1985. 149–68.

Carroll, Lewis. *Alice in Wonderland.* Ed. Donald J. Gray. Norton Critical Edition. New York: Norton, 1971.

———. "Alice on the Stage." *The Lewis Carroll Picture Book.* Ed. Stuart Dodgson Collingwood. London: Unwin, 1899. 163–74.

———. *Alice's Adventures in Wonderland.* London: Macmillan, 1866. Facsimile ed. London: Macmillan, 1984.

———. *Alice's Adventures under Ground.* Ed. Martin Gardner. New York: Dover, 1965.

———. *The Annotated Alice: Alice's Adventures in Wonderland and Through the Looking Glass.* Ed. Martin Gardner. New York: Potter, 1960.

———. *The Letters of Lewis Carroll.* Ed. Morton N. Cohen. 2 vols. New York: Oxford UP, 1979.

———. *The Nursery "Alice."* London: Macmillan, 1890. Facsimile ed. Ed. Martin Gardner. New York: Dover, 1966.

——— . *A Selection from the Letters of Lewis Carroll (The Rev. Charles Lutwidge Dodgson) to His Child-Friends.* Ed. Evelyn M. Hatch. London: Macmillan, 1933.

——— . *Through the Looking-Glass, and What Alice Found There.* London: Macmillan, 1866. Facsimile ed. London: Macmillan, 1984.

Clark, Anne. *The Real Alice: Lewis Carroll's Dream Child.* London: Joseph, 1981.

Cohen, Morton N., and Anita Gandolfo. *Lewis Carroll and the House of Macmillan.* Cambridge Studies in Publishing and Printing History. Cambridge: Cambridge UP, 1987.

Collingwood, Stuart Dodgson. *The Life and Letters of Lewis Carroll.* New York: Century, 1898.

Cripps, Elizabeth A. "*Alice* and the Reviewers." *Children's Literature* 11 (1983): 32–48.

Foulkes, David. *The Psychology of Sleep.* New York: Scribner's, 1966.

Freud, Sigmund. *The Interpretation of Dreams.* Trans. James Strachey. New York: Avon, 1969.

Grotjahn, Martin. "About the Symbolization of *Alice's Adventures in Wonderland.*" 1947. Phillips 308–15.

Hancher, Michael. "Humpty Dumpty and Verbal Meaning." *Journal of Aesthetics and Art Criticism* 40 (1981): 49–58.

——— . *On the Writing, Illustration, and Publication of Lewis Carroll's "Alice" Books.* London: Macmillan, 1984.

——— . "Pragmatics in Wonderland." *Rhetoric, Literature, and Interpretation.* Ed. Harry R. Garvin and Steven Mailloux. Lewisburg: Bucknell UP, 1983. 165–84.

——— . *The Tenniel Illustrations to the "Alice" Books.* Columbus: Ohio State UP, 1985.

Harrison, Colin. *Readability in the Classroom.* Cambridge: Cambridge UP, 1980.

Ingarden, Roman. *The Cognition of the Literary Work of Art.* Trans. Ruth Ann Crowley and Kenneth R. Olson. Evanston: Northwestern UP, 1973.

MacDonald, Greville. *George MacDonald and His Wife.* New York: Dial, 1924.

Madden, William. "Framing the 'Alices.'" *PMLA* 101 (1986): 362–73.

Matthews, Dorothy Otterman. "The Literary Reputation of Lewis Carroll in England and America in the Nineteenth Century." Diss. Western Reserve U, 1962.

Natov, Roni. "The Persistence of Alice." *The Lion and the Unicorn* 3 (1979): 48–61.

Norvell, George W. *The Reading Interests of Young People.* N.p.: Michigan State UP, 1973.

Page, Jane Izzard. "Enduring Alice." Diss. U of Washington, 1970.

Phillips, Robert, ed. *Aspects of Alice: Lewis Carroll's Dreamchild as Seen through the Critics' Looking-Glasses, 1865–1971.* New York: Vintage-Random, 1977.

Porter, Katherine Anne, Bertrand Russell, and Mark Van Doren. "Lewis Carroll: *Alice in Wonderland.*" *The New Invitation to Learning.* Ed. Mark Van Doren. New York: Random, 1942.

Rackin, Donald. "The Critical Interpretations of *Alice in Wonderland:* A Survey and Suggested Reading." Diss. U of Illinois, 1964.

"The Reviews of *Alice's Adventures in Wonderland.*" *Jabberwocky: The Journal of the Lewis Carroll Society* 9 (1979–80): 3–8, 27–39, 55–58, 79–86.

Rheinstein, Phyllis Gilia. "Alice in Context: A Study of Children's Literature and the Dominant Culture in the Eighteenth and Nineteenth Centuries." Diss. Yale U, 1972.

The Right Book for the Right Child: A Graded Buying List of Children's Books. New York: Day, 1933. 3rd ed. New York: Day, 1942.

Schilder, Paul. "Psychoanalytic Remarks on *Alice in Wonderland* and Lewis Carroll." 1938. Phillips 283–92.

Spacks, Patricia Meyer. "The Yale Curriculum." *The Future of Doctoral Studies in English.* Ed. Andrea Lunsford, Helene Moglen, and James F. Slevin. New York: MLA, 1989. 25–29.

Sunderland, Zena, et al. *Children and Books.* 6th ed. Glenview, IL: Scott, 1981.

PHYLLIS BIXLER

Gardens, Houses, and Nurturant Power

in The Secret Garden

rances Hodgson Burnett's *The Secret Garden* (1911) has elicited a considerable body of appreciative explication; the book has been praised for psychological realism in its portrayal of ill-tempered children, for example, and for its use of pastoral imagery to symbolize the children's physical and psychological healing. Recently, however, the book has undergone a feminist critique by Elizabeth Lennox Keyser. Keyser laments that after Mary Lennox's healing process is well under way, the book shifts its focus to the recuperation of her cousin Colin Craven, while Mary herself "slips into the background until she disappears entirely from the final chapter" (9). Keyser asserts that the book's imaginative power diminishes with this shift in focal character. The now conventional Mary and the "self-centered" Colin never engage the reader as did the earlier "contrary," "independent, self-contained" Mary (2, 7, 9). According to Keyser, *The Secret Garden* reflects Burnett's own "ambivalence about sex roles" (12); like women writers such as the Brontës, George Eliot, Louisa May Alcott, and Mrs. Humphry Ward, Burnett was uncomfortable with the self-assertion of her writing career and chastened herself by chastening "her self-assertive female characters" (10). Even more, by ending her book with a description of "the master of Misselthwaite with his son, Master Colin," Burnett "seems to be affirming male supremacy" and suggesting "a defense of patriarchal authority" (12).

Keyser has described a response to characterization in *The Secret Garden* which, I have discovered, other readers share; and the gender-role conflicts Keyser identifies as the source of Burnett's portrayal of Mary and Colin are easily documented by looking at Burnett's other fiction as well as her life, as I have argued in my book. However, if

208

one is to explain why *The Secret Garden* continues to fascinate readers and elicit critical explication, if one is to describe the deeply female voice many readers hear in the text, one must move beyond "Images of Women" criticism, as Toril Moi has observed (42–49). One must look not only at the book's portrayal of individual characters but also at its configurations of characters and webs of symbolic imagery. My essay attempts this task by discussing as focal centers of meaning not Mary and Colin but the secret garden—the book's title "character"—and Misselthwaite Manor. An examination of these images shows Burnett's masterpiece to be a celebration of nature's power as a primarily female power, a gender designation provided earlier by canonical Romantic poets, who "troped" nature as "female," as Anne Mellor has pointed out (8). To highlight the nearly utopian vision of female nurturant power to be found in *The Secret Garden*, comparisons will be made with Burnett's other fiction, Charlotte Brontë's *Jane Eyre* (1847), and Charles Dickens's *Great Expectations* (1861). Burnett loved and was clearly influenced by Charles Dickens, as I have earlier pointed out (22, 31, 126–27); and the parallels between *The Secret Garden* and *Jane Eyre* have been noted by others besides myself (100), for example Burnett's biographer Ann Thwaite (220).

In using the secret garden's transformation from seeming death to blossoming health as an image for the parallel transformation of the two children, Burnett was following well-established Romantic precedents. In *Emile* (1762), Jean-Jacques Rousseau said the child should be given a garden to cultivate (bk. 2, p. 98), and he described the child itself as a young plant to be carefully tended (bk. 1, p. 38). Catherine Sinclair used garden imagery in the preface to *Holiday House* (1839), which anticipated many late-nineteenth century children's classics in its appreciation for high-spirited, "contrary" children. Sinclair lamented that current methods of education suppressed in the child "the vigour of natural feeling, the glow of natural genius, the ardour of natural enthusiasm" (iv); she hoped instead for a child-garden in which "some lively blossoms that spring spontaneously in the uncultivated soil, might still be cherished into strength and beauty" (iv). The association of child and garden stirred the imagination of many. Michael Cohen has noted a considerable number of paintings from the 1770s through the 1850s which portray children in a garden, often suggested by part of a wall; poor children were sometimes portrayed as being outside a garden, perhaps deprived of the Edenic innocence that should have been their birthright (94–112).

A garden can provide an image of not only childhood but also motherhood; as Sinclair's metaphor implies, a garden reveals as much about its gardener as about the composition of its soil and the kinds of plants that can grow there. According to the nineteenth-century ideology of separate gender spheres, mothers are the primary caretakers of the young child; the home is a primarily female sphere, isolated and protected from the competitive male world outside. In his earlier articulation of this ideology, the epistolary novel *Julie; or, The New Eloise* (1761), Rousseau suggested the holiness of a woman's calling and the isolation of her home by comparing it to both a convent and a walled garden. Through an extended description of the secluded garden "Elysium," which Julie tends on her husband's estate (pt. 4, letter 11, pp. 304–15), Rousseau suggests not only that a married woman chooses a domestic garden over the courtly love garden of illicit passion, but also that she creates this "Elysium" especially for the sake of her young children. The birds in Julie's garden demonstrate a "zeal for domestic duties, paternal and maternal tenderness" (309) as do the birds in *The Secret Garden*, published over a century later. That gardens provided images for motherhood as well as for childhood during the nineteenth century is suggested by Michael Waters's recent survey of the garden in Victorian literature. According to Waters, "it is virtually impossible to say anything about the garden in Victorian fiction without reference to the concept of home and the place of women within it" (227).

The use of a garden as an image for both childhood and motherhood figures prominently in the mid-century adult classic *Great Expectations*. Near the Gargery home, where Pip is reared as a young child, there is a garden in which he later has several crucial conversations with Biddy, his childhood friend and the bride nature probably intended for him, had not his aspirations and passions been diverted elsewhere by his visits to Miss Havisham's Satis House and his residence in London; Pip appreciates this childhood garden only after it is too late to return to it. In contrast is the garden on the Satis House grounds, where Pip often converses with Estella, Miss Havisham's adopted daughter. Frequently described as "neglected" and "rank," this walled garden provides an image of Estella's childhood much as Burnett's garden mirrors the childhood of Mary and Colin. Being fashioned as a tool for Miss Havisham's revenge on the world, Estella has been deprived of "the lively blossoms" of "natural feeling," to use Sinclair's words. Dickens underscores the importance of this garden by setting his concluding scene there; after their various misadventures in London, Estella and Pip meet on the Satis House grounds where nothing is left "but the wall of the old garden" (491; ch. 59). In this abandoned garden, however, lies any hope Estella may have for a better future. Just as Pip has recently relived and reaffirmed his childhood by allowing Joe to nurse him back to health after a serious illness has reduced him to virtual infancy, Estella must find and nuture the dwarfed plants of natural feeling surviving from her childhood if she and Pip are to go forth in a mature, adult relationship.

If the Satis House garden provides an image of Estella's childhood, it similarly speaks of Miss Havisham's motherhood. Having grown up without a mother as well as having been rejected by her lover, she neglects to foster Estella's natural feelings even as she neglects the garden she herself never enters. The garden's walls shade the daylight from her garden as she has shut it out of her rooms. Pip finds snow in the garden after it has melted outside (108–9; ch. 11), snow that is as cold as Estella has become under the tutelage of her white-haired, bridal-garbed mother. Shortly before she dies, however, the snow in Miss Havisham's heart does melt; she shows that her own feelings are not dead. Still capable of suffering as Pip does from Estella's coldness and recognizing in Pip's suffering a mirror of her own, Miss Havisham asks his forgiveness and offers to make financial restitution. Perhaps it is because Miss Havisham eventually repents and attempts to compensate for her earlier abuse of a mother's role that she is allowed to leave at least the remnant of a garden to her adopted daughter. This garden's survival and Miss Havisham's late repentence offer a remnant of hope in a book filled with mothers who fail their high calling. Pip's biological mother fails him by dying, and the sister who takes his mother's place tyrannizes him with her switch, "Tickler"; before giving her up for adoption, Estella's natural mother threatens to kill her in revenge against Estella's father; Mrs. Pocket would allow her babes to swallow pins and tumble into the fire had she not the help of her older children and a nurse.

It is likely, as Keyser observes (11), that Burnett also felt she had sometimes failed her children. She often left them with their father while she pursued her career; and, watching her older son die, she felt keenly a mother's powerlessness. However, when she wrote *The Secret Garden* in late middle life (she was in her early sixties, two decades had passed since Lionel's death, and Vivian was an adult), she allowed herself to rewrite this page in her history, and she left future child readers a healing legacy in her portrayal of the garden as an image of powerful motherhood.

Like the children in *Great Expectations*, Mary and Colin begin without mothers. Mary's mother neglects her for social gaieties and then, along with Mary's father, dies in a cholera epidemic, all in the book's first chapter; Colin's mother died when he was born. In *The Secret Garden*, as in *Great Expectations*, fathers are unable to compensate for the children's lack of adequate mothering. Archibald Craven is incapacitated by his excessive grief and avoids both Colin and Mary. Joe Gargery has insufficient psychological strength to intercede between his wife's switch "Tickler" and Pip. Until shortly before his death, Magwitch does not know that his daughter Estella has survived, and his efforts to make a gentleman out of Pip warp Pip just as Miss Havisham's rearing distorts Estella. Unlike Dickens, however, Burnett provided her children with a community of mothers, who work effectively with nature in the secret garden.

When Mary arrives at Misselthwaite Manor, she learns about the garden from the first caregiver to offer her psychological as well as physical nurture, the servant Martha. In the first part of the book, Mary is still a child who needs mothering, especially because she is too "independent" and "self-contained" (Keyser 9); psychologically unconnected to others, she is also detached from her own feelings. Mary then learns more about the garden—and herself—from the gardener Ben Weatherstaff and from the robin, which eventually points her to the garden's buried key and hidden door. Once Mary is inside the garden, Martha's brother Dickon helps her prune and plant with tools and seeds she had arranged to have him buy for her. Finally, Mary and later Colin are assisted by the mother of Martha and Dickon. Mother Sowerby— that "comfortable wonderful mother creature" who has birthed and reared twelve children of her own (250; ch. 24)—sends Mary a jump rope, and she later sends both Mary and Colin nourishing food to provide energy for their garden work. Working largely behind the scenes on their behalf, this archetypal earth mother eventually appears in the garden to praise what the children have done.

In *The Secret Garden*, effective motherhood means giving children tools to help themselves rather than making them tools for satisfying one's own egoistic desires, as Miss Havisham and Magwitch did—or as Burnett herself was accused of doing when she publicly described her

younger son as the model for Little Lord Fauntleroy. Effective motherhood is not limited by gender—the gardener Ben Weatherstaff, Dickon,
and the male robin, who helps his mate with their eggs in the garden,
as well as Martha and Mother Sowerby, can nurture. Finally, effective
motherhood, like gardening, is a shared, communal venture.

Once this nurturant "Magic" power has set Mary on the path toward
health, Mary herself joins this mothering community. By bringing
Colin and the garden together and then stepping back to let the garden and Colin do their work, she gives the kind of mothering she
has received. This kind of mothering may not be "contrary" nor "self-
assertive," but it need not be seen as totally self-sacrificial; it has its
own rewards, the joy of working cooperatively with nature and other
human beings, the sense of individual empowerment that can come
when one participates in a nurturant power greater than any of its
agents. The last part of *The Secret Garden* may be disappointing if one
attends primarily to the characterization of Mary and Colin, and if
one values primarily expressions of anger and dramatizations of self-
assertion in texts written by women. However, if one regards the book's
"heroes" to be neither Mary nor Colin but rather its community of
mothers centered in the secret garden, and if one values also the ideals
of empathy and connection which Carol Gilligan identifies as women's
"different" moral "voice," the last part of *The Secret Garden* need not
be considered disappointing.

Indeed, all of *The Secret Garden* can be deeply satisfying if one
notices Burnett's portrayal of how the nurturant power of the garden
gradually comes inside and transforms Misselthwaite Manor. A first
glance at Misselthwaite Manor as a center of meaning does seem to
suggest that Burnett's book is, at the least, avoiding criticism of "patriarchal authority" as well as the class system. The estate upon which
both secret garden and manor rest is owned by Archibald Craven and
will be inherited, presumably, by his male heir Colin. Working-class
males like gardener Ben Weatherstaff and Dickon may join the mothering community in the garden but, like Martha, Mother Sowerby, and
probably Mary, they do not own it. Women and working-class males
may have nurturant power, but they have limited economic power. (The
1987 television-movie version suggests that Mary, if not Dickon, may
eventually inherit the Misselthwaite estate along with Colin; portraying
them as having no family relationship, it suggests that they will marry,
in a scene reminiscent of the end of *Great Expectations*. After World

War I has killed Dickon and injured Colin, the young adults meet in the garden to exchange a promise to marry.)

It would be difficult to find in *The Secret Garden* a critique of the class system. Ben Weatherstaff has an acerbic temperament but he readily adopts the obeisant role of Colin's servant. Unlike Ben, Mother Sowerby calls Colin "dear lad" rather than "mester Colin" (275; ch. 26); also, the text does refer to her difficulties paying the cottage rent and giving her children enough food (30–34; ch. 4). But neither Mother Sowerby nor her children seem to suffer much—she finds that "th' air of th' moor fattens" her children, and "they eat th' grass same as th' wild ponies do" (30; ch. 4). Indeed, it was only in Burnett's realist adult fiction of the 1870s that she seriously addressed the economic inequities of class. By the time she wrote *The Secret Garden*, she had turned to popular adult romances such as *A Lady of Quality* (1896), *The Making of a Marchioness* (1901), and *The Shuttle* (1907), which purveyed a nostalgic, sentimental vision of Britain's landed aristocracy and its relationship to the virtuous, appreciative poor.

Throughout her career, however, Burnett's fiction did imply a critique of patriarchal restraints on women, often through the portrayal of houses and house ownership. In *The Shuttle*, for example, Burnett asserted emphatically that women should be allowed to maintain control of their own fortunes. When two American heiresses marry British aristocrats, one is tyrannized by her husband until her sister rescues her; and the romance emphasizes how the sisters' wealth restores the decaying British halls and estates. Burnett's own early childhood had provided her an example of houses as images of typical discrepancies in male and female economic power. She was born into a family made materially comfortable by her father's business, which sold household furnishings in Manchester, England. However, her father died when she was four, and her mother was unable to keep the business profitable in Manchester's mercurial economy. In her childhood memoir, *The One I Knew the Best of All* (1893), Burnett dramatized the resultant change in family fortune by comparing the smoggy, inner-city home they moved into after her father died with the suburban estate owned by relatives she sometimes visited (251–53; ch. 14; 29–31, ch. 3). Not surprisingly, when her writing brought her wealth, Burnett spent much of it on houses and estates; beginning in 1898, for example, she rented Maytham Hall in Kent; in 1909, she built a mansion at Plandome, Long Island, and later she bought another home in Bermuda.

Before she herself enjoyed the power of home ownership, however, Burnett offered a poignant portrayal of houses as images of male power and female dependence in *Through One Administration* (1883), based in part on her own unhappy married life with Swann Burnett in Washington, D. C. Bertha Amory's husband uses her social graces and fortune in his lobbying and money-making schemes; when these schemes are exposed, he goes abroad, leaving her to face the resulting financial ruin and social disapprobation. Her own economic resources depleted by one male authority, she becomes dependent on another. She moves with her children back to the home of her father, and the book's final lines depict her unhappy retreat to this home. Bertha climbs the stairs to the nursery—"the only safe thing . . . for a woman who is unhappy," she had earlier said (465; ch. 34)—and then shuts the door. The book ends with this image of a patriarchal house as imprisoning retreat.

In *Little Lord Fauntleroy* (1886) and *A Little Princess* (1905) as well as in *The Secret Garden*—the three romances which carry Burnett's reputation as a classic children's author—large houses remain images of economic, primarily patriarchal, power. However, these romances also suggest that if houses are not filled with nurturant power, they are essentially empty; they are not really homes. In *Little Lord Fauntleroy*, little Cedric's patrimony is epitomized by his British grandfather's estate and hall. As in *The Secret Garden*, women have limited economic power. Having relatively little money of her own, Mrs. Errol agrees to give her son to his grandfather; initially placed in a lodge on the grandfather's estate, she must rely on her son as an entrée to the patriarchal hall. Mrs. Errol does have considerable nurturant power, however; it is in no small part because of the kind of rearing she gave Cedric that he is able to soften his grandfather's heart. *A Little Princess* (1905; an enlargement of "Sara Crewe," a tale published in 1887–88, and a play produced in 1901–2) similarly portrays male characters as having the "magic" economic power to create a good life for a child. Sara's mother is dead and it is her father's money that causes her to be treated as a "princess" at Miss Minchin's school until he dies, apparently penniless; it is her father's wealthy business partner, Mr. Carrisford, who frees Sara from servant life in the school, restores to Sara her father's great wealth, and becomes her guardian.

By comparison to Sara's biological and adopted fathers, Miss Minchin has a relative lack of economic power and social station; if she and her sister have an inheritance, they apparently need to supplement it by running a boarding school for girls. Moreover, if Burnett's book suggests any motive for Miss Minchin's malignancy toward Sara, it is her jealousy of Sara's class and wealth. Their first trial of wills comes when Sara's fluency in French publicly embarrasses Miss Minchin, who lacks that index of class (19–25; ch. 2). Miss Minchin's preoccupation with money blinds her to Sara's princess-like nature, and the scene in which Miss Minchin tries to retrieve Sara from Mr. Carrisford's house contains a hint of the schoolmistress's economic vulnerability. When she threatens not to allow her pupils to visit Sara, Mr. Carrisford's lawyer reminds her that the pupils' parents are unlikely to refuse such visits. Miss Minchin immediately recognizes the veiled threat this reminder represents to the economic well-being of her establishment. She knows that "if Mr. Carrisford chose to tell certain of her patrons how unhappy Sara Crewe had been made, many unpleasant things might happen." Burnett's narrator calls Miss Minchin a "woman of sordid mind" for believing "that most people would not refuse to allow their children to remain friends with a little heiress of diamond mines" (213; ch. 18). If Burnett had wanted to make Miss Minchin a sympathetic character, her narrator could have added that Miss Minchin was probably right that "most people" would probably share her overvaluation of Sara's wealth and thus might similarly be described as being "of sordid mind."

Clearly, however, Burnett did not intend Miss Minchin to be a sympathetic character. In this variant of the Cinderella tale, Miss Minchin is cast in the role of the wicked stepmother; thus, it is her lack of nurturant rather than economic power that Burnett stresses. (In her fiction, Burnett chastised female characters far more harshly for a lack of nurturance than for self-assertion. *A Lady of Quality* scandalized critics because its heroine goes unpunished for having in a fit of rage killed her former lover, while in her last romance, *Robin* [1922], Burnett mercilessly embroiders the sins of a neglectful mother before having her obliterated in a World War I bombing raid [312].) In *A Little Princess*, Burnett portrayed a female establishment diametrically opposed to the mothering community found in *The Secret Garden*. Sara herself knows how to mother, as Mary learns to do; but Sara, unlike Mary, does not find adult women who effectively mother her—Miss Amelia is too much dominated by her sister to act on her softer feelings and sense of justice. While Mother Sowerby offers Mary and Colin nourishing food and praise for good work, Miss Minchin withholds both food and appreciation from overworked Sara. Finally, Miss Minchin's lack of nurturant power is imaged by her school, a large urban house devoid of gardens or other signs of nature's creatures other than the rats Sara tries to domesticate. For a reviving glimpse of nature, Sara must peer at the birds and sky outside her attic room. And, since Miss Minchin proves unable to become a nurturant mother, her house itself is unredeemable and Sara must leave it in the end. In *A Little Princess,* it is male adults who nurture—Sara's father and his friend Mr. Carrisford; Mr. Carrisford's servant Ram Dass, who enters Sara's attic room to transform it; and Mr. Carrisford's lawyer, a doting father of many children, who travels to the continent to find her. In Burnett's utopia, as suggested by her romances for children and adults, neither nurturant nor economic power would be the province of one gender; men would nurture and women would own houses.

Women do not own houses in *The Secret Garden;* inasmuch as they can nurture, however, they fill houses with a power without which the signature on a deed of ownership brings little happiness, as is dramatized by the life of Archibald and Colin Craven at the beginning of the story. By its end, *The Secret Garden* does fall far short of the utopian vision in its portrayal of economic distribution according to gender and class; however, if one examines Misselthwaite Manor as well as the secret garden as a center of meaning, Burnett's masterpiece is nearly utopian in its portrayal of the power of nurturance. For Burnett portrays this male-owned manor, with its almost one hundred, mostly empty rooms, as being gradually entered and revived by the same nurturant forces that transform the garden.

In dramatizing this transformation of Misselthwaite Manor, Burnett used gothic elements like those found in *Jane Eyre* and *Great Expectations.* (The gothic elements in *The Secret Garden* were heightened in the 1987 television movie.) Miss Havisham's Satis House, Edward Rochester's Thornfield Hall, and Archibald Craven's Misselthwaite Manor are all patrimonial mansions with large unused portions and ghostly hidden residents. Pip witnesses Miss Havisham's nocturnal wanderings; twice, he has a vision of her hanging from the rafters, foreshadowing her death from injuries incurred during a fire (94, ch. 8; 325, ch. 38; 413, ch. 49). Jane Eyre has several nocturnal encounters with Edward's wife Bertha before that woman's fiery death. During the night, Mary Lennox first follows a cry in the corridor to find Colin, and, at first, each child considers the other a ghost (124; ch. 13). In all three books, the hidden inhabitants represent some past victimization which prevents present and future happiness. Victimized by a father who spoiled her and by a brother and lover who swindled her, Miss Havisham victimizes Estella and Pip. Having inherited madness with her wealth and, like Edward himself, having been married to solidify a family fortune, Bertha impedes the hopes Edward and Jane have for a happy marriage. Rejected by his father because he resembles his dead mother and because he has apparently inherited his father's crooked back, Colin proves destructive of himself and others; believing he will soon die, Colin refuses to go outside, and his tyrannical tantrums make the rest of the household as unhappy as he is.

Gothic manor and ghostly resident have different fates in the three books, however. In the adult novels, manor and resident prove unredeemable and are destroyed. Satis House is dismantled and sold as old building lumber, apparently at Estella's order (482; ch. 58); perhaps, since the house was never a home, its value to her is primarily monetary, unlike the grounds themselves with their remnant of a garden. This alone Estella struggles to maintain during her unhappy years of marriage to the abusive Drummle, when she relinquishes "little by little" all other possessions she has received from Miss Havisham (492; ch. 59). At the end of the novel, the grounds will again be built upon, though apparently not by Estella, for she declares that she has come to take "leave of this spot"; and the book's final paragraph describes Pip and Estella going out of that "ruined place" (493; ch. 59). Dickens remains as silent about what is to be built on the Satis House grounds as he is about the future home of Pip and Estella. At the end of *Jane Eyre*, Thornfield Hall, like Satis House, is a "ruined place," destroyed by Bertha's fire. Its proud battlements and chimneys have crashed in, just as its proud owner is now "stone-blind" and without one of his hands (377; ch. 36). Unlike Dickens, however, Brontë offers her characters an alternative; she describes the house where a humbled man and a now economically independent woman can be happy. The "manor-house of Ferndean," unlike Thornfield Hall, is of "moderate size, and no architectural pretensions"; moreover, it is "deep buried in a wood" (378; ch. 37). Earlier, an orchard-garden had allowed the love of Jane and Edward to blossom relatively free from those reminders of their economic inequity and of Edward's past that they found inside Thornfield Hall. In a more modest house totally enveloped by nature's green, however, past inequities and injuries can be healed in a fruitful marriage; Edward recovers at least enough sight to recognize that the firstborn in his arms has "inherited his own eyes, as they once were" (397; ch. 38).

At the end of *The Secret Garden*, Misselthwaite Manor does not have to be abandoned or replaced because it is in the process of being transformed by the same nurturant power at work in the garden. The natural forces that lead Mary to enter the secret garden also prompt her to explore the house and find its secret inhabitant. The wind that blows aside the ivy to reveal the secret garden's hidden door also first reveals to her Colin's cry. At first, she can hardly distinguish his cry from the wind, but the cry becomes clear when a draft comes from his door through the passages and blows her door open (50; ch. 5). Later, it is because the "wuthering" wind and rain keep her awake one night that she decides to follow the cry through the corridors and finds Colin (122; ch. 8). Rain also plays a role in filling the empty house with the children's noisy life; rainy days prompt Mary, and later Colin with her, to explore and use as runways the manor's many unused rooms and corridors. Also, before Colin himself enters the garden, its natural healing force comes inside to him through Mary's lyric descriptions; similarly, Dickon brings his assorted animals which dart in and out of an open window in Colin's room.

Burnett's text emphasizes the opening of the manor to nature's healing influences by portraying this change as occurring simultaneously with those occurring in the garden. Her narrative cuts back and forth between garden and house, highlighting the parallel developments in what is occurring in the two places. In chapters 5 and 6, for example, Mary first hears Colin's cry and makes her first exploration of the house; in the next two chapters, Mary discovers the garden's key and door. The next three chapters describe her entrance and early work in the garden, followed by three chapters set inside, depicting Mary's first visit with Archibald Craven and her discovery of Colin. The book continues this pattern until the last two chapters, when Mother Sowerby and finally Archibald Craven enter the garden. The book's concluding paragraphs conflate the two settings by placing the reader inside a house now fully open to the garden's nurturant influence, a house ready to receive a father and son who can now truly live in the house as well as own it. For the first time in the book, Ben Weatherstaff— whose "duties rarely took him away from the gardens" (297; ch. 27)— is inside the house. It is by looking out the window with Ben that the reader receives the book's final vision of Colin and his father walking from the garden, across the lawn, and into the house.

Burnett uses not only narrative structure but also linking imagery to suggest that the garden's nurturant power is also filling the house. When Mary first enters the garden, Burnett's chapter title calls the garden "The Strangest House"; inside, Mary finds this "house" to have "arches," "alcoves," and "stone seats." Mary is obviously fascinated by the garden's secrecy, but she also feels alone; "I am the first person who has spoken here for ten years," she muses (76–79; ch. 9). Soon after, in speaking to Martha, she associates the garden with the loneliness she has experienced elsewhere on the estate. "This is such a big lonely place," Mary says. "The house is lonely, and the park is lonely, and the gardens are lonely. So many places seem shut up" (82; ch. 9). Neither house nor garden, however, is entirely empty of life. Both contain nests. During Mary's first exploration of the house, she sees "nothing alive" until she finds in a hole in a sofa cushion "six baby mice" "cuddled up asleep" in "a comfortable nest" (57; ch. 6). The garden also contains a nest. During Mary's initial visits, the robin who showed her the garden's key and door is still courting; later, however, the robin and his mate build a nest and tend their eggs there. Both garden and house not only contain nests but are suggested to be nests. When Dickon first enters the garden, Burnett's chapter title calls it "The Nest of the Missel Thrush" (100; ch. 11); later, through a picture and note that he leaves for Mary, Dickon identifies the garden as "her nest" and suggests that she is "like a missel thrush" (121; ch. 13). Dickon's note reminds the reader that, because of its name, Misselthwaite Manor can also be considered a nest for Colin—if Mary's first exploration of the house leads her to the nest of mice, her second trip leads her to a similarly hidden Colin. That Misselthwaite Manor is Colin's nest is further suggested by a conversation between the nesting robins in the garden. Watching Colin's strange behavior, the mother bird fears for her eggs until the father bird recalls that he had behaved similarly when his parents made him learn to fly; he tells her that Colin is like a bird just out of its nest and "learning to fly—or rather to walk" (261–62; ch. 25). Appropriately, later in the same chapter, the children find an empty nest in the manor; "the mice had grown up and run away and the hole [in the sofa cushion] was empty" (266; ch. 25).

Several paragraphs later, Mary makes a discovery that begins to reveal one of the most important secrets in Burnett's masterpiece, a secret fully revealed in the next two, concluding chapters: The "Magic" power at work in both house and garden is Colin's dead mother. Mary notices in Colin's room that the curtain over the portrait of his mother is now open; this curtain provides yet another link to the garden, since it has been earlier described as "rose-colored" (132; ch. 13), while the ivy covering the garden door has, in turn, frequently been called a "curtain." Colin had shown Mary the portrait the night Mary found him; he had told Mary that he kept the curtain closed because he hated his mother for dying, because she smiled too much when he was miserable, and because "she is mine and I don't want everyone to see her" (133; ch. 13). Now that Colin is healthy and happy, however, it does not make him "angry any more to see her laughing" (267; ch. 25). Apparently, his garden experience of a power larger than his own has made him more willing to share. Finally, perhaps Colin is no longer driven by anger at her death because he senses that she is still somehow alive in his room. He tells Mary how, two nights ago, the moonlight had come in the window and made him pull the curtain's cord; it "felt as if the Magic was filling the room," he says, and he associates this Magic with his mother by adding that she "must have been a sort of Magic person." Mary's reply suggests that Colin's mother is alive in his room also in that her own soul at last shines through his face. Viewing the mother's laughing portrait, Mary tells Colin, "You are so like her now . . . that sometimes I think perhaps you are her ghost made into a boy." "If I were her ghost—my father would be fond of me," Colin observes (267; ch. 25).

Colin's observation points toward the final reunion of son and father in the garden, where his mother's Magic, now acknowledged in the manor, had first begun its work. The garden and garden community members have for some time been her living hands. It was because her orders to tend the garden preceded Archibald Craven's orders to have it locked that Ben Weatherstaff continued to prune the garden after she died (229; ch. 22). Similarly, it was Colin's mother who told Mary and Dickon to bring Colin to the garden, according to Mother Sowerby (217; ch. 21). Now, in a chapter titled "It's Mother," Colin's mother is given not only hands but voice by Mother Sowerby, who finally visits the children in the garden. When Colin says he wishes Mother Sowerby were his mother, she embraces him and says, "Thy own mother's in this 'ere very garden, I do believe. She couldna' keep out of it." Adding, "thy father mun come back to thee—he mun" (279–80; ch. 26), Mother Sowerby sends a letter telling Archibald Craven to return to the garden, a letter he receives just as he wakes—one moonlit night—

from a dream in which his wife called him back to her "in the garden" (287; ch. 27).

The final chapter, "In the Garden," describes Archibald Craven's return as a reprise of the earlier, more fully dramatized experiences of Colin and Mary. Without his knowing it, the garden had been at work within the father while it had worked within the son; he began to feel its "awakening" power while gazing at a forget-me-not on the same day Colin first entered the garden and declared, "I am going to live forever" (285–86; ch. 27). As he makes the trip home, Craven acknowledges that, in his earlier anger that "the child was alive and the mother was dead," "he had not felt like a father at all" (289; ch. 27). Perhaps aware that he needs to learn how to nurture, he stops at Mother Sowerby's cottage; she is away helping a woman with a new baby, but he recognizes, apparently for the first time, that the Sowerby children are "a healthy likable lot," and he gives them "a golden sovereign" (291; ch. 27). Craven must learn also to receive, however, if he is to give of himself as well as of his money. Still an isolate as Mary was at the beginning of the book, he must retrace her steps. After a brief visit to the manor, feeling "on earth again," Craven takes "his way, as Mary had done, through the door in the shrubbery and among the laurels and the fountain beds" to the garden (293; ch. 27). There, like Mary before him, he himself can be nurtured and thus learn how to nurture.

Some of the deepest satisfactions Burnett's masterpiece affords can be explained if one perceives that the reunion that occurs when Craven reaches the garden is not just paternal but maternal. The book's configuration of characters and webs of imagery have already suggested that it is the soul of Colin's mother that has been transforming the garden and the house with nurturant power; now, language of birth suggests that garden, and perhaps also house, are her maternal body. As the "rose-colored" curtain has recently been opened to reveal her portrait in the house, the door to the garden is now "flung wide open, the sheet of ivy swinging back"; "the uncontrollable moment" has arrived; with "quick strong young breathing," "a boy burst[s] through it at full speed and, without seeing," dashes "almost into his [father's] arms" (294; ch. 27).

By perceiving house and garden as images of not only the transforming power of nature and a mothering community but also of a mother's nurturant body, one uncovers a secret plot within *The Secret Garden* that breaks through its patriarchal sociology. Keyser points to this plot when she includes the following in her description of what she remembered of the book before rereading it to write her article: "I remembered Mary exploring the winding paths and gardens within gardens, and indoors the winding corridors with their many locked rooms" (2). At some level, the reader, along with Mary, Colin, and finally even Archibald Craven, reenacts the usually repressed desire to explore the secret mysteries of the mother's body as well as her soul. It may be this plot which above all identifies *The Secret Garden* as what the French feminists call *écriture féminine*. According to Toril Moi (114), Hélène Cixous describes "the mother as the source and origin of the voice to be heard in all female texts." In *The Secret Garden*, we hear this voice, this voice of the mother who "physically materializes what she's thinking," who "signifies it with her body."

WORKS CITED

Bixler, Phyllis. *Frances Hodgson Burnett*. Boston: Hall, 1984.

Brontë, Charlotte. *Jane Eyre*. 1847. New York: Norton, 1971.

Burnett, Frances Hodgson. *A Lady of Quality: Being a Most Curious, Hitherto Unknown History, as Related by Mr. Isaac Bickerstaff But Not Presented to the World of Fashion Through the Pages of the Tattler and Now for the First Time Written Down*. New York: Scribner's, 1896.

————. *Little Lord Fauntleroy*. New York: Scribner's, 1886.

————. *A Little Princess*. 1905. Harmondsworth: Penguin, 1961.

————. *The One I Knew the Best of All: A Memory of the Mind of a Child*. New York: Scribner's, 1893.

————. *Robin*. New York: Stokes, 1922.

————. *The Secret Garden*. 1911. New York: Dell, 1962.

————. *The Shuttle*. New York: Stokes, 1907.

————. *Through One Administration*. 1883. Ridgewood, NJ: Gregg, 1967.

Cohen, Michael. *Engaging Art: Entering the Work in Two Centuries of English Painting and Poetry*. Tuscaloosa: U of Alabama P, 1987.

Dickens, Charles. *Great Expectations*. 1861. Harmondsworth: Penguin, 1965.

Gilligan, Carol. *In a Different Voice: Psychological Theory and Women's Development*. Cambridge: Harvard UP, 1982.

Keyser, Elizabeth Lennox. " 'Quite Contrary': Frances Hodgson Burnett's *The Secret Garden*." *Children's Literature* 11 (1983): 1–13.

Mellor, Anne K. "On Romanticism and Feminism." *Romanticism and Feminism*. Ed. Mellor. Bloomington: Indiana UP, 1988. 3–9.

Moi, Toril. *Sexual/Textual Politics: Feminist Literary Theory.* London: Methuen, 1985.

Rousseau, Jean-Jacques. *Emile; or, On Education.* 1762. Trans. Allan Bloom. New York: Basic, 1979.

——— . *Julie; or, the New Eloise: Letters of Two Lovers, Inhabitants of a Small Town at the Foot of the Alps.* 1761. Trans. Judith H. McDowell. University Park: Pennsylvania State UP, 1968.

Sinclair, Catherine. *Holiday House: A Series of Tales.* 1839. New York: Carter, 1869.

Thwaite, Ann. *Waiting for the Party: The Life of Frances Hodgson Burnett, 1849–1924.* New York: Scribner's, 1974.

Waters, Michael. *The Garden in Victorian Literature.* Aldershot: Scolar, 1988.

E. Nesbit's Romantic Child in Modern Dress

*H*ad E. Nesbit (1858–1924) written no children's books at all, her life would fascinate the student of social history. With her quick wit, lively sense of humor, keen intelligence, commitment to social issues on one hand and attraction to aesthetic escape on the other, as well as her famous friendships and love affairs, Nesbit's life reflected many of the best and worst traits of her era. Her ideas and her life often contradicted one another. Her commitment to social change, for example, did not always mesh with her taste for elegance. Her interest in children of all social classes did not quite square with her frank admission that she wrote for middle-class children and usually about them as well. Although she posed liberated identities for children, she was sometimes guilty of cruel and unjust treatment of her own children. Despite her advanced social views, she could not support women's efforts to secure essential rights because of her somewhat domineering husband, Hubert Bland. Nor did Nesbit's desire for social justice and a humane order quite coalesce with her sometimes conservative idealization of the past.

The trait that seems most abiding in Nesbit's children's books and in her interesting life is her vitality, her enormous zest for living and being in a world that her humor, imagination, and spirit allowed her to experience as a continuing and compelling adventure. Nesbit's passionate attention to life, to books, people, games, and creative work of all kinds, her close observation of the natural world, as well as her generosity and capacity for friendship, remained with her all of her life. As Nesbit grew older, her sensibility was marked with an increasing spirituality even as she continued her avid interest in the social and material world.

An heir to Romantic conceptions of nature, art, imagination, and the child, Nesbit celebrated creative activity of all kinds and stressed the imagination's capacity to infuse life with meaning and value. Hostile to the industrial invasion of England, Nesbit often expressed nostalgia for the past. She explored the limits of time and space, dimensions which take an inward turn in her children's stories, just as they do in many Romantic works of literature. While Nesbit abhorred the ugliness of industrial England and praised the value of life close to nature, she nevertheless exhibited an enduring fascination with science and a decided taste for a sophisticated cultural life available only in great cities.

Despite the numerous oppositions readily apparent in her life and children's stories, Nesbit managed to liberate herself and children's books from Victorian constraints. She became the most famous Edwardian writer for children and breathed new and vital life into the Romantic child with the publication of her "Bastable Stories"—*The Story of the Treasure Seekers* (1899), *The Wouldbegoods* (1901), and *The New Treasure Seekers* (1904). *The Story of the Treasure Seekers* stands squarely between Victorian and modern children's literature and has been acclaimed by critics as ushering in the "Nesbit Tradition" in twentieth-century children's literature, a vision that owes much to Romantic conceptions of childhood and imagination (Crouch). By the end of the nineteenth century, however, the Romantic child had found expression in many fine children's stories and in novels for adults as well and had begun to lose much of its vitality in overly sentimental works such as James Barrie's *Peter Pan*, Frances Hodgson Burnett's *Little Lord Fauntleroy*, and countless ephemeral children's stories in which the Romantic child had become escapist and regressive (Coveney). At the same time another Romantic vision of the child emerged, one that did not idealize the capacity of the child to redeem and to reconcile a community of adults but that celebrated childhood as a time of special, Pan-like vitality and pleasure (Avery, Koppes). In this Romantic idealization of the child, the attitude represented was much more emphatically modern, as it stressed that children may realize themselves most fully when free from adult intrusions. Childhood in such works was itself a community, one often located in a free green setting in which adults are regarded as enemies. In this vision of childhood, to grow up was to be forever severed from its joyous freedom except through memory.

Memory and imagination were for Nesbit the only vehicles which could enable the sympathetic adult to reach across the gulf of childhood. To write about "the Child" would inevitably lead the adult writer to nostalgic sentimentality. Like William Wordsworth, Nesbit felt that vivid memory of one's own childhood experience could indeed enable the adult to renew both the spirit and the senses, as she explained in her book on childhood education, *Wings and the Child:* "Do you remember the world of small and new and joyous and delightful things? Try to remember it . . . try to look at the world with the clear, clean eyes that once were yours in the days when you had never deceived a friend. You will then be able to see again certain ideals, unclouded and radiant . . . Look back and you will see that you yourself were also able to distinguish these things—once" (14). Nesbit, like many other Romantic writers and such Victorian writers for children as Lewis Carroll and George MacDonald, deplored the emphasis upon facts in education. She believed that "liberty of thought, word, and deed was one of the rights of children," and she inveighed against an older method of education designed to break the child's spirit, citing a *Punch* cartoon, the legend of which read, "Cissy, go and see what Bobbie's doing and tell him not to" (11). She also wrote in ringing and urgent tones about the follies of modern mechanistic education which treated children as a class (or mob) rather than as individual human beings: "I would have every man and woman in whom the heart of childhood still lives, protest, however feebly and haltingly, yet with all the power of the heart, against machine-made education—against the instruction which crams a child with facts and starves it of dreams" (8). Education should instead be the "unfolding of a flower"; yet she argued that the last three hundred years of education "has led, in all things vital and spiritual, downhill all the way. We have gone on frustrating natural human intelligence and emotion, inculcating false doctrine, choking with incoherent facts the soul which asked to be fed with dreams come true—till now our civilization is a thing we cannot look at without a mental and moral nausea. We have, in our countryside, peasants too broken for rebellion, in our cities, 'The mortal sickness of a mind / Too unhappy to be kind' " (15).

In educating the child, Nesbit agreed with Wordsworth that nature is the best teacher. Since the "prime instinct of the child at play . . . is to create," natural playthings—clay, sand, acorns, shells, sticks, and stones—best nourish the creative imagination. While Nesbit argued that modern toys distorted the child's imagination and spirit, these natural playthings were "the thousand adjuncts to that play which is dream and reality in one" (17).

The imagination, according to Nesbit, was the most important faculty to be encouraged in the child's education. Imagination and faith were closely related in her view. Like John Ruskin and George MacDonald, Nesbit believed that imagination promotes the development of virtue and uproots the worst sins: "Imagination, duly fostered and trained, is to the world of visible wonder and beauty what the inner light is to the Japanese lantern. It transfigures everything into a glory" (26).

Nesbit was well aware that because most children's books were written, published, and purchased by adults, children were all too easily imprisoned in and by the text. Victorian writers for children tended to freeze the good pious child in a frail angelic image, a powerful sepia found in the works of adult writers as well. Charles Dickens's Tiny Tim, George MacDonald's Diamond in *At the Back of the North Wind*, Dinah Mulock's Little Lame Prince, even Louisa May Alcott's Beth March—such characters are legion in Victorian fiction, and they often earn the contempt of Nesbit's child characters, who refer to narratives featuring such characters as "goody books" since they are often given as school prizes. Nesbit's characters avoid such books whenever possible in favor of fairy tales, adventure stories, and detective stories.

If Nesbit's Bastable children broke free of the imprisoned pious child, Nesbit herself succumbed to that seductive image at least once in depicting the angelic character of lame Dickie Harding in *Harding's Luck* (1909), a plucky boy who inspires world-weary deceitful adults, rescues his uncle from incredible danger, and in a generous gesture surrenders his inheritance and title to his cousins before returning to another life as stalwart Richard Arden, the son of a wealthy nobleman in the court of James I. Despite her conventional use of the pious child figure in this fantasy, however, Nesbit manages to achieve a complex unified aesthetic and social vision in *The House of Arden* and *Harding's Luck*.

In her book *The Story of the Treasure Seekers*, however, Nesbit liberates her child characters and, by implication, her child readers from this static myth of childhood. Nesbit's Bastable children—Dora, Oswald, Noel, Dicky, Alice, and H.O.—express their liberation from adults' nostalgia and aggression in several important ways. Their mother's death and their father's struggles with bankruptcy and poverty afford the Bastables exceptional freedom. They cannot afford either school or a governess. They live in a seemingly safe community, where they can explore and enjoy picnics. They even ride the train into the city alone. Although their house has grown shabby, the children nevertheless preside in their own nursery, establish their own rules, and evade adult constraints. They learn most from experience in the natural world, but they also learn from books and from Albert-next-door's uncle, a writer who retains empathy for children because he remembers his own childhood so vividly and has managed himself to evade such adult institutions as marriage.

The Bastables are perpetually on holiday. Like young William Wordsworth, they revel in their "glad animal movements" ("Tintern Abbey" 74) and in their own inventiveness. Unlike many Victorian child characters, however, the Bastable children are by no means persecuted by adults. Oswald, Nesbit's child author and narrator, explains the Bastable attitude towards adults:

> The author of these few lines really does hope to goodness that no one will be such an owl as to think from the number of things we did when we were in the country that we were wretched, neglected little children, whose grown-up relations sparkled in the bright haunts of pleasure, and whirled in the giddy what's-its-name of fashion, while we were left to weep forsaken at home. It was nothing of the kind, and I wish you to know that my father was with us a good deal—and Albert's uncle—And we had some very decent times with them; and enjoyed ourselves very much, thank you. In some ways the good times you have with grown-ups are better than the ones you have by yourselves. At any rate they are safer . . . But these secure pleasures are not so interesting to tell about as the things you do when there is no one to stop you on the edge of a rash act. It is curious, too, that many of our most interesting games were when the grown-ups were all away. (*The Story of the Treasure Seekers* 201)

Thus Nesbit liberates the child from its image as victim of adult cruelty. Her child characters have good parents who understand their children's needs for freedom to enjoy adventures on their own.

Nesbit also overturns the Victorian stereotype of pious childhood by imbuing her Bastable children with spirited naughtiness. They have all of the appeal Leslie Fiedler ascribes to the "good bad boy" and the "good bad girl." Although the Bastables (except for the elder sister, Dora, who behaves according to Oswald "like the good elder sister out of books") are in fact incurably naughty, they are not liars or sneaks. They are quick to "own-up" when they are wrong. Most readers can scarcely fail to respond with pleasure to Oswald's opening statement in *The Wouldbegoods:* "This is the story of one of the most far-reaching and influentially naughty things we ever did in our lives. We did not mean to do such a deed. And yet we did do it. These things will happen with the best-regulated consciences" (75). Oswald concludes with an address to the reader: "If you have never done any naughty acts, I expect it is only because you never had the sense to think of anything" (75). Thus Nesbit's presiding voice in the Bastable books marks a radical departure from the condescending tones of most adult narrators in Victorian children's books.

While the spirited naughty child eventually became a stereotype itself in children's books and in popular culture, it still allowed Nesbit to break free from stifling Victorian conventions for writing for and about children. *The Wouldbegoods* in fact contains a strong element of parody of the moral tale. When the Bastables set out to be "good children," they wind up outdoing themselves in naughtiness. "Goodness" for Nesbit, as for William Blake, Wordsworth, and MacDonald, was not a matter of following a narrowly conceived set of social and moral rules.

Oswald-as-writer-and-narrator is a narrative strategy enabling Nesbit to evade the Victorian looking-glass of childhood, to create new images of childhood, and to endorse new modes of being and knowing. Wordsworth and Coleridge had tried and perhaps failed to speak to men and women in their own language. Most children's books also displayed a false idiom of childhood speech. Nesbit, however, succeeds brilliantly in speaking to children in their own language. Oswald cannot speak like characters in a "goody book" even when he tries. As a novice writer in *The Wouldbegoods*, Oswald decides to imitate conventional Victorian children's writers, explaining his experiment:

> let me do my narrating. I hope you will like it. I am going to write it a different way, like the books they give you for a prize at a girl's school—I mean a "young ladies school," of course—not a high school. High schools are not nearly so silly as some other kinds. Here goes. "'Ah, me!' sighed a slender maid of twelve summers, removing her elegant hat and passing her tapery fingers lightly through her tresses, 'how sad it is—is it not?—to see able-bodied youths and young ladies wasting the precious summer hours in idleness and luxury!' The maiden frowned reproachfully, but yet with earnest gentleness, at the group of youths and maidens who sat beneath an Umbragipeaous beech tree and ate black currants". (113)

At this point Oswald breaks off his narrative and exclaims, "It's no use.

I can't write like these books. I wonder how some authors can keep it up. What really happened was that we were all eating black currants in the orchard out of a cabbage leaf and Alice said, 'I say, look here. Let's do something. It's simply silly to waste a day' " (113).

The Bastable children are steeped in fairy tales, adventure stories, and books by Charles Dickens, Rudyard Kipling, William Shakespeare, and other writers. They also read the newspaper, see plays, and read poetry. Noel writes and publishes poetry. The Bastables are altogether more literate and sophisticated than Wordsworth's rustic child characters. Like other late-nineteenth-century Romantics, Nesbit envisions nature as art. The sophistication and intelligence of her child characters are also features which allow them to escape entrapment in the text and to evade the adult writer's nostalgia as projected in many sentimental depictions of childhood. In the end, however, the Bastables do not break free. In *The New Treasure Seekers*, the last book about the Bastables, Oswald admits that he feels grown-upness creeping up on him, as he and his siblings must leave the green freedom of the country and submit to such adult institutions as school. As Oswald notes at one point in *The Wouldbegoods*, "We began to feel as if we had forgotten something and did not know what it was" (11). Nesbit does not spell out what the Bastables are forgetting, but we can guess: that timeless ability of young children to play and to be without looking to past and future with regret and anxiety—eternity in the world of here and now.

If, like the Romantic poets before her, Nesbit was unable to sustain her revolutionary stance, if she did not entirely escape Victorian nostalgia for the lost golden age of childhood, she eventually found a solution to the dilemma by internalizing the child's quest for liberation. For Nesbit one solution to the problem—how to sustain the vision and to maintain the joy of childhood in a world of painful experience—lay in turning from the realistic to the fantasy mode.

Nesbit had always written and published literary fairy tales, some of which exhibit her best writing, defy deadening conventions, and advocate radically transformed modes of being and knowing. In 1901, though, she began to publish a series of tales under the title of "The Psammead," illustrated by H. R. Millar. Eventually these stories evolved into Nesbit's first series of full-length fantasies for children— *Five Children and It* (1901), *The Phoenix and the Carpet* (1903), and *The Story of the Amulet* (1905). In the first two of these fantasies Nesbit cleverly dramatizes the conscious wishes of children: the wish for wealth and beauty, the desire to fly, etc. In *Five Children and It* and *The Phoenix and the Carpet* Nesbit cleverly manipulates and parodies convention to create what C. N. Manlove describes as fantasy in which "narratives are organized not by themes or deep meanings but by comic schemata which make witty conceits out of magic" (114). In these first two fantasies of the series Nesbit attempts to naturalize the supernatural. Magic becomes accessible for child characters through conscious acts of will. They may be seen as products of what Samuel Taylor Coleridge called "fancy" rather than the imagination (*Biographia Literaria* 378). Nevertheless, Nesbit reveals again her desire to free children from stereotyped images; her child characters in these books subvert stereotypes of childhood through their displays of wit and humor. Moreover, these two works of fantasy enable Nesbit to discover a richer ore to mine—a mode of fantasy which issues from a more expansive vision of art and society. In the first two books of the series, the children's wishes are obvious and material. In *The Story of the Amulet*, though, the child characters' concerns center not upon material gain and gratification but upon the mysteries of time and space.

In some significant respects *The Story of the Amulet* displays what Harold Bloom has described as the Promethean or socially active phase of Romantic rebellion. Nesbit ardently believed in social reform. She and her husband, Hubert Bland, were founding members of the Fabian Society and remained socialists all of their lives. In *The Story of the Amulet* the characters—Cyril, Robert, Anthea, and Jane—visit civilizations in ancient Egypt and Babylon; they even locate the lost continent of Atlantis. They have found one half of a magical amulet. The quest which organizes their adventures into past civilizations is to find the missing half of the magical charm and to reunite their family, as both parents have had to travel far away from home. Nesbit uses these visits to ancient civilizations to reveal social ills in Edwardian England. Eventually Nesbit proposes a Utopian vision of society when the children travel into the future. In this enlightened and humane society people wear brief, comfortable clothing of bright colors and soft textures. Cities display the finest achievements of art and the best of nature as well. Architecture is functional as well as aesthetically pleasing. The institution of the family has been reorganized in order that both men and women participate in rearing children. Nesbit also envisions reforms in health care, education, and class structure.

The fantasy ends with a powerful vision. When the children at last find the missing half of the amulet and join the two halves, it becomes a brilliantly radiant arch through which the soul of the children's friend, an Egyptologist, unites with that of Rekh-Mara, a priest from ancient Egypt. Nesbit describes the union: "Then the great double arch glowed in and through the green light that had been there since the Name of Power had first been spoken—it glowed with a light more bright yet more soft than the other light—a light that the children could bear to look upon—a glory and splendour and sweetness unspeakable" (622–23). While Nesbit describes this event in transcendent terms, she makes clear that the result will be enacted within the context of social reality. She also underscores the vital connections and potent links between the present and the past. Nesbit believed that human beings may participate in eternity, but this participation appears profoundly natural, rather than supernatural. *The Story of the Amulet* includes many such moments of vision which strongly resemble Wordsworth's "spots of time" (*Prelude* [1850] 12.208) or similar moments of vision in the poetry of William Blake and Percy Bysshe Shelley. Such moments, according to the children's old magical friend from *Five Children and It*, the wise and crotchety Psammead, allow us to "see everything happening in the same place at the same time" (435).

One important way that Nesbit reveals significant connections between past and present is through story itself. The magical creatures in *The Story of the Amulet* all narrate their histories. Yet this storytelling capacity seems aligned with some larger creative power expressed in the amulet's exquisite music, light, and voice, just as Shelley's west wind, Coleridge's Aeolian harp, and Wordsworth's correspondent breeze (*Prelude* 1.35) seem to unite these Romantic poets' imaginations to some mysterious creative force.

We have noted that *The Story of the Amulet* is "Promethean" in exploring the child characters' penetration of time and space and in Nesbit's use of narrative to express revolutionary views on reforming her society, one which she increasingly viewed as destructive to imagination, beauty, health, and life. In *The Enchanted Castle* (1907) and *The Magic City* (1910), the quest turns increasingly inward. Northrop Frye has written "that the metaphorical structure of Romantic poetry tends to move inside and downward instead of outside and upward, hence the creative world is deep within, and so is heaven or the place of the presence of God" (16). For Nesbit, as for her late-century Romantic contemporaries, this "center" was increasingly expressed in art itself—

art as the reality, not art as the vehicle for apprehending a transcendent reality. During this period Nesbit had become increasingly interested in spiritual matters; for example, she was received into the Roman Catholic Church in 1906. Yet, unlike George MacDonald and C. S. Lewis, Nesbit does not express her religious faith and feeling through fantasy. Nesbit's mature fantasies—*The Enchanted Castle* (1907), *The House of Arden* (1908), *Harding's Luck* (1909), and *The Magic City* (1910)—celebrate the primacy of the human imagination and reveal the role of the arts as a center of value and meaning in human civilization. In all of these books creative acts of reading, writing, imagining, and building are all closely associated with magic. At such creative moments the child characters are at once their most totally human selves and also participants in eternity.

In *The Enchanted Castle* three siblings—Gerald, Jimmy, and Kathleen—remain at school with their French governess during the summer holiday because their cousin is seriously ill. The governess allows them to explore freely, and they soon discover an "enchanted castle," replete with a garden in which Greek statues and stone dinosaurs magically come to life. In this garden they find a "sleeping beauty," who turns out to be only Mabel, a servant's niece. Mabel plays tricks on the children but is shocked to find herself invisible because her ring really is magic. Nesbit structures several adventures and misadventures connected with the magical ring. A subplot concerning the French governess's long-lost love, Lord Yalding, finally unifies the adventures and brings them to a close. When Lord Yalding and the young governess rediscover each other, they both wish "that all the magic this ring has wrought may be undone, and that the ring itself may be no more and no less than a charm to bind thee and me together forevermore" (228).

Throughout *The Enchanted Castle* Nesbit links art, the imagination, nature, literature, magic, and belief. She describes nature as art and art as nature. Nesbit also investigates the nature of fiction, lies, and truth. In contrast to Wordsworthian children who never seem to read, Gerald reads so much that he loses the vividness of actual experience by rendering it almost immediately into conventional and rather shallow literary language. Mabel's aunt has damaged her mind by reading too many novels in pink wrappers. The experience with magic, however, transforms Gerald's storytelling ability. He encounters radically new modes of being, knowing, and perceiving. Though Gerald believes his experience is merely a dream, he still makes good use of it as he narrates it to the other children: "As he told it some of the white mystery and magic of the moonlit gardens got into his voice and his words, so that when he told of the statues that came alive, and the great beast that was alive through its stone, Kathleen thrilled responsive, clutching his arm, and even Jimmy ceased to kick the wall with his boot heels and listened open-mouthed" (75). Gerald's practice in using fictional language, his visionary experience in the castle garden, and his encounter with burglars clearly enliven and enhance his stories. Not only do Gerald's tales now resonate with mystery and magic; they also exhibit more exciting plots and more vivid concrete details. As Gerald's narrative skills develop, he blends literary conventions, practices his stories on a real child audience, and enlarges his plots with the mythic dimensions of dreams and fantasy.

One of the most potentially terrifying incidents in *The Enchanted Castle* occurs when the children find themselves transformed into stone. To become a stone statue, they learn, is not to become dead and lifeless but to be alive in a new and exciting way. Inside the stone dinosaur Kathleen was "just the same as ever, only she was Kathleen in a case of marble that would not let her move. It would not have let her cry, even if she wanted to. But she had not wanted to cry. Inside, the marble was not cold or hard. It seemed, somehow, to be softly lined with warmth and pleasantness and safety" (171–72).

As living statues, the children swim on an enchanted island with other living statues. Significantly, these statues are characters from Greek and Roman mythology: Janus, Phoebus Apollo, and Hermes are among the mythological figures prominent in the scene. The higher reality in which the children participate, then, is not really a transcendent one, but profoundly human. The Greek and Roman characters seem to symbolize the best achievements of human civilization. Appropriately, the character of Phoebus Apollo plays a central role in this magical scene. The god of medicine, music, and poetry, the bringer of light, Apollo had conquered the dark unfathomable forces in the underworld and secured the basis of civilization. In juxtaposing the statues of Apollo and the dinosaur, Nesbit reveals opposing Apollonian and Dionysian dimensions in the human psyche. The children seem to experience magically these powers in their own imaginative lives and to integrate them through art. As they raptly listen to Apollo's music, the children enter a timeless realm of art:

> Then Phoebus struck the strings and softly plucked melody from them, and all the beautiful dreams of all the world came fluttering

> close with wings like doves' wings; and all the lovely thoughts that
> sometimes hover near, but not so near that you can catch them, now
> came home as to their nests in the hearts of those who listened. And
> those who listened forgot time and space, and how to be sad, and
> how to be naughty, and it seemed that the whole world lay like a
> magic apple in the hand of each listener, and that the whole world
> was good and beautiful. (188)

This magical adventure within the protected oasis of the enchanted garden represents and celebrates artistic creation as a supreme value. The highly poetic texture of Nesbit's prose throughout the chapter emphasizes that the world of art and the creative imagination are the deep centers of magical enchantment. Mabel's human story, though shyly told, nevertheless exerts a hushing spell even upon the gods: "The marble Olympians listened enchanted—almost as enchanted as the castle itself, and the soft moonlit moments fell past like pearls dropping into a deep pool" (186). Nesbit contrasts a highly realistic scene with this visionary garden of art. As the sun rises, the statues flee to their pedestals, and the children cease to be marble and become flesh. From an island of brambles and coarse grass, the children climb down into a passage ending in the Temple of Flora, "a great hall, whose arched roof was held up by two rows of round pillars, and whose every corner was filled with a soft, searching, lovely light, filling every cranny, as water fills the rocky secrecies of hidden sea-caves" (194).

In this deep illuminated space, each child perceives a perfect vision differently; the narrator explains, "I won't describe it, because it does not look the same to any two people" (195). The statue of Psyche presides over the cave and serves as the source of light. The secret of the magic, Nesbit implies, lies deep within the self, the creative center which enables each child to imagine "the most perfect thing possible" (195). In Psyche's cave, the children enjoy viewing splendid artistic achievements from different cultures and eras, all framed as if pictures in a gallery and each depicting "some moment when life had sprung to fire and flower—the best that the soul of man could ask or man's destiny grant" (195). For Nesbit, as for the English Romantics before her, the arts are the center of civilization, just as the creative imagination is the center of the self. Her heavenly vision thus becomes profoundly imbued with the imaginative products of human culture, the only hope, Nesbit seems to imply, whereby her characters and her readers may sustain themselves in an increasingly mechanistic and materialistic world.

Between the publication of *The Enchanted Castle* and *The Magic City*, Nesbit turned her energies once more to writing about fantastic voyages in time with *The House of Arden* (1908) and *Harding's Luck* (1909). These two volumes exhibit Nesbit's outrage with the social conditions of Edwardian England, as well as her enduring fascination with the literary potential of fairy tales. In *The House of Arden* and *Harding's Luck* Nesbit experiments with fairy tale structures and the possibilities of time fantasy to pose a mature social and aesthetic vision. She also investigates the interpenetration of the past and present, while revealing the significance of the past and of place in the imaginative and emotional lives of children. Both of these splendid books resonate with the power of an imagination which can fuse dream and reality, the ordinary and the fabulous. Again Nesbit suggests that apparently transcendent realms may be apprehended through the creative acts of reading, writing, making, and imagining.

The House of Arden centers upon the time travels of Edred and Elfrida Arden, heirs to an ancient castle now fallen from former glory. When they move to Arden Castle, they learn from an ancient servant, Old Beale, that the last Arden treasure is hidden somewhere in the castle. Inspired by Old Beale's legend, the children search for and finally locate a fragile sheet of parchment on which is written a spell for finding the treasure:

> Hear, Oh badge of Arden's house,
> The spell my little age allows;
> Arden speaks it without fear,
> Badge of Arden's house, draw near,
> Make me brave and kind and wise,
> And show me where the treasure lies.

> (24)

When Edred utters the spell, the "badge of Arden's House" appears in the form of a Mouldiwarp, a little animal resembling a mole whose emblem had been stamped in gold above the chequered shield on the cover of the white book in which the children had found the spell. This curious and comical creature initiates Edred and Elfrida into a series of magical journeys into the past: to the early nineteenth century when France is about to attack England in 1807; to the period of James I in 1605, when Elfrida inadvertently chants a rhyme about Guy Fawkes and the Gunpowder Plot and finds herself in the Tower of London, where she and Edred meet their cousin Richard Arden;

and, perhaps the most perilous of all, to the sixteenth century in the period of Henry VIII's marriage to Anne Boleyn (1533–36). With the help of several characters from the sixteenth century—their old nurse, a wise woman, the Mouldiwarp, and Richard—the two children rescue their father and uncle from imprisonment in twentieth-century South America. Although this experience marks the end of their adventures into the past and their quest to find the treasure, Edred and Elfrida choose the true treasure—the happiness of a reunited family.

In the sequel to *The House of Arden, Harding's Luck*, Nesbit introduces Dickie Harding, a lame child who lives with a cruel woman in an impoverished little house in Deptford. (Nesbit knew the condition of such children well, as she devoted much time and energy to the poor children of Deptford.) Dickie amuses himself with a coral and bells and a seal, both bearing the image of a curious little mole-like creature. Dickie's father had instructed him never to part with these treasures, the emblems of his true noble identity. Dickie amuses himself by playing with these treasures and by reading. He also longs, like Mary Lennox in Frances Hodgson Burnett's *The Secret Garden*, to make a little garden of his own. From the cornchandler, Dickie purchases a packet of Perrokett's Artistic Bird Seed, which produces exotically beautiful moonflowers. Later Dickie attaches himself to a tramp, Beale, and travels about the country side. Beale is a crook and uses Dickie to beg from passersby. Beale's true nature is clear to the reader, but not to the innocent Dickie. Eventually, however, Dickie reforms Beale and makes an honest man of him, and the two establish a household together.

In alternating chapters Nesbit creates Dickie's fantastic travels to the past. Arranging silver seeds from the moonflowers in crossed triangles, Dickie falls into a trancelike sleep and awakes in the reign of James I, where, no longer lame, he enjoys the privileged status as Sir Richard Arden's son. In this stately home Dickie studies Latin and Greek, learns to dance and to fence, and meets his cousins, Edred and Elfrida. He also learns the art of wood carving in this past life. When he returns to Beale, Dickie uses this craft to establish a business and an honest stable household for himself and Beale. Like many of Charles Dickens's characters, Dickie is quite literally father to the man. Later Dickie, who turns out to be the true heir of Arden Castle, finds the ancient treasure and relinquishes it all to his cousins in order to return permanently to his past life as the stalwart young Richard Arden. Nesbit clearly implies that the past is preferable in all ways to the present, though she also reveals the social problems of the past.

One of Nesbit's purposes in writing the Arden fantasies was clearly to enliven the study of history. Like Lewis Carroll's Alice, Nesbit had been forced to learn history out of a "horrid little book, called somebody's *Outlines of English History*" (Preface, *Children's Stories from English History*). She also wished to contrast the idea of "Arden" (actually a dense forest which covered the English Midlands in ancient times) with what Nesbit viewed as a corrupt and inhumane society. Nesbit's Arden suggests the values represented in William Shakespeare's comedy, *As You Like It*—the timelessness of the pastoral world, its unity of being, its sense of community where all social classes meet to bask in the green enchantment of the forest. Nesbit's Arden books ultimately celebrate literature itself as a living reality; it is therefore fitting that her Arden should resemble Shakespeare's more than it does the actual historical forest.

As Shakespeare's play is laced with verse and song, so too are Nesbit's fantasies. The timeless pastoral world of Arden is not only a green sphere of leisure; it is also the realm of creative energy and imaginative labor. Just as *As You Like It* simultaneously idealizes the pastoral life and calls it into question, so too Nesbit's Arden fantasies simultaneously idealize the past and reveal its flaws. Most important, both the play and Nesbit's Arden books end with a restored and revitalized order which offers hope for an ideal society. It is fitting, for example, that Lord Arden in contemporary times rescues ancient Arden lands from the Tallow King, a vulgar industrialist who abuses tenants and whose only concern is profit.

The Romantic elements of Nesbit's Arden fantasies owe much to such Victorian fantasy writers as Charles Kingsley, Jean Ingelow, Mary Louisa Molesworth, Dinah Mulock, and most especially, George Mac-Donald. Dickie Harding strongly resembles MacDonald's Diamond of *At the Back of the North Wind*. Dickie's goodness, innocence and resourcefulness transform everyone he encounters. His magical adventures are contrasted with chapters dealing with his poverty-ridden life in Deptford, just as Diamond's voyages contrast with his everyday existence in illness as the son of a poor cabman. The fantastic journeys of both Dickie and Diamond are presided over by strong, goddess-like maternal figures, who protect the children but who also teach them and help them to grow. Yet both of these saintly children are finally too good for this world. As Diamond disappears into that mysterious place "at the back of the North Wind," so Dickie retreats into the time of James I. But Dickie does not retreat until he has transformed the present. Elfrida, Edred, and Dickie change the past; in turn those past actions transform the present. Thus, while Nesbit's Arden books do indeed reveal a conservative turn to the past somewhat at odds with her advanced social views, it is not merely an uncritical and idealized treatment of the past. The Arden books provide a thorough critique of both past and present. In so doing the books reveal Nesbit's sophisticated sense of history and the interpenetration of past and present.

In both Arden books Nesbit celebrates the activities of play, reading, composing, and creating. Literature in these books provides children with potent links to the past. The Mouldiwarp may only be summoned by an act of composing poetry. When Edred doubts his magical experience, the Mouldiwarp reminds him of the magical toadstools in Charles Kingsley's *Hereward the Wake,* and that less likely events had taken place in *The Story of the Amulet.* He chides Edred for not realizing that he is in a fairy tale, where anything is possible. Mouldiwarp himself can speak the languages of other creatures and control natural elements with the sweetness of his music and the power of his voice. In fact Mouldiwarp seems to be a powerful symbol of the creative imagination. As a mole, he is close to the earth but nevertheless summons pigeons and swans; hence he unifies heaven and earth, the physical and the spiritual. His abilities in fact resemble strongly Nesbit's own practice of blending the ordinary and the magical. A speaker of country dialect and a master of the most elegant French, Mouldiwarp dissolves social and cultural barriers and implies that art comes from folk and cultivated cultures. Although Mouldiwarp's relative, "Mouldierwarp," controls space and the "Mouldiestwarp" of all presides over some still higher and unattainable reality, Mouldiwarp remains the center of the magic and provides the vehicles for apprehending the other two levels.

In the course of his adventures Dickie Harding becomes a creative artist. Not only does he read, imagine, and grow magical moonflowers; he entertains his friends with stories and steadily polishes his art of wood carving. Similarly, Edred and Elfrida become storytellers, and Elfrida's skill as a poet develops throughout the fantasies. In the Arden books, then, Nesbit integrates her social and aesthetic vision. She advocates careful analysis and imaginative immersion in the past in order to use one's creative gifts in the present and to make society itself a work of art—a garden where human beings may work, play, and love in joyous fellowship. In such an ideal society, Nesbit suggests, barriers of social class dissolve. Living itself becomes an art where greed, ugliness, and the indignities of poverty and social oppression have no place. Like William Morris, William Butler Yeats, and other late-century Romantics, Nesbit would unify labor and art in order that a true community could flourish. She was deeply aware of how alienated English workers were from their labor and how divided were the social classes; however conservative her books may appear from some perspectives, Nesbit never stopped dreaming that human effort and intelligence could establish a more just order of society. Thus Nesbit's child characters do not merely retreat into the past. She clearly intends for both her characters and her child readers to appropriate knowledge from the past, "lessons" in fact. In this sense Nesbit's later fantasies are indeed "didactic," but they are expansively, not narrowly, didactic.

In her last great fantasy for children, *The Magic City*, Nesbit expresses her natural supernaturalism most explicitly. In this complex book Nesbit explores the imaginary adventures of Philip Haldane. Through these adventures Philip adjusts to the marriage of his half-sister, Helen, to Peter Graham, her childhood sweetheart, now a widower with one daughter, Lucy. While the happy couple departs for an extended honeymoon in Europe, Philip remains with Lucy in Graham's spacious mansion. Fearful of a cruel and rather insensitive nurse, Philip amuses himself by building a magic city from books, toys, candle sticks, blocks, dominoes, and other common household items. This activity comforts him because it had been one of his favorite pastimes with Helen. At the Grange, however, Philip's creation results in punishment rather than the praise to which he has been accustomed. The unpleasant nurse accuses the child of being "naughty, wicked, and untruthful" and "whirled him off to bed" (23) without supper.

Later in the night Philip awakens to brilliantly radiant moonlight and creeps downstairs for a last glimpse of his wonderful city. Instead he finds himself on a vast flat plain. He has entered his magic city. Soon Lucy joins him, and guardsmen apprehend both children. Lucy and Philip are told of an ancient prophecy foretelling that both a Destroyer and a Deliverer will enter the city by the route they have used.

Mr. Noah, apparently the ruler of the magic city, explains that one enters by building something. Philip also meets his old friend, Mr. Perrin, the master builder who made Philip's beloved and highly useful oak blocks. To be a Deliverer, Mr. Perrin explains, Philip must accomplish seven great deeds, the first of which is the slaying of an enormous green dragon. Philip's adversary arrives in the form of a "Pretenderette," though she is really only the unpleasant nurse who has also gotten into the magic city, perhaps in the act of trying to destroy it. In any event the nurse eventually proves herself to be the Destroyer, just as Philip, with the help of Lucy, becomes the Deliverer. Philip's most significant quest is not the seven brave deeds but the struggle to overcome his selfish and possessive feelings for Helen and to learn to love Lucy. The seven deeds serve this larger purpose.

Philip's first two heroic tasks are simple. He settles the dreadful dragon (only a windup toy) by removing the key. Nesbit hints that technology must serve humane purposes; to achieve this worthy end, Philip must be master of it. One of the most important events in the quest occurs when Philip is mysteriously kidnapped, since he joins Helen on an imaginary island during this episode. Helen explains that she had come to the island by walking in "at the other side of the dream" (245). In an unselfish gesture, Philip yields his happy island to displaced islanders and also supplies the kingdom with fruit.

After Philip and Lucy have completed all the deeds, they return to the Magic City, where they must free the people from the Pretenderette, who has demolished the Hall of Justice, opened a book, and in the process released invaders into the magic city. To quell the invaders, Philip merely opens another book and calls upon Caesar to drive out the invaders. In the end the Pretenderette is condemned to make herself loved by someone, while Helen and Philip realize that they must return home. As in so many of Nesbit's children's books, the reunited family marks the end of the narrative. In building their own magical cities, Philip and Lucy not only solve their emotional problems but also create an order characterized by peace, satisfying labor, books, art, and the finest of cultural artifacts. Again, all barriers between people dissolve, evil spells dissipate, and a new era is ushered in. Nesbit implies that Lucy and Philip will take these same values back to the primary world and that they will create such a beneficent world at the Grange.

Nesbit herself was famous for building magic cities, a process she describes in *Wings and the Child*. In the foreword to this book, Nesbit explains that it "took shape as an attempt to contribute something, however small and unworthy, to the science of building a magic city in the soul of a child, a city built of all things pure and fine and beautiful." The child will, she says, "use the whole force of dream and fancy to create something out of nothing" (vii).

In *The Magic City* Nesbit truly celebrates this human instinct to create something out of nothing. In discussing the complex philosophical structure of *The Magic City* Stephen Prickett has placed E. Nesbit in the Christian Platonic tradition of Charles Kingsley and George Mac-Donald, noting that *The Enchanted Castle* and *The Magic City* "involve the discovery not so much of magic creatures in this world, as of the existence of other worlds along-side this one" (229). While Nesbit shared many spiritual and artistic convictions with Kingsley and MacDonald, *The Enchanted Castle*, the Arden books, and *The Magic City* do not celebrate the discovery of other worlds so much as the creation of an ideal human world. Hence, Nesbit, unlike Kingsley and MacDonald, stresses the human rather than the divine forces as the grounds of the magic world. Plato had felt that artists could only imitate shadows or reflections of the Ideas which existed in the mind of God. Plotinus and other Neoplatonists believed that the artist could through the creative imagination reach these Ideas and bypass the concrete world of objects. The English Romantic poets had in various ways attempted to "naturalize the supernatural and to humanize the divine" (Abrams 68). Nesbit's major fantasies show that she believes the way to create this human order is with creative acts within the context of the concrete world.

In *The Enchanted Castle* Gerald and Mabel appropriate visions and become storytellers. Even the Greek gods and goddesses listen to these stories. At the end of the fantasy, Lord Yalding yields supernatural magic for human love and determines to restore his castle through active human effort. Similarly in *The Magic City* the basis of Philip's magical world lies in the material world. The magic city's existence depends upon his creative labor. As Mr. Perrin explains: "All the cities and things you ever built is in this country. I don't know how it's managed, no more'n what you do. But so it is . . . *Making's* the thing. If it was no more than the lad that turned the handle of the grindstone to sharp the knife that carved a bit of a cabinet or what not, or a child that picked a teazle to finish a bit of the cloth that's glued on to the bottom of the chessman—they're all here" (106). Similarly in the Arden fantasies the children use art and creative activities to enter the magical past and to restore the House of Arden; in so doing they establish a more progressive society for all who inhabit the estate.

Art and creative work, then, allow one to participate in a visionary city and to build an ideal community. The magic city is Nesbit's complex symbol for an ideal civilization. *The Magic City* thus resembles other Romantic expressions in making the highest claim for the place of art. Northrop Frye has written, "In the Romantic construct there is a center where inward and outward manifestations of a common motion and spirit are unified, where the ego is identified as itself because it is also identified with something which is not itself. In Blake this world at the deep center is Jerusalem, the city of God that mankind or Albion has sought all through history without success because he has been looking in the wrong direction, outside" (17). In *The Magic City* and in her other fantasies, Nesbit suggests that the potential for magical creation, for making oneself a "Deliverer" rather than a "Destroyer," lies within each of us. Philip's quest involves his acceptance of help from Lucy and also reveals him on the boundary between the two worlds of the conscious and the unconscious, the ideal and the actual, the real and the imaginary. Just as magical creatures, rivers, and characters spill out of books in the magic city and profoundly affect events and characters, so art itself interacts with social and historical reality, at once reflecting and shaping it.

Towards the end of his adventures, Philip journies to Somnolentia with Lucy to awaken the Great Sloth. Here the children encounter a monstrous creature similar to the dinosaurs in *The Enchanted Castle*. This creature has put the people to sleep. They neglect their city and allow their clear stream to become clogged with gold (an analogy perhaps for what Nesbit saw happening to her own society). The sloth represents not just laziness, but a regressive refusal to create and thus to become fully human. It is humanity at an arrested state of development, since it only requires sleeping, eating, and soothing lullabies. One of the ways that Lucy and Philip awaken the Somnolentians and liberate them from the sloth's tyranny is to remind the citizens of their true names and thus of their human identities. At Lucy's insistence, they work at restoring the buildings, gardens, and fields, just as Philip had worked to create his magic city. The city and the garden represent the human imagination at work on the mineral and vegetable worlds. The orderly beauty of the magic city is a heavenly vision against chaos. Such creative endeavor, Nesbit implies, requires both imagination and humanity. Thus Philip learns to share his adventure and his labor with Lucy. In the final scene Philip and Lucy cooperate as equals to build a model of the Grange and thus return home to be reunited with their family.

The most significant way that Nesbit's child characters liberate themselves from static myths of childhood is by seizing control of their own stories to become makers and creators. Unlike Wordsworth's child characters, Nesbit's are highly literate. Although they retain intuitive ways of knowing, the activities of reading, thinking, fabricating, and even artful lying help them to evade sentimentality, constraints, and aggressions of adults. While Wordsworth and MacDonald celebrate the simplicity and innocence of children, Lewis Carroll and Nesbit rejoice in their complexity, intelligence, and experience. Nesbit encourages her child characters and her readers to transcend literary and social convention, to speak in radically new voices, and to create new idioms and myths of childhood, just as Nesbit herself broke free of some rather stifling conventions of Victorian children's literature. We have seen that children in Romantic and Victorian children's literature have been entrapped in texts; it is a telling metaphor that Philip Haldane frees creatures from texts in *The Magic City*—frees both monsters and marvels, transforms them, and sends them back again. Similarly Nesbit releases her child characters and her child readers from such imprisonment. While Oswald Bastable had feared "grown-upness," Philip Haldane and Lucy of *The Magic City* and Gerald of *The Enchanted Castle* just grow. In her later fantasies Nesbit does not lock magic behind the golden gates of childhood but makes it available within the context of mundane reality. Her characters make the magic for themselves through the creative acts of storytelling and art. Finally, each of these fantasies ends with a reunited family experiencing a sense of renewal and anticipating a future of creative labors together. Implicit in all of Nesbit's children's stories is her profoundly optimistic belief in the human capacity for transformation. New societies may emerge from the ruins of the old, she suggests, just as new stories may be constructed from the worn-out fragments of literary convention.

WORKS CITED

Abrams, M. H. *Natural Supernaturalism: Tradition and Revolution in Romantic Literature.* New York: Norton, 1971.

Avery, Gillian. *Nineteenth Century Children: Heroes and Heroines in English*

Children's Stories, 1780–1900. London: Hodder and Stoughton, 1965.

Bloom, Harold. "The Internalization of Quest Romance." *Romanticism and Consciousness.* Ed. Bloom. New York: Norton, 1970. 3–24.

Coleridge, Samuel Taylor. *Biographia Literaria.* New York: Allison, 1882.

Coveney, Peter. *The Image of Childhood.* London, 1967; originally published as *Poor Monkey: The Child in Literature.* London: Rockliff, 1957.

Crouch, Marcus. *The Nesbit Tradition: The Children's Novel in England, 1945–1970.* London: Ernest Benn, 1972.

Fiedler, Leslie. "The Eye of Innocence." *No! In Thunder: Essays in Myth and Literature.* Boston: Beacon, 1960. 251–82.

Frye, Northrop. "The Drunken Boat: The Revolutionary Element in Romanticism." *Romanticism Reconsidered.* Ed. Frye. New York: Columbia UP, 1963. 1–25.

Koppes, Phyllis Bixler. "The Child in Pastoral Myth: A Study in Rousseau and Wordsworth, Children's Literature and Literary Fantasy." Diss. U. of Kansas, 1977.

MacDonald, George. *At the Back of the North Wind.* New York: Airmont, 1966.

Manlove, C. N. "Fantasy as Witty Conceit: E. Nesbit." *Mosaic* 10 (Winter 1977). 110–30.

Moore, Doris Langley. *E. Nesbit: A Biography.* London: Ernest Benn, 1933. Rev. ed. with new material, Philadelphia: Chilton, 1966.

Nesbit, E. *Children's Stories from English History.* With Doris Ashley. Illus. by John H. Bacon, Howard Davie, and others. London: Raphael Tuck and Son, 1914.

———. *The Enchanted Castle.* Illus. by Cecil Leslie. 1907. London: Dent; New York: Dutton, 1964.

———. *Five Children and It.* Illus. by H. R. Millar. London: Unwin, 1902.

———. *Harding's Luck.* Illus. by H. R. Millar. 1909. New York: Coward-McCann, 1961.

———. *The House of Arden.* 1908. New York: Coward-McCann, 1958.

———. *The Magic City.* Illus. by H. R. Millar. 1910. Boston: Gregg, 1981.

———. *The New Treasure Seekers.* Illus. by Gordon Brown and Lewis Baumer. London: Unwin, 1904.

———. *The Phoenix and the Carpet.* Illus. by H. R. Millar. London: George Newnes, 1904.

———. *The Story of the Amulet.* Illus. by H. R. Millar. London: Unwin, 1906.

———. *The Story of the Treasure Seekers.* Illus. by Gordon Brown and Lewis Baumer. London: Unwin, 1899.

———. *Wings and the Child.* London: Hodder and Stoughton, 1913.

———. *The Wouldbegoods.* Illus. by Arthur Buckland. London: Unwin, 1901.

Prickett, Stephen. *Victorian Fantasy.* Bloomington: Indiana UP, 1979.

Wordsworth, William. "Lines Composed a Few Miles Above Tintern Abbey."
The Poetical Works of William Wordsworth. Ed. Ernest De Selincourt. 2nd
ed. Vol. 2. Oxford: Clarendon, 1952.
————. *The Prelude: 1799, 1805, 1850.* Ed. Jonathan Wordsworth, M. H.
Abrams, and Stephen Gill. New York: Norton, 1979.

CONTRIBUTORS

PHYLLIS BIXLER, a professor of English at Southwest Missouri State University, is the author of *Frances Hodgson Burnett* (G. K. Hall, 1984), as well as various articles on Burnett and other children's authors. She has taught women's literature and ethnic literature in addition to children's and young adult literature.

PATRICIA DEMERS is a professor of English at the University of Alberta, where she teaches courses in Renaissance literature, the Bible, and children's literature. She has edited two anthologies of children's literature for Oxford University Press: *From Instruction to Delight* (with R. G. Moyles, 1982) and *A Garland from the Golden Age* (1983).

MICHAEL HANCHER, a professor of English at the University of Minnesota, has published *The Tenniel Illustrations to the "Alice" Books* (Ohio State University Press, 1985), as well as many articles and reviews about interpretation, speech-act theory, and the law.

JAMES HOLT MCGAVRAN, JR., is a professor of English and assistant dean of the College of Arts and Sciences at the University of North Carolina, Charlotte. He has published articles on William and Dorothy Wordsworth, Samuel T. Coleridge, Virginia Woolf, and children's and adolescent literature. McGavran teaches courses in the Romantic era and modern British fiction.

RODERICK MCGILLIS, a professor of English at the University of Calgary, is the editor of the *Children's Literature Association Quarterly*. He has recently published an edition of George MacDonald's *The Princess and the Goblin* and *The Princess and Curdie* (Oxford World's Classics, 1990).

ANITA MOSS is a professor of English at the University of North Carolina, Charlotte, where she teaches children's literature and British literature. She is the editor, with Jon C. Stott, of *The Family of Stories: An*

Anthology of Children's Literature (Holt, Rinehart, and Winston, 1986) and the author of numerous articles and reviews.

MITZI MYERS teaches writing and children's and adolescent literature at the University of California, Los Angeles. She has published numerous essays and reviews on women writers and children's literature.

JUDITH PLOTZ is a professor of English and coordinator of the humanities program at George Washington University. She is the author of *Ideas of the Decline of Poetry* (Garland, 1987) and various articles on romanticism and childhood. She teaches nineteenth-century English literature, Commonwealth literature, and children's literature.

ALAN RICHARDSON, an assistant professor of English at Boston College, is the author of *A Mental Theatre: Poetic Drama and Consciousness in the Romantic Age* (Pennsylvania State University Press, 1988), as well as numerous articles on Romantic literature.

JEANIE WATSON is a professor of English and dean of the College of Liberal Arts at Hamline University. She has published *Risking Enchantment: Coleridge's Symbolic World of Faery* (University of Nebraska Press, 1990) and has edited or coedited *Children's Literature of the English Renaissance: Essays by Warren W. Wooden* (University Press of Kentucky, 1986), *Ambiguous Realities: Women in the Middle Ages and Renaissance* (Wayne State University Press, 1987), *The Figure of Merlin in the Nineteenth and Twentieth Centuries* (Edwin Mellen Press, 1989), and *Approaches to Teaching the Arthurian Tradition* (Modern Language Association, 1991).

ROSS WOODMAN, a professor emeritus of English at the University of Western Ontario, has authored *The Apocalyptic Vision in the Poetry of Shelley* (University of Toronto Press, 1964), *James Reaney* (McClelland and Stewart, 1971), and numerous articles on the Romantic poets and Canadian art.

INDEX